See How
We Roll

See How
We Roll

GLOBAL INSECURITIES

A series edited by Catherine Besteman and Darryl Li

Enduring Exile
between Desert
and Urban Australia
Melinda Hinkson

DUKE UNIVERSITY PRESS
Durham and London 2021

Designed by Courtney Leigh Richardson
Typeset in Portrait and Helvetica Neue by Westchester Publishing Services

Library of Congress Cataloging-in-Publication Data
Names: Hinkson, Melinda, author.
Title: See how we roll : enduring exile between desert and urban Australia /
Melinda Hinkson.
Other titles: Global insecurities.
Description: Durham : Duke University Press, 2021. | Series: Global
insecurities | Includes bibliographical references and index.
Identifiers: LCCN 2021000891 (print)
LCCN 2021000892 (ebook)
ISBN 9781478013846 (hardcover)
ISBN 9781478014775 (paperback)
ISBN 9781478022077 (ebook)
Subjects: LCSH: Warlpiri (Australian people)—Social conditions. | Women,
Warlpiri—Social conditions. | Women, Aboriginal Australian—Social
conditions. | Aboriginal Australians—Urban residence. | Migration,
Internal—Australia. | Adelaide (S.A.)—Ethnic relations. | BISAC: SOCIAL
SCIENCE / Anthropology / Cultural & Social | HISTORY / Australia & New
Zealand
Classification: LCC DU125.W37 H56 2021 (print) | LCC DU125.W37 (ebook) |
DDC 305.48/89915 [B]—dc23
LC record available at https://lccn.loc.gov/2021000891
LC ebook record available at https://lccn.loc.gov/2021000892

Cover art: Kangaroo tail picnic. Photo courtesy the author.

Contents

Acknowledgments

One of the many constraints of writing a book in which the identities of people and places are disguised is that those same people cannot be named in gratitude. This book would never have been imagined let alone brought into being without the friendship, generosity, and care Nungarrayi has shared with me across two and a half decades. In relation to the work we have undertaken together for this book, I am grateful for her creative energy, hospitality, forbearance, patience, and trust. I am also indebted to Nungarrayi's many close and extended relatives, and to other Warlpiri friends, who make appearances throughout this book and who in other ways have contributed to and supported my research. Beyond friendship, these relationships provide a singular anchor point in my life—a constant reminder of the remarkable strength, wit, and humor with which subjugated people pursue lives of dignity and purpose.

I have wrestled with the dilemmas of how to write this book in the company of close friends, Jennifer Deger, Ute Eickelkamp, Eve Vincent, and Paul Carter, whose various forms of support, stimulation, and responses to drafts of writing have been vital. Nicolas Rothwell made a generous and inspired intervention—the idea that this book was about friendship—at a crucial juncture. More generally the project has benefited from discussions with Lucas Bessire, Sarah Holcombe, Mandy Paul, Kalissa Alexeyeff, Yasmine Musharbash, Fred Myers, Åse Ottosson, Nicolas Peterson, Lisa Stefanoff, Frank Baarda, Andrew Stojanovski, and Cecilia Alfonso, as well as with Deakin University colleagues Gillian Tan, Rohan Bastin, Roland Kapferer, Andrea Witcomb, Victoria Stead, David Giles, Tanya King, Sarah Hayes, Anita Harris, Rose Butler, Maree Pardy, Sam Balaton-Chrimes, Tim Neale, Emma Kowal, Cameo Dalley, Billy Griffiths, and Michele Lobo. Ben Scambary and Sophie Creighton of the Aboriginal Areas Protection Authority committed generous resources in support of a disastrous desert expedition that was formative in shaping my analysis. David Jeffrey facilitated access to collections at the Australian Institute of Torres Strait Islander Studies in Canberra. The community of scholars and activists associated with the Arena project in Melbourne have long provided a vital base for thinking and working through underlying ethical commitments and social analysis with which this book is concerned.

Place has been much more than an intellectual concern throughout this research. I commenced this project after returning to my hometown of Melbourne after sixteen years in Canberra. The joyous but uncanny experience of taking up residence in a familiar neighborhood on the other side of its neoliberal restructuring as well as with much-transformed personal circumstances has been a constant spark for thinking on the significance of place and its transformation. Reestablishing a second home on a bush block with long and changing associations enabled deeper probing of these matters, as well as invaluable opportunities for solitary writing retreats.

An Australian Research Council Future Fellowship enabled the rare privilege of four years of research-intensive time. The Alfred Deakin Institute of Citizenship and Globalisation at Deakin University, under the directorship of Fethi Mansouri, has been a most supportive and collegial environment in which to think, read, and write.

Sections of this book draw on previously published work. Chapter 1 is a revised and expanded version of "In and Out of Place: Ethnography as 'Journeying With' between Central and South Australia," *Oceania* 88, no. 3 (2018). Ethnographic material and analysis throughout the book has appeared in "Locating a Zeitgeist: Displacement, Becoming and the End of Alterity," *Critique of Anthropology* 39, no. 3 (2019); "Turbulent Dislocations in Central Australia: Exile, Placemaking and the Promises of Elsewhere," *American Ethnologist* 45, no. 4 (2018); "Beyond Assimilation and Refusal: A Warlpiri Perspective on the Politics of Recognition," *Postcolonial Studies* 20, no. 1 (2017); and "On the Edges of the Visual Culture of Exile: A View from South Australia," in *Refiguring Techniques in Digital Visual Research*, ed. S. Pink, S. Sumartojo, and E. Gómez Cruz (London: Palgrave Macmillan, 2017).

My thinking about exile was stimulated in multiple ways in two months spent roaming, reading, and writing in New York. As a visiting fellow in the Department of Anthropology and the Center for Religion and Media at New York University, I, along with my partner, Jon Altman, and our son, Oskar, were generously hosted by Faye Ginsburg and Fred Myers. Valuable further prompts for de-parochializing my thinking about displacement came from stimulating discussions convened by Heath Cabot and Georgina Ramsay at the European Association of Social Anthropologists meeting in Stockholm in

2018 and an extended workshop in Pittsburgh in 2019. Annual meetings of the American Anthropological Association and the Australian Anthropological Society, as well as work-in-progress presentations at New York University, the University of Melbourne, Sydney University, and Deakin University, have provided important opportunities for further critical engagement. I am grateful to Elisabeth Yarbakhsh for her eagle eye and elegant editing assistance.

It was my good fortune to meet Catherine Besteman in Pittsburgh and to find strong affinities between our interests and her enthusiasm for this project. Perceptive and generous feedback from Duke University Press's anonymous readers encouraged me to make this a better book. Gisela Fosado, Liz Smith, and Alejandra Mejía at Duke have been warm, supportive, and efficient in shepherding the work through editorial production.

Finally, this has not been an easy project to live through. I have been blessed with the interest and unwavering support of my family, my four parents, John Hinkson and Alison Caddick and Meryl and Nigel Taylor, and especially the forbearance of those in my immediate household—my son, Oskar, and partner, Jon, who not only read multiple versions of the manuscript as it took shape but worked hard to offset and alleviate the shape-shifting anxieties and uncertainties I have wrestled with along the way. My stepdaughter, Tess Altman, the third anthropologist in the family, hovered ever interested from her more distanced vantage of London. For the love of family and friends, I say thanks.

Introduction

In and Out
of Place

Unsettling Country

We have been driving for four hours when I suggest we pull off the road to light a fire and make a cup of tea. Nungarrayi looks at me as if I'm mad. "We can't stop, Nangala," she says. "That country gives me the creeps." In the wake of The Troubles—protracted feuding and related anxieties—the desert has become dangerous. Most people are disinclined to venture out of the town and into the desert to go hunting. Many are reluctant to break a journey for any purpose aside from the need to relieve full bladders, and on those brief stops keep as close as possible to the roadside. Two decades ago the situation could not have been more different. As a doctoral fieldworker in the mid-1990s,

FIGURE I.1 Tanami Desert, the road between the Big Town and the Tiny Town
(photo by author)

I observed bush roads abuzz with cars—cars funded by government grants
and issued to community organizations, cars purchased by individuals with
the proceeds of mining royalty payments, cars owned and driven by white
friends—people would leap at any opportunity to get out bush. But now I cannot convince my friend to pause for a tea break as we drive the well-worn bush
road between two Central Australian Warlpiri towns. Disheartened, I drive on,
taking in, through the car window, fleeting glimpses of the abundant plant life
that thrives in the wake of recent heavy rains.

My traveling companion, Nungarrayi, is a close friend of twenty-five years
and a woman my age. She currently lives in the South Australian capital of Adelaide, two thousand kilometers (more than one thousand miles) south of the
area through which we are driving, which is adjacent to her ancestral lands and
the town in which she was born and lived for most of her life. She and I once
wandered through the desert she now finds unsettling on hunting trips, chasing goannas and digging up bush potatoes in the company of several women
she called mother, all since deceased. She is a "traditional owner" of Jukurrpa—
ancestral dreaming tracks and places that traverse the desert—but is only at ease
on her deceased father's and grandfather's country, another twenty kilometers
(twelve miles) down the road. Three days later, Nungarrayi and I visit her coun-

try, where she walks confidently in the haze of midday heat, newly invigorated, a woman in her place, calling out to her ancestors with great emotion, announcing our presence. She bathes at the sacred water hole and guides me up the rock face to peer at and photograph faint traces of ocher-drawn pictures. But she dismisses my suggestion that we camp overnight. Several hours later, we are on the road again and heading toward the Big Town. We are visiting on her suggestion, but as we approach the outskirts of her hometown, she becomes increasingly agitated. As I slow down and pull the car up outside the house of one of her sister's sons, she has what appears to be a panic attack. She folds into herself in the passenger seat and screams, "No room! No room!" declaring the imminent presence of a person with whom she has an avoidance relationship. But to my eyes there is no such person, nor indeed any person, to be seen.

We had planned to spend the weekend here visiting her family but end up making the briefest of visits to one sister who resides in a house perched on the eastern edge of town. Nungarrayi instructs me to park our rental car behind the house, out of view of the road. We enter the house through the back door. Camila is lying in bed, watching television. She is a retired schoolteacher and daughter of the woman who was the most formidable ceremonial leader of her generation. She is also the grandmother of a renowned football player and has spent lengthy periods living in southern cities in support of his career. Her hair has recently been cut severely short in ritual mourning following the death of a close brother. Camila is diabetic and was forced to have one of her lower legs amputated the previous year, after an infection went untreated and turned gangrenous. Her Irish Australian partner, an "ex–stick man" (former intravenous drug user), as Nungarrayi describes him, is in the kitchen preparing to cook a large piece of meat. Two children are curled up asleep on a mattress on the lounge room floor. We join Camila on her bed and cursorily exchange news. After fifteen minutes of edgy chat, Nungarrayi gets up and announces that it is time for us to leave. Before I know it, we are back in the car and on the road, heading in fading light toward the regional center of Alice Springs. The more distance we put between the town and ourselves, the more the mood within the car thaws and then lifts.

FOR TWO AND A HALF DECADES I have watched Warlpiri friends perilously navigate the volatile circumstances of their lives. In a decisive move, Nungarrayi left the desert following a turbulent set of events and is pursuing a new life for herself in the city. It is a move with profound implications for herself, for her family, for the larger Warlpiri community, and ultimately for those abstract assemblies we identify as Australian society and humanity at large. This book attempts to tease out and make partly visible the constellation of forces at work in her situation. It pays particular attention to the influences and pressures with which former hunter-gatherers, such as Central Australian Warlpiri, have had to contend over several decades as they ceaselessly adjust to shifting governmental and public attitudes to their place-based orientations and ways of life. *See How We Roll* tracks the creative and energetic work pursued by a determined woman who is highly competent and respected in one social world, as she tries to establish a new life for herself in another. It explores her attempt at upholding an appropriate exilic code of conduct, a "proper way" of being a Warlpiri woman at a distance from the places and intense sociality where such ways are shaped and adjudicated. My approach in telling this story emerges from a driving need to make sense of major ruptures in the life of a friend, with a sense that the singularity of her situation reveals related, dispersed stresses that traverse her community, and ultimately implicate national and international communities at large. I grapple with these circumstances through the prism of relationships—the evolving and attenuated relationships to country and kin that both confound and sustain life at a distance from the desert, as well as the new kinds of relationships that displacement and metropolitan life make possible and create an urgent need for. The mediating pivot point is the friendship between the two of us.

After much back-and-forth discussion, my primary interlocutor agrees with me that the best approach for the telling of this story is to refer to her by her Warlpiri "skin," or subsection, name, Nungarrayi. We could have settled on a pseudonym in order to more fully disguise her identity, but to adopt the name Nungarrayi enables a double move that speaks directly to this book's concerns. At birth, a Warlpiri person acquires one of eight possible "skin" names.[1] There is nothing arbitrary in one's skin name. Skin names pass patrilineally, via a father to his children; they repeat in alternate generations, so that in Nungarrayi's case she is born Nungarrayi on account of her father being a Japaljarri, and the female and male children of her Jungarrayi brothers will at birth inherit the names Napaljarri and Japaljarri, respectively. And so the mortal coil cycles around. The entire Warlpiri community of some five to six thousand people figure their close and distant relationships to each other through "skins" and the father-child patri-couples the terms instantiate. These terms ultimately denote a moral order that enfolds all such related people and places. One's "skin" indexes the places one owns and associated bodies of knowledge for which one may acquire responsibility; potential persons one might consider as marriage partners; those whom one calls mother, niece, daughter; those whom one must avoid; and so on. This extended web radiates outward, across desert communities interlinked by ceremonial, marriage, and other exchange relationships, and ultimately, albeit at a more abstract level, across Aboriginal Australia at large. The centrality of this web is indicated in the pages that follow by interactions with numerous kin I describe as "extended." This extended relational order is at play when Nungarrayi addresses me as Nangala, my adoptive "skin," which establishes us as *jukana*, female cross-cousins, women who marry each other's brothers, or, in her more recent cosmopolitan mode of address, simply as "sis." Warlpiri attribute and use names and nicknames in highly dynamic and context-specific ways. But without a skin name one is literally no one. Nungarrayi is a highly meaningful identification in the desert, not so in the city. Away from the desert, Nungarrayi is a name out of place. To deploy Nungarrayi in the pages that follow is to invoke the social world marked by this name. In the city, Nungarrayi is a name that marks a difference that is dissolved in its conventional use in the desert. The name Nungarrayi is both distinctive resource *and* hindrance in her navigation of the turbulence of displacement. Where it makes sense to do so, other people who appear in the pages that follow are referred to by skin name. All other names are pseudonyms.

Significantly, Nungarrayi has moved away from the places that historically anchored her identity and pursues self-transformation at a time when the Australian government encourages Aboriginal people from "remote" areas to do exactly as she does. An ascendant discourse would see people from the bush loosen their place-based commitments to kin and country and move in order to seek improved employment and life prospects elsewhere. Such visions are deployed in support of arguments for reducing government funding for "unviable" small towns. Outstations, the smallest decentralized living areas on land under Aboriginal ownership that were encouraged and indeed acquired iconic significance in the previous policy era of "self-determination," have come to be disparaged as "cultural museums," places that lock their residents out of any prospect of engagement in the "real economy."[2] A renewed government push to "develop the north" coincides with heated public and political contestation over potential locations for planned nuclear waste dumps, and over active transnational and national interests in resource extraction and fracking across the Australian interior.[3] The most explicit state threats to Aboriginal residential living arrangements in the desert have come from the state of Western Australia, where a reform "road map" presents the idea of withdrawing government resourcing for small communities altogether.[4] The Western Australian government's strikingly literal Move to Town program has to date presided over the relocation of thirty-seven Aboriginal families to regional centers.[5] Aboriginal residents of the mineral-rich Pilbara, the region at the heart of Australia's mining boom, battled long-standing government neglect only to watch in horror as their homes were classified as uninhabitable and demolished.[6] Newly profound challenges wrought by overextraction and climate change—water scarcity and record-breaking searing temperatures—now hover over any future-focused debates about the "viability" of desert inhabitation.[7] For the people who call these places home, questions of viability, such that they arise, are experienced in terms of profound threat. I avoid agitating a suite of pressing real-world matters by referring to Nungarrayi's hometown simply as the Big Town. Similarly, I disguise related significant places.

The mobility for improvement logic that sits at the heart of current government imaginaries aims to produce *placeless* Aboriginal subjects, people who will move to maximize their chances of finding employment and accessing resources, educational opportunities, and government services. This kind of mobile subjectivity reverses the vision for remote-living Aboriginal people of the previous policy era that implemented land rights legislation and "self-determination," where decentralized movement from government settlements to smaller kin-based residential arrangements on ancestral land was tolerated and indeed became a centerpiece of government reform.[8] Warlpiri and other desert people's distinctive place-based associations and their related cultural production figured in a national imaginary for that period that celebrated the relatively isolated small towns of Central and North Australia as locations that fostered and sustained "traditional" Aboriginal culture, language, art, and ceremony. In the transition from a mode of governance characterized by social welfare to security, the Australian state no longer couches such alterity in terms of positive value.[9] This shift in vision is not just decreed by governments. High-profile Aboriginal commentators have lent their voices in support of capital-led "orbiting" and the modes of cosmopolitan subjectivity that are anticipated will follow.[10] Anthropology is also implicated in these debates.[11] Peter Sutton sparked a vigorous debate among disciplinary colleagues with the publication of *The Politics of Suffering*, a book that excoriated a generation of anthropologists for their complicity in what he dubbed the "liberal consensus" of the self-determination era.[12] In Sutton's view the pervasive ideological force of self-determination delivered a more or less wholesale trade in positive, abstract depictions of Aboriginal "culture," at the expense of addressing the brutalities and traumas being endured by living persons. Sutton offered bleak judgments of Aboriginal cultural practice, kinship, and community life as inherently violent and ill-equipped for modern conditions. These judgments were seized upon and deployed by advocates of a newly punitive governmental regime.[13]

Meanwhile, Aboriginal people whose lives are subject to these debates and punitive social experiments long to break out of grinding poverty and constrained possibilities. "This is no way to live," one stressed friend tells me as she describes her struggle to provide for the needs of five grandchildren living in her care, as she navigates the punishing new demands to access family support payments. When the notion that there is no future in the desert gains traction, the idea of leaving—whether for a finite period or for good—has strong appeal. But what happens when desert people heed these calls and get up and move?

Mobility and Its Containment

See How We Roll tells the incongruous story of Warlpiri being newly encouraged to move amid ever-tightening control over their lives. Simultaneously, it tracks those same people's vigorous pursuit of lives beyond the terms of securitized governance regimes and beyond the lands over which they were recognized as "traditional owners" under land rights law. This is a process of displacement—forced *and* voluntary—the broad shape of which is not new but rather has been unfolding since Warlpiri people's earliest settler colonial encounters. Warlpiri felt the full intensity of colonial power as recently as the 1920s, as they were progressively driven from their arid desert lands and hunter-gatherer mode of life by encroaching pastoralists and prospectors.[14] As with elsewhere in Australia, the worst atrocities of this period involved mass killings, exploitation of Aboriginal bodies, malnutrition, and the spread of chronic disease, resulting in the devastation of entire residential groups.[15] By the 1940s, the great majority of Warlpiri had been relocated onto government settlements and subjected to a new sedentary existence. Part of this relocation occurred voluntarily, as Warlpiri assessed their situation pragmatically and were drawn to settlements as places offering respite from the grueling demands of hunter-gatherer subsistence.[16] But settlement would not bring to an end the vigorous reproduction of Warlpiri modes of authority and ways of relating. Across the subsequent decades, senior men and women led several remarkable episodes of creative dissent to collectively reorient large congregations of people to their new environments and living arrangements, on their own terms. In one significant mid-twentieth-century episode, overcrowding, "tribal fighting," and insufficient water supply in the southern Warlpiri settlement led the minister for native affairs to order the relocation of 130 Warlpiri to a new settlement, six hundred kilometers (almost four hundred miles) north on the lands of the Gurinji. In the months that followed, at a partially built settlement that was dangerously underequipped to cater to the basic needs of so many people and amid the homesickness and mental and physical trauma of dislocation, senior men embarked upon an intensified period of ceremonial activity and ritual exchange with local landowners. Through this activity they acquired and activated symbolic resources and legitimacy with which to refocus the newly assembled group.[17]

While the superintendents of the mid-twentieth century exercised considerable control over the movement of people in and out of settlements, this control was by no means total.[18] Following the Hooker Creek relocation, a distressed mother, whose young baby had died, walked with her extended family hundreds of kilometers through the desert back to the southern settlement from which they had been removed. They would not be the last to do so. Sedentarization also involved new kinds of government-condoned mobility, all tied to emerging Warlpiri participation in the wider economy. From the 1930s, men walked into the desert on foot to shoot dingoes and collect their scalps; from the 1940s, they were deployed to pastoral stations to work in the cattle industry; from the 1960s, children were taken on interstate school excursions; and from the 1970s, Warlpiri traveled increasingly farther afield to attend boarding school and higher education institutions, to exhibit their art, to play football matches, to lobby politicians, and to visit city-based kin and friends.[19]

Prior to colonization, masterful navigation of the desert and its seasonal resources was a matter of life and death. The deep-time mythopoetic order of Jukurrpa—the body of ancestral law embodied in ceremony, song, and iconography through which the world-making endeavors of ancestral beings are narrated and reenacted—premises a distinctive form of mobility that made the desert both sentient and inhabitable. Nancy Munn has shown that movement is itself instantiated in the primary symbol of Warlpiri iconography: the coupling of circle and line, or site and path, figured in Warlpiri and broader Central Desert visual culture as $\bigcirc\!\!=$.[20] This icon enacts the spatiotemporal intersection between place and movement: most basically between *ngurra*/site/camp, as the place where vital activities of nurturance and reproduction occur; and *kuruwarri*/track/ancestral potency, as the dynamic movement forward and away from the camp in pursuit of sustenance and world-making adventure. The recursive relationship between camp and movement insists that any journeying outward is followed by a return to camp—by no means always to the same place, but to the same set of nurturing arrangements and practices a camp sustains. Events or happenings occur in specifically located places.[21] These are named and known places, places linked through eventful travel, ancestral places glossed in English as "country," owned by and associated collectively with intergenerational lineages of peoples. Places are inextricably involved in the making of persons; places confer particular qualities and characteristics on people. In return, places demand to be looked after. This reciprocal conjuncture, signaled in the pages that follow by the concept of emplacement, is, as numerous anthropologists have observed, the primary medium of transgenerational inheritance.[22] Yet, the assured authority with which I can draw from an earlier generation of compelling and richly detailed anthropology to rehearse the lineaments of such a social order is cut across by more recent observations. These make clear that the symbolic order, practices, and processes through which intergenerational inheritance occurs are under extraordinary pressure.[23]

The force of movement, as people accede to the call of journeying kin and other needs and attractions, constitutes a primary dynamic of life in the desert. Older people's memories and modes of storytelling are stacked with rich details of travels made, the order of places visited, meals that were taken, all in the company of specific persons.[24] Such detailed recall continues to be a characteristic feature of Warlpiri attention, as is taking pleasure in journeying itself. The idea of "kinship riding" conjures the dense and dynamic assemblies of travelers who spontaneously fill a car as it departs one place for another.[25] Prior to the introduction of laws prohibiting such modes of transport, extended families would enthusiastically pile onto the open traybacks of trucks and utility vehicles in order to travel together. For as long as Warlpiri have had access to motorcars, senior men have orchestrated *jilkija* (initiation journeys), which bring together many hundreds of dispersed male kin traveling by vehicle across a vast area.[26] These large convoys mobilize and visibilize patrilineal authority; they enact the regional workings of Aboriginal law, following pathways laid down by ancestors, demonstrating knowledge of country, ritual status, and relationships of shared responsibility across space and time. Simultaneously, these journeys restrict the movement of others, especially women, in earlier times on threat of death. At the level of the everyday, desert towns experience constantly fluctuating populations as people flee boredom and the pressures and responsibilities of home for short periods of adventure, drinking, gambling, chasing love interests, and visiting family in other towns, regional centers, or farther afield.

If emplacement predicated on mobility is a primary force in Warlpiri life, another kind of movement occurs in long-term and permanent departures from the desert. Extended separations commonly occur as a result of chronic illness necessitating intensive medical care; the sending of children away to boarding school; incarceration; and removal of children by government authorities. Since the 1970s, it has been increasingly easy for individuals, especially

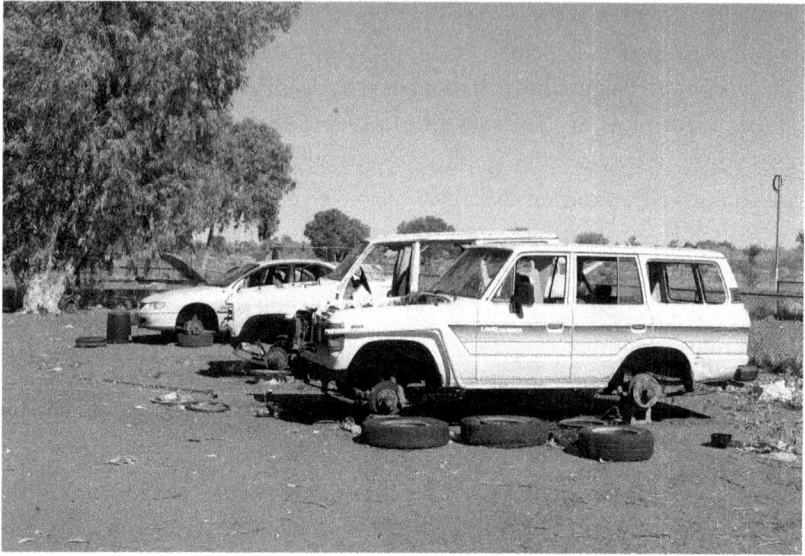

FIGURE I.2 Tiny Town backyard workshop (photo by author)

women, to leave of their own volition, whether fleeing situations of physical abuse by domestic partners or for other reasons.[27] In his study of what he dubs the Warlpiri "diaspora," Paul Burke estimates 23 percent of the total Warlpiri population live outside the "homeland." Beyond those who leave are those who dream of leaving. Departure fantasies are fed by social media feeds, intimate relationships struck up with new "friends," and images promising that better lives can be lived elsewhere. Thus, the history of Warlpiri mobility is multifaceted and contradictory, at once enforced by settler colonial dispossession and more recent episodes of governmental fiat, and also vigorously pursued by Warlpiri themselves. Movement is distinctively inscribed in dynamics of the everyday, as well as being what many recognize is a deeply held cultural impetus.[28] As one senior man put it to me glibly, "We have always moved around." The pages that follow are attentive to the complex interpenetration of these competing cultural logics—to the need to differentiate *kinds* of movement and to understand the implications of acceleration and stasis.

It is a cunning paradox that against this picture of incessant movement the Australian nation-state recognition of Warlpiri ownership of one hundred thousand square kilometers of the Tanami Desert works to fix desert people in place and time. Through the lens of land rights and "traditional ownership," Warlpiri are recognized as having place-based "culture" but not future-focused civilization. This recognition serves to legitimize the conditional nature of the legal title granted to Warlpiri: they are owners of land but not the valuable mineral deposits that lie beneath its surface. They can live on and adjacent to their ancestral places, they can "maintain" their "cultural practices," but in doing so they must forgo many of the resources and citizenship entitlements taken for granted by Australians living in metropolitan regions. Land rights legislation entitles those recognized as "traditional owners" to receive their share of mining royalty distributions paid as compensation for damage done to country and communities. These royalty payments translate into desperately needed income, but they also establish new tensions and highly charged politics for the public identification of entitled kin. This is the pincer movement in which Warlpiri are caught: intergenerational inheritance of country remains a primary ontological anchor, but that distinctive relationship is cut across by commodity capitalism's competing logic and the settler colonial state's governance of Indigenous difference. Four decades after the establishment of land rights and its associated regime of "traditional ownership," the generation of senior men and women who acquired place-based knowledge while living in the desert have passed on. The ever-voracious commodity-extraction regime compels Warlpiri to relate to their ancestral places not as sites of sustaining, taken-for-granted identity but as containing a different kind of transformative potency, one that might enable or force them to become different people. If they so choose, they can leverage their places in order to go elsewhere.

Displacement in the Time of The Troubles

The preceding discussion makes clear that from the perspective of Warlpiri history, Nungarrayi's displacement, per se, is by no means exceptional. But the historical moment and the character of her displacement are distinctive. At the heart of the more recent events with which this book is concerned sit ten years of protracted fighting and distress, which Nungarrayi and other Warlpiri would prefer to shield from public view. The Troubles, as I shall refer to them— and here I consciously borrow the term that invokes the pervasive and protracted political terror of Northern Ireland's extended period of conflict—are a cluster of volatile tensions that pervade the southern Warlpiri community, running along lines of kinship (rather than religion), erupting sporadically and with terrifying force.[29] Triggered initially by the death of a much-loved young man and the sorcery allegations that followed, The Troubles evolved as an extended period of intermittent and spontaneous large-scale fighting and episodes of arson, leading to injury, more deaths, banishments, displacements, and many lives irreparably broken. The Troubles have become *the* causal narrative of the times—they are ceaselessly invoked and talked over and freshly ignited with news of every mishap, accident, diagnosis of chronic illness, and death that befalls this community. The Troubles have had dramatic spatial effects, at times enforcing new restrictions on the movement of residents in the largest Warlpiri town, igniting pervasive fear of the desert, and causing families to bury deceased loved ones three hundred kilometers (almost two hundred miles) away from home, outside of Warlpiri country, in the Alice Springs cemetery. This vigorously pursued, sorcery-fueled set of disputes galvanizes Warlpiri attention, constituting a dispersed space for wielding power and inflicting damage.

How to deal with these forces at the level of ethnographic writing is a challenge. In the context of such volatile eruptions, which are watched and reported on with voyeuristic fascination by mainstream media outlets and feed public perceptions of remote Aboriginal towns as places of violence and pathology, to produce a detailed account of The Troubles would be an exercise in doing violence by re-presentation.[30] In requesting that I not write directly about The Troubles, Nungarrayi flags one of anthropology's enduring neocolonial dilemmas. The revelatory narrative that was the hallmark of one kind of classical anthropological project resulted in the publication of finely grained description of intimacies, practices, and forms of knowledge that otherwise moved through restricted circuits. The anthropological endeavor thus became imbricated with colonial violence, secret stealing, and spying. As a community with nearly a century of experience as subjects of and participants in research, film, and media projects, many Warlpiri have a sophisticated understanding of the disconnects between their own circuits of exchange, their inwardly focused public sphere, and the complex politics of representation through which depictions of Warlpiri circulate more widely. Descriptive writing *about* life does not stand airily above our outside life. In eruptive circumstances writing can be hurled like petrol bombs.

In the pages that follow I do not seek to tell the "truth" about The Troubles, and I deliberately avoid the term Warlpiri use to invoke them. Rather, I attempt to understand something of their dispersed effects and the broader context in which they have been unleashed.[31] From one perspective my approach might be interpreted in terms of ethnographic refusal.[32] But there is also a basic analytic impulse at work here, a commitment to approaching life as lived through the myriad social forces that constrain and enable it. To approach life thus is to refuse parochialism, and relatedly the idea that Warlpiri circumstances can be "understood" by delving ever more deeply into a set of inwardly focused, apparently locally ordered phenomena. As Daniel Goldstein argues, in the time of the security state there is a pressing task for anthropologists to analyze how a truly global reality is played out in local contexts.[33] Moreover, displacement occurs by way of dispersed, confusing, countervailing forces that can never be fully gotten hold of, let alone mastered.

While Warlpiri themselves do not make the connection, The Troubles were initially ignited a year after a dramatic federal governmental incursion, the 2007 Northern Territory Emergency Response, otherwise known as "the Intervention." The Intervention was delivered into the public domain spectacularly, on prime-time television, along with a new image-world that characterized bush towns as sites of pervasive child sexual abuse, domestic violence, dysfunction, and corrupt culture. The prime minister's initial deployment of the army and subsequent introduction of a plethora of new legislation, including a new income management regime, new land tenure arrangements, strict new housing tenancy agreements, and new school attendance strategies, were closely followed by the Northern Territory government's replacement of Aboriginal community government councils with spatially massive regional shires and the disbanding of bilingual education programs. From one angle, the Intervention was a textbook case of a security state deploying dispersed fear to "fill the ruptures that the crisis of neoliberalism has engendered."[34] The implementation of these policies was experienced by Warlpiri in the form of slow-moving misery rather than dramatic event, but also, unmistakably, as an outright attack on the slender vestiges of power they tenuously held over their own affairs.[35] Most keenly felt by community leaders and political activists was the decisive removal from the town of any structure through which they could exercise authority over the matters that most concerned them.[36] Moreover, every aspect of Warlpiri lives was now subject to government and police scrutiny.

As I watched The Troubles unfold in tandem with the implementation of this militarized, world-changing shift in governance, one possible interpretation of Warlpiri agency emerged as compelling. At a time when authority was comprehensively being taken from them, The Troubles appeared as a vigorous effort by Warlpiri to hold on to the one kind of power that arguably remains theirs: the power to tell stories, to constitute the order of things in their own narrative terms. The Troubles disrupt the dominant governmental representation of Aboriginal "dysfunction" and supplant a Warlpiri understanding of the workings of power and world (dis)order. At times, the forces that appear to swarm and congeal in The Troubles assume a magnetism and shadowy terror similar to the allegorical black caiman that stalks Lucas Bessire's stirring navigation of end-of-world violence in the Chaco, with its composite image of Indigenous "senses of being in the world, ongoing destruction, and the re-animated legacies of colonial and ethnographic projects of all kinds."[37] If The Troubles constitute not simply a series of incursions and counterincursions but also the kind of storytelling that Michael Taussig writes of, where stories themselves constitute "the ether" in which violence operates, this storytelling occurs as a complex series of movements.[38] There is the story that circulates, the story told to the anthropologist, the story the anthropologist apprehends, and the story the anthropologist herself presents.

In the wake of the violent retribution unleashed by The Troubles, in late 2010, one hundred members of Nungarrayi's extended family fled two thousand kilometers (more than one thousand miles) to the South Australian capital of Adelaide. Their decision to leave was made after police intervened in the families' attempts to resolve the dispute locally, via customary punishment. It is telling that they felt they needed to go so far to reach a place of relative sanctuary. Ironically, on arrival in Adelaide the "refugees" were initially provided accommodations and sustenance by the local police academy. Leaving these orderly premises, a large number of people moved to the parklands on the edge of the city in an area frequented by itinerant Aboriginal drinkers, where they set up tents and camped for three weeks. By all accounts a great time was had by all, but the very public ways in which these Warlpiri live stirred the anxieties of local residents and precipitated the group's eventual repatriation to Central Australia the following March, in two buses funded by the Northern Territory government.[39] Nungarrayi returned home to face the customary punishment that awaited her as mother of a man implicated in the death of another man. This "payback" was finally carried out—a remarkable feat given that the practice of such customary authority had been outlawed by the new federal legislation. According to Warlpiri edicts, this should have been the end of the matter. But it wasn't. Four years later Nungarrayi tells me she feels like she has been sung, that she has been the subject of a sorcery attack. When she sets foot on the land of the town in which she was born and lived most of her life, *it pushes her back*.

Nungarrayi's banishment from her hometown could, from one angle, be explained as an outcome of protracted feuding between two extended families with primitivist commitments to arcane sorcery beliefs. "Rioters Seek Enemies' Exile," screamed the headline on the front page of Australia's only national newspaper, the Murdoch-owned *Australian*, on September 28, 2010. Attention to the feud and separately to "the Intervention" brings certain features into view but not others. As I draft this book, the twinned governmental forces of welfare and policing/incarceration bear down upon Aboriginal people in the

Northern Territory with exceptional punishing reach.[40] Premature deaths as a result of accident, chronic illness, and suicide generate pervasive grief and transform weekends into a relentless schedule of funeral attendance.[41] It is chillingly common for middle-aged friends to have lost siblings, children, and grandchildren as a result of premature death. Chronic health conditions such as diabetes, heart disease, acute rheumatic fever (eradicated decades ago for the wider Australian population), and obesity are widespread. The shrinkage of spaces in which Aboriginal authority can be meaningfully enacted constrains any future focused work of the imagination. Governments, meanwhile, proliferate all manner of inquiries, royal commissions, "Closing the Gap" targets, and interventions that entrench rather than shift these circumstances. Yet, on the ground, despite the constant presence of grief and trauma, and below the radar of statistical measurement, life is lived vigorously, with humor. Remarkably, as Achille Mbembe observes, "something in the principle of life defies all ideas of the end."[42]

In mid-2016, when Nungarrayi and I reunite in Adelaide, she is not only grieving the lost possibilities of her earlier life in Central Australia and much consumed by concern for the welfare of her beloved son who was incarcerated in Darwin prison. She is also rejoicing in her survival and in a new life she is making with Ram, a Bhutanese man who has been in Australia for just two years following the Australian government's acceptance of his family's application for asylum. The two met at the house of one of Nungarrayi's cousins, a place where diverse marginalized people come together to find company, to score and smoke marijuana. Ram is twenty years younger than Nungarrayi, the same age as her son. As she describes it to me, with a sparkle in her eye, he pursued a relationship with her with some determination. For a year they have lived together in the modest transitional housing provided to Nungarrayi after she accessed the South Australian government program in support of survivors of domestic assault.

Friendship on the Move

Displacement not only fractures a person's assured relationship to place. Relatedly, displaced persons confront unprecedented pressure on the social relations through which they know places. Under these conditions it is not surprising that friendship emerges as promise as well as problematic. Philosopher Hans-Georg Gadamer, reading Aristotle, provides a fleeting, intriguing sense of the resonances between friendship and at-homeness that bears directly upon the concerns of this book. True, complete friendship, Aristotle argues, turns upon self-love: the state of effectively being a friend for oneself is the condition for all possible bonds with others. Friendship is closely linked with ideas of home and homeland. It derives from the ancient Greek term *oikeion*, variously defined in relation to ideas of affinity, familiarity, and endearment. The implication is that friendship involves a special state of connectedness, a taken-for-granted solidarity, genuine at-homeness.[43] Situations of displacement present an urgent existential need for genuine friendship, for relationships that foster and support a sense of being at home, enduring but flexible relationships, familiar anchor points in the midst of dislocation.

So, what then of cross-cultural friendship? What additional challenges of empathy and understanding are encountered by persons who pursue friendships across differences of language and ethnicity, place-based orientations, and social inequality? Zooming out, does friendship offer a potential ideal for relations at a distance, for transformative relations between stranger-citizens, passersby, at the level of neighborhoods, regions, and nations? Such questions are commonly posed in migration studies, and they become pressing as Nungarrayi and I travel around together and encounter others. Her shifts in demeanor reveal a great deal about the racialized expectations and presumptions that mark the ground of dislocated existence in contemporary Australia. I have become alert to the stark change in mood that often occurs as we leave the easy, open space of walking the streets together and climb into the back seat of a taxi, especially one driven by an Indian man. How, by what means, and in whose company we journey matters.

Axel Honneth, pressing further with Gadamer's ideas, observes that authentic friendship breaks down at a distance where the thinned-out attitude of respect (or disrespect) is the starting point of engagement between self and other.[44] In Honneth's reading, respect—whether in positive or negative modes—is a reflective attitude, a deficient form of intersubjectivity that requires no genuine engagement with or openness to a response from the other. Honneth, by way of social psychologist George Herbert Mead, reminds us that every person is dependent on the possibility of constant reassurance by the other. The experience of disrespect is a direct affront to expectations of such reassurance. Ultimately, the experience of disrespect "poses *the risk of an injury that can cause the identity of the entire person to collapse.*"[45]

The specter of this risk hangs over the journeying that unfolds in this book, as Nungarrayi navigates her precarious situation: banished from her hometown, not fully accepted in her new place of residence. Undertaking research for this book, Nungarrayi and I travel together in and between all manner of places and social assemblies. As we do, her vigorous wrestling between the terms and associations of the city and the desert comes into view, as do creative conjunctions she makes between the experience of dislocation and new placemaking practices, along with situations that trigger her differently geared and emergent subject positions. Getting stuck is as much a feature of these circumstances as is mobility itself. Free physical movement and rapid-paced mediated communication coexist with the containment, misery, and slow grind of poverty and oppressive governmental oversight. Myriad factors intervene in the pace of life. The larger framing of this project in terms of our journeying together foregrounds the two and a half decades in which Nungarrayi and I have known each other, and relatedly the shifts in governance, public attitudes, Warlpiri circumstances, and anthropological theory that have unfolded across that period. Our movement at times stimulates a dynamic back-and-forth engagement between the immediacy of a situation and older associations. Memory and nostalgia are often at work in our conversations. Journeying in this way is not a seamless flow of mobility, of immanence, but rather an uneven, volatile, and at times discordant mix of relational, temporal, and spatial elements. The conjunctions here resonate with dynamics Henrik Vigh describes as "motion squared," when he observes interactions on the streets of Bissau, Guinea, between marginalized men who are themselves undergoing transformation, in places marked by volatility, insecurity, and uncertainty.[46] Attention to moments of stasis and rupture, to a change of pace, provides a glimpse of what is at stake in distinctively ordered relationships between people and places at a time when such relationships are everywhere under unprecedented pressure.

Becoming, from Where?

The affective call of the desert and the relationships it indexes register strongly in the pages that follow. It thus strikes me as paradoxical that at a time when displacement is identified as a generalized human condition, and a matter of urgent concern for social movements and research, there is a corresponding waning of interest in difference. In much recent anthropology, place-based alterity is commonly a casualty of cultural critique, dismissed as the product of colonial imaginaries, more recent forms of governmental domination, or totalizing social theory. In one influential project that wholeheartedly embraces a Deleuzian orientation to "becoming," João Biehl and Peter Locke put forward a schema for contemporary ethnography that destabilizes the "primacy of being" and privileges the terms of open-ended movement, emergence, and immanence.[47] Biehl and Locke's analysis attributes a normative status to mobile, future-focused, flexible subjectivities, against what are identified as coercive nativist imaginaries of unchanging difference. Such a line of argument has broad appeal in the present. Against the brutality of border protection regimes, passionate arguments are made in support of the hypermobile and future-focused migrant.[48] Yet, such a bifurcation of becoming from alterity has the effect of closing down attention to the distinctive place-based practices and orientations that are invariably a target of state interventions, and that displaced persons themselves actively draw upon as they push back against the terms of dislocation.[49]

Across the history of settler colonial Australia, as elsewhere, primitivist categories and imaginaries of fixed and reified Aboriginality have played and continue to play a crucial role in channeling logics for governance of, and public attitudes to, Aboriginal people.[50] Disentangling the recursive politics of Indigenous recognition and representation—the space where the terms of Indigeneity as well as self-recognition are produced and reproduced—is a complex exercise. A thread running through this book attempts to tease apart fetishized deployments of Aboriginality from the place-based practices that structure and sustain shared orientations between persons, their environments, and the world at large. The imperative to follow this line of inquiry does not derive from a romantic proclivity for keeping people fixed in time and place, but rather from observing Warlpiri friends formulate creative responses to the challenges they face. Strategic Warlpiri campaigns, whether personal or collective, inevitably seem to involve drawing concepts and practices from older social formations. Any Warlpiri politics of becoming turns upon the ability to reenact symbolic forms that are authorized as "proper," masterfully reproduced, or deliberately refashioned for new circumstances.

The recursive nature of this process calls to mind the dynamic structure of the self described by Mead. Mead figures the relationship between the "I" and the "me" that a person ceaselessly cycles through in the give-and-take of social interchange. A self, Mead eloquently writes, is "an eddy in the social current," actively engaged in registering and internalizing attitudes of specific and generalized others, taking on those ideas as one's own.[51] Social integration proceeds through this internal "conversation of gestures," the "me" absorbing social convention, a process that makes a coherent and organized self possible, just as the "I" calls out one's individualized distinction and the pursuit of innovative conduct. In this approach, "becoming" can only proceed through conscious awareness of where and what one has been. Mead's "conversation of gestures" offers an especially apt metaphor for Nungarrayi's negotiation of the subjective possibilities that emerge in her new life in Adelaide, as well as the conversations I have with myself from time to time, as I wonder out loud on the page about the baggage and blinkers that attend to my observations.

Nungarrayi's exile and the possibilities and challenges it entails are distinguished from the forced displacement of her grandparents and great-grandparents in the 1940s and 1950s in several ways. To be *displaced*, in the sense of being physically distant from a particular place or social assembly, no longer straightforwardly involves separation and certainly not isolation. Mobile phones, many times lost and replaced, enable Nungarrayi's exilic existence, sustaining spontaneous and intense interactions with kin, and especially daily conversations with her son during his lengthy periods of incarceration. The methods and means of communication afforded by mobile phones differ markedly from the dense bodily engaged sociality that is a requirement of human intimacy and vital to desert modes of interaction. In this sense, the widespread take-up of mobile phones and related social media by those who live in the desert might be identified as an uncanny generalized displacement, including of people from the physical environments they continue to inhabit.[52] If this is the case, elements of Nungarrayi's exile are closely shadowed by the transforming lives of her kin who stay at home. In one scene that conjures some of these distinctively contemporary cleavages of people from place, in early 2011, I visited the Big Town during an intense flare-up of The Troubles and was concerned for the well-being of a friend who was mourning the death of his father and worrying over the recent imprisonment of his son. I found him on more than one occasion in the back room of the community arts center, huddled over a computer monitor and peering hard at a Google Map image, trying to locate the place deep in the desert where his father was born.

While fiber-optic cable and digital communication provide the vital means by which Nungarrayi continues to participate in the sociality from which she is physically separated, the governance of Warlpiri lives in the present increasingly occurs via the networked databases and case files of government departments and CCTV footage. The same digital networks that Warlpiri enthusiastically plug into as mechanisms for keeping in contact with their hypermobile relatives and for entertainment are also conduits of their own surveillance. Digital circuits disgorge other kinds of information, including disparaging images of Warlpiri that circulate in the wider world. Mobile phones and social media apps are vehicles of jealous fights and sorcery accusations; they are mechanisms of profound agitation that reconstitute sensory and temporal orders of people-place relationships.[53]

The Cultural Politics of Writing Close to Life

I have written this book at a time when the politics of storytelling about Aboriginal life at large and Central Australian Aboriginal life in particular has become highly charged and newly divisive. There are many fault lines to these politics. A small number of Aboriginal voices, two of those belonging to Warlpiri women, mother and daughter, have the ear of national media and government. The stories told by these women support a vision for a radical transformation of desert life. Their voices are lauded in the public domain but create distress and anger among some of their own kin.[54] The two-decade arc of my friendship with Nungarrayi shadows the systematic disbandment of Aboriginal representational politics. Under the circumstances, there is a fresh onus on those of us who trade in forms of storytelling to give careful consideration to the narrative forms we adopt. In one innovative recent contribution, acclaimed Waanyi essayist and novelist Alexis Wright created a tribute to her close friend and comrade in arms, the late Bruce "Tracker" Tilmouth, a former director of Central Australian Aboriginal people's regional organization, the Central Land Council, by marshaling and assembling the voices of those who had worked alongside him.[55] In *Tracker*, Wright mobilizes a new cultural politics of storytelling, one that enacts an ethos of Aboriginal sociality, where everyone gets a voice, everyone speaks for themselves. Wright's collective memoir is diametrically opposed to a form of storytelling she identifies elsewhere as "the national narrative."[56]

By extension, Wright's approach is also opposed to the classical style of ethnographic writing that assumes all voice, all authority for the anthropologist as master author/authority. In the 1980s, when postmodernism made a strong claim on anthropology, dialogic ethnographies performed one kind of compelling response to postcolonial critique.[57] Yet to decenter the presumed authority of the anthropologist and the structured inequalities between those of us who write and those whose lives are written about is a challenge that continues to trouble and ultimately elude most cultural writing. One remarkable recent exception is the jewellike production *Phone and Spear: A Yuta Anthropology* by cross-cultural creators Miyarrka Media, which proposes the relationship-making possibilities of a revitalized anthropology.[58] In the terms of one influential Indigenous critique, decolonization is not a metaphor.[59] Eve Tuck and K. Wayne Yang's critical manifesto proposes what they call an ethic of incommensurability, a mode of Indigenous/non-Indigenous solidarity that is and always will be uneasy, unsettled, unresolved. These terms resonate strongly with one end of the plane of my friendship with Nungarrayi, but they entirely miss the other end, the space where transformative interactions, responsibility, mutuality, love, and care enfold. Nevertheless, I have no wish to conjure this research venture in the terms of "collaboration." The prism of friendship insists upon a particular kind of relational vantage, but it does not dissolve the dilemmas of anthropology and its publishing forms. Ultimately, this book is an account told, with Nungarrayi's consent, through my eyes and words.

Journeying involves distinctive conjunctions of time and space. For Nungarrayi and me, our journeying is anchored in the present and charged by the challenges, tragedies, and hopes that swirl around her and sometimes catch me in their net, as well as the interpersonal encounters and knotty conundrums of Indigenous affairs policy and larger governmental processes that come to register in our midst. Journeying assumes a distinctive pace: the starts, stops, and forces of emotion and attitude that cause people to dawdle, cruise, or barrel along, whether on foot, or traveling in a car, on a bus or train, or by taxi. Journeying is punctuated by changes in pace, sparks of memory, shifts in emotional register, stark switches in mood. The journeying Nungarrayi and I have undertaken between 2016 and 2019 is shadowed by the longer tail of the time of our friendship, and especially the two years 1995 and 1996 when I lived in her hometown. We traveled together then, too, but our journeying then seemed much more contained and straightforward. Then, there was no question of where home was.

The ambiguous social distance between the lives of anthropologists and the lives of the people with whom we work is foundational for the discipline. Distance is a vital prerequisite for grappling with flows of experience and observation and for making something cogent of strands of life that attract our attention. But in its reflexive posture, the anthropological enterprise also creates a special kind of relational zone that can be mutually transformative. In the process of journeying around together doing research for this book, I have often been reminded of the particular social space Nungarrayi and I create when we come together. Traveling with Nungarrayi, I am drawn into all manner of densely social situations, immersed in the intensity of Warlpiri ways of noticing things, responding to circumstances, living with others. With her, I am exposed to a style of life that evades conventional expectations in ways that are at once exhilarating and distressing. Warlpiri live with a spontaneity and fervor that is starkly at odds with the relatively ordered, planned, law-abiding, and routinized style of the Anglo-Australian middle class. Traveling with me, she in turn is exposed to radically different attitudes and experiences to those she often encounters and indeed expects to encounter on her own or traveling with her own kin. In the respectable terms of white metropolitan sociality, she is treated politely. Traveling with me, she enters places, spends money, and consumes in ways that she would never do if she were not in my company and supported by my income. The structured inequalities between us—my relative economic wealth, her poverty—intervene decisively at times, mirroring larger social forces at play, threatening to reduce our friendship to a thinned-out conduit of financial transaction. For each of us these terms can shift instantly, in a misplaced interaction with others, in a frustrated refusal to meet a demand, in circumstances of great stress, in the moment we part company.

The confidence and pride with which Nungarrayi carried herself, directed our work, and engaged with all manner of people as we traveled together around Alice Springs one afternoon in October 2016 were dramatically recast later that same evening. She and her extended daughter came to meet me at a community concert and were turned away by a security guard who judged them as being inebriated and thus potential public nuisances. Such thresholds of intercultural encounter are spaces where desert people routinely confront sedimented expectations of their unruliness. These racialized exclusions constitute volatile flash points where anything can happen. They expose the conditional nature of Warlpiri citizenship as well as vulnerabilities of our friendship. *See How We Roll* follows Nungarrayi's—and my—precarious navigation of these conditions.

1

Journeying
With

Unsettling Relations

We had spoken on the phone only intermittently over the past four years. Nungarrayi lost mobile phones frequently, so although she always seemed to be able to locate my number whenever she wanted to make contact, my ability to contact her was constrained by circumstance and contingency. Her two adult daughters, mothers themselves, were much more adept at holding on to their phones, so between these women and several kin who frequented Facebook, I did have ways of tracking her down. My impression at a distance, supplemented by snippets of gossip from Warlpiri friends, was that her life had gone off the rails since she had left Central Australia.

When we first became friends in 1995, Nungarrayi was a committed non-drinker. She was a proud and doting mother of two young children, a regular churchgoer, and an accomplished translator who had been employed at the local school for several years. She was a woman born into families of considerable authority and carried herself with dignity and pride: a leader in the making. We met in Warlpiri language classes. At the end of the intensive course she promised to teach me more, but in the weeks that followed, our cursory attempts at structuring one-on-one tuition gave way to a looser and more intensively engaged friendship. Her English was too sophisticated to lead our dialogue in the direction of language lessons. I was a slow learner. There were more pressing matters to talk about and explore. We were the same age and became firm friends. We hung out at each other's houses, attended football matches and discos, and traveled together to Alice Springs. I became part of an extended network of carers for her children, although she rarely spent time away from them. We danced together ritually at the ceremony where her son went through the first stage of initiation into manhood. In the years after my doctoral fieldwork, I saw her on infrequent return visits. The last time we were together was during a short visit I made with my family to the Big Town in mid-2009. Following a period of sporadic movement between the town and Alice Springs, she had left her long-standing job at the school and was employed by a government department to monitor the welfare of "at-risk" children.

Her husband, Daniel, who was also a close friend of mine and alongside whom I had worked at the local media association, was now employed in the newly created position of community translator. In this high-profile role, he was charged with mediating between government service providers and the town's residents in the intense period of new program implementation that followed the Northern Territory Emergency Response.[1] In short, both Nungarrayi and her husband were occupied in frontline government employment at a time of considerable destabilization for their community.

Daniel, like many of his male kin, had always struggled with alcohol. Nungarrayi bore the brunt of his infrequent grog-fueled incidents of fury and distress. But something must have ruptured the night in 2009 when he let rip and nearly killed her. When she rang me from an Adelaide hospital to tell me about the attack, about the nature of her life-threatening injuries, and about surgery she had undergone to have a plate implanted in her skull, I was dumbfounded. Over time that sentiment shifted to quiet, burning anger. I decided I could never speak to Daniel again. But when Nungarrayi and I visited Alice Springs together seven years after the attack, it was she who encouraged me to go and visit him in jail. Daniel was now on remand awaiting trial on charges of domestic assault laid against him by a new partner. Nungarrayi, along with his sisters and other close female kin, blamed the woman who "put him in jail." Sitting with him at a metal table in the visitor's room of the prison one day in October 2016, I try, without success, to get Daniel to talk about why it is that he and so many of his male kin are getting stuck in cycles of incarceration for violent assaults of women they purportedly love. Why the descent from responsible community-based work to the ravages of town camp drinking circles? His deflection of my questions and long silences between us made it clear this line of conversation would go nowhere.

Anthropologists have long struggled with the challenge of how to best do justice on the page to the circumstances we observe and to the lives of the people with whom we form close relationships. *See How We Roll* approaches writing as a mediation of relationships and shifting circumstances through time. The challenges of ethnographic writing most often emerge in debates about large-scale social transformation and the efficacy or otherwise of particular theoretical and methodological approaches. In an influential essay published in 1991, Lila Abu-Lughod urges anthropologists to write "against culture" and, in so doing, pursue a new "tactical humanism."[2] She argues that "culture" has become a concept for the enforcement of difference and hierarchy rather than a prism to enable the exploration of relatedness.[3] The challenge for anthropologists, in reasserting the discipline's humanist foundations, is to write "close to life." The present book is at one level an experiment in writing close to life at a time of "dissolving assurances," dispersed uncertainties, and volatile identity politics.[4] Anthropologists confront such uncertainties everywhere they work in the present. In Australia, vigorously contested debates indicate that the practice of anthropology in the field of Aboriginal Australia particularly—its authority, truth claims, and appeals to public relevance—has been newly destabilized.[5] The two-and-a-half-decade period that frames the time of this book provides a distinctive vantage on these shifting conditions as well as a related emergent zeitgeist.

This chapter lays some foundations for those that follow. It introduces an analytic frame of *journeying with*, a perspective anchored in an individual person's life, and one that keeps constantly in mind the relationships through which she navigates unfolding circumstances, including the relationship that enables this story to be told: the friendship between the two of us. *Journeying with* provides a prism through which to glimpse myriad social forces and creative responses that cycle through and congeal in the life that Nungarrayi lives. It is a space of contingent mutuality for grappling with destabilizations as well as stabilities. Simultaneously, this prism will be brought to bear upon the circumstances of Nungarrayi's life, the transforming world of desert people, changes in anthropological knowledge production, and our long-standing research-mediated friendship.

Beware the Obituary Mode

My adoption of a single-person focus as a means to explore transformations at large is variously influenced by earlier experiments with the form. Six decades ago, Australian anthropologist W. E. H. Stanner published "Durmugam: A Ngangiomeri," an essay that has since been much celebrated for its combination of deep humanistic understanding with fine-grained attention to world-changing social transformation, while paying homage to a formative research relationship.[6] Stimulated by Joseph Casagrande's invitation to contribute an essay to a book celebrating anthropological friendships, Stanner, who had been a journalist before he become a student of Alfred Radcliffe-Brown, found a new writerly mode in which to figure his deep appreciation of Aboriginal culture, his observations of the perceptiveness and frailty of actual Aboriginal persons, and the fracturing of social organization.[7] Stanner took up biography for an open-ended exploration of the human condition, a kind of writing that was not easily pursued from within the frame of 1930s structural functionalism in which he had been schooled. Yet, for all this, Stanner's "Durmugam" is not without limitations. In his critical appreciation of the essay, Jeremy Beckett draws attention to Stanner's narration of a naturalized arc of decline: "Having Durmugam in his prime, with his superb physique and commanding stature, embodying a still vital Aboriginal way, prepares the reader for the inevitable decline of both; as the body becomes infirm, so too does the Aboriginal way . . . here we are to understand the man and the social order going down together before a misguided policy."[8]

"Beware the obituary mode," Beckett perceptively alerts anthropologists who venture near biography.[9] However, we can immediately note that the arc of decline is more than a pitfall of biographical writing; it pervades the history of anthropology's engagement with Aboriginal Australia more broadly. Daisy Bates's *Passing of the Aborigines* surmised that the role of benevolent government policy was to "smooth the pillow of a dying race."[10] T. G. H. Strehlow left a remarkable legacy in his monumental transcription of Arrernte song and ceremony, but late in life controversially anointed himself as the last holder of Arrernte high culture.[11] More broadly, the "before it's too late" assimilation era mantra shaped decades of salvage anthropological fieldwork, as well as the establishment of the Australian Institute of Aboriginal Studies in 1961.[12] And most recently Peter Sutton proposed that a "liberal consensus" entangled anthropologists and politicians alike in a distinctive "politics of suffering."[13]

Beckett's warning also presents a quandary for those of us who work closely with Aboriginal people in the present, confronted as we are with the distress and misery of frequent premature deaths, chronic illness, hunger, economic stress, incarceration, and existential crisis. In short, students of the post–"crisis of representation" turn that gave rise to Abu-Lughod's proclamation that we should "write against culture," are very much alive to the obituary mode as reductive anthropological trope.[14] But we are also aware of life in Aboriginal communities being, as Ute Eickelkamp puts it, "under siege."[15] How, in such circumstances, can anthropological writing transcend the debates in which it has been embroiled, debates that would reduce our work to contributing to one or another policy-making trajectory?

Biographical and autobiographical modes have been adopted by anthropologists with varied intentions and effects across the discipline's history. Life writing most broadly appeals to writers who are keen to transcend the abstraction of conceptual models that foreground social institutions and higher-scale units of analysis. One genre of the biographical idiom emerged as anthropologists were moved to write creative companion volumes to their formal ethnographies, dissatisfied as they were with conventional formats of scholarly writing that effectively disappeared the flesh and blood, complex emotions, and uncertainties of their fieldwork experiences.[16] In this context, Vincent Crapanzano alerts us to a second pitfall—that of sentimentality—as well as to a certain tendency to apply a naive empiricism to the biographical endeavor rather than to approach it as the critical, distinctively located outcome of "the interplay between demand and desire" of anthropologist and informant/interlocutor.[17]

On either side of the 1980s "crisis of representation" and the new interpretivist attention to writing, anthropologists experimented with modeling dialogical engagement, individual creativity, autobiography, and life writing as social history.[18] Just as anthropologists turned to history to inflect their ethnographic accounts with an enlarged sense of transformation and political economy, life writing became alluring for its inevitable considerations of human agency, individual aspiration, intention, and affect. In this sense, ethnographic life writing inevitably speaks, consciously or otherwise, to prevalent themes and pressing concerns of the times in which it is written.[19]

Experiments with life writing have occurred more or less on the margins of the discipline. In observing this, Nigel Rapport criticizes anthropology's commitment to "impersonalisation" as a particular kind of scholarly strategy: "a rhetoric, an instrument to denaturalise the world" deeply rooted in social scientific method.[20] Rapport points out that personal relations are the ground from which any larger social formations and objectifications are produced.[21]

He argues that anthropologists should give greater attention to the practices through which individuals, as boundary riders and bricoleur interpreters, interpret themselves and their own societies.[22] Notably, Rapport's critique is mounted as an appeal for appreciation of the universal figure of the individual, not an anthropology of the contemporary. He seems not at all interested in the interplay between an anthropologist's strategic focus on individual persons or subjectivity and the formulation of social analysis or critique. Abu-Lughod's work, by contrast, is a methodological outcome of her critique of reified models of cultural difference and their tendency toward homogeneity, coherence, and timelessness.[23] Taking up Pierre Bourdieu's critique of structuralism, she argues powerfully for anthropologists to grasp social processes at the level of their lived reality, via close attention to particular situations and particular women's lives. Further, Abu-Lughod's biographical frame works across different scales of civic association, from kinship, to community, to region, and nation. She draws attention to transformations as well as qualitative differences in social relationship and subjectivity, and the identities and identifications they call out. She presents rapport with actual persons as the ground of ethnography, and biography or life story as the method for building narratives that interleave what she describes as the "contrasting cosmopolitanisms" of differently socially located women.[24]

More recent single-person-focused writing tends to enact a shift in the figuring of subjectivity, such as in João Biehl's celebrated *Vita: Life in a Zone of Social Abandonment*, which examines practices and processes governing the mentally ill in contemporary Brazil.[25] Through his discussions with one woman, Caterina, and his reading of the remarkable dictionaries she keeps, Biehl explores the "complex network of family, medicine, state, and economy in which her abandonment and pathology took place."[26] Through the specificity of Caterina's situation, he elucidates a contemporary cultural attitude toward dealing with those who have been assessed as unable to care for themselves. Biehl was drawn to a single-person-focused approach as he grappled with the problem of how to restore context and meaning to the lived experience of abandonment. How is one to produce a theory of the abandoned subject and her subjectivity that is ethnographically grounded?[27] Vitally, Biehl observed that

ethnography makes visible the intermingling of colloquial practices and relations, institutional histories, and discursive structures that—in categories of madness, pharmaceuticals, migrant households, and disintegrating services—have bounded normalcy and displaced Caterina on the register of social death, where her condition appears to have been "self-generated." . . . From the perspective of Vita and from the perspective of one human life deemed mad and intractable, one comes to understand how economic globalization, state and medical reform, and the acceleration of claims to human rights and citizenship coincide with and impinge on a local production of social death.[28]

Biehl's project builds upon the body of work by Veena Das, Arthur Kleinman, and colleagues, to read social suffering—the brutalities born out of large-scale forces—through the intimate lens of personal experience.[29] In both Abu-Lughod's and Biehl's projects, a focus on single persons opens out to a consideration of wider webs of relationships and social processes through which individuals negotiate life's constraints and possibilities. However, there is an important distinction to be made between these works. Where Abu-Lughod is concerned to give shape and form to diversely situated individual lives, Biehl more explicitly pursues the kind of opening out that I wish to pursue, where the biographical mode is transcended by an overt concern to understand large-scale processes that can be glimpsed in terms of their human consequences through a focus on a single person. The key difference here is in fact a paradigmatic one. Where Abu-Lughod flags attention to discursive power as one avenue for "writing close to life," two decades later Biehl deploys the interpretive frame of biopower to reveal the intimate workings of myriad techniques for subjugating bodies and minds. If Abu-Lughod's life writing is methodologically geared toward the coming into being of the nation-state through the vantage of differently socially and geographically located women, Biehl's project makes visible a subjectivity that is cultivated bodily, through the intimate play between state governance of mental illness, constraints of familial care, and transnational biomedical regimes.

Suffering in an Expanded Field

My project with Nungarrayi is influenced by these recent experiments and also coincides with renewed interest in life writing, following a reinvigorated humanitarian impulse in public politics. In Australia, the federal government's declaration of a "national emergency" in respect of Aboriginal child abuse in the Northern Territory followed a year of alarming public reportage and commentary that suggested child sexual abuse, pedophile rings, and domestic violence were rife in "remote" Aboriginal communities.[30] In the debates that swirled around these allegations, the rights of the individual child were often starkly pitted against the rights of cultural difference. Australian anthropologist Peter

Sutton had made a dramatic intervention in these debates in 2001, with a presentation to the annual society conference of a paper titled "The Politics of Suffering," in which he offered a vivid account of brutal domestic violence in the communities in which he worked and accused colleagues of having been complicit in shielding from view the desperate conditions of Aboriginal people's lives.[31] Sutton's intervention in Australian politics coincided with but largely ignored a wider transnational turn in anthropology in which the ethnography produced by Biehl is also situated, a shift identified by Joel Robbins as a turning away from "the other," from "the cultural point" to "the suffering other," to the universal space of humanity, or more succinctly, "from the savage to the suffering slot."[32] Didier Fassin provides a wider vantage on a new moral economy centering on humanitarian reason that came into being toward the end of the twentieth century.[33] At stake in this transformation are the very terms by which domination is conceived and located; "inequality is replaced by exclusion, domination is transformed into misfortune, injustice is articulated as suffering, violence is expressed in terms of trauma."[34]

The rise of humanitarianism followed the critiques of cultural studies that had mired the study of difference in colonial practice and ways of seeing. Distanced observation was being transposed with empathy and human feeling. With the appeal to anthropologists to produce lucid, intimate accounts of personal trauma rather than coolly observed descriptions of social organization, with certainty and solidity of analysis giving way to flux, the anthropological project shifts to a new kind of human ground. Suffering takes on a newly dispersed life of its own. Politically engaged ethnographers are compelled to produce work that aims to move the reader to act, urgently, just as visual scholars have observed the circulation of images of distant suffering subjects similarly operates.[35] A generalized closeness to suffering, through social proximity as well as mediated exposure, leads Fassin to describe it as contagious and as a distinctive language of the present that refigures our vision of the world.[36] Yet it is also a hallmark of immersive accounts to eschew systematic attention to the processes by which suffering, in either specific, embodied, or broader, processual terms, is produced.

I completed my doctoral thesis on the cusp of this paradigm shift, but the writing I produced contains little evidence of any wrestling with such issues. My doctoral project was framed very much at the level of "community," with a focus on new Warlpiri media organizations as sites of creative production and tension. Individuals were not visible and certainly not named. My primary concern was to make sense of the fraught politics of Aboriginal self-determination and the perpetual deferral of its arrival in tangible form—a framing that with the benefit of hindsight might be criticized as being unreflexively entangled with the very conditions of governmental production of that period. "Community" was the primary unit for the governance of self-determination, just as the individual is the central focus of the neoliberal regime that replaced it. How was this shift introduced locally? I can still vividly recall scenes captured on video by Warlpiri media workers of a large meeting held in 1996, where a visiting senior bureaucrat aggressively delivered the news to local residents that the federal government was bringing to an end the unconditional payment of unemployment benefits, known locally as "sit down money." People would henceforth have to *work* for their welfare payments and would suffer the consequences if they refused. The video is a remarkable artifact; the bureaucrat's hostile style of presentation strikingly conveys the change in government attitude from nanny to daddy state, a transformation in the personality of governance, from relation that Warlpiri called upon to look after them, to hard master they now expect to be tricky and cruel.[37]

Before this shift came to pass, every second Thursday residents would assemble on the lawns outside the post office, waiting patiently for the delivery of their welfare checks. Such a congregation, which would grow slowly over several hours, was from time to time spontaneously mobilized for a "community meeting" to address whatever antagonisms were reverberating through the body politic. Soon after the implementation of the federal government's "emergency response" legislation in 2007, new processes were introduced for governing the unemployed. A new, large building was erected on the edge of the old town square, a new office for Centrelink, the agency whose expanded staff were tasked with more actively administering the unemployed and disabled individuals, as well as those receiving child, family, or other government support payments—most of the town's Aboriginal residents. Henceforth, the organic public gatherings ceased to occur. As the federal government ratcheted up its punitive approach, new cruel punishments were introduced for those who "breached" the requirements of their Job Active, or Remote Jobs and Community Program, or Community Development Program: a loss of payments for up to eight weeks. In time, further breaches were introduced, with parents and guardians whose children failed to attend school or "improvement programs" punished with suspended payments.

Navigating the terms of one's own governance under the arrangements of the security state is extremely stressful and time-consuming. The pressures on primary carers to meet the basic needs of feeding and clothing those in their care are intense. The cost of food in remote community stores is commonly 50 percent higher than in metropolitan supermarkets, while the base rate of unemployment payments has not increased since 1994.[38] People commonly run out of money before the end of a fortnightly payment cycle and struggle to feed their families and keep metered power running to their houses. Compounding these mundane stresses of economic poverty is what might be described as the remote political economy of premature death. Premature deaths occur at a staggering rate in desert communities, devastating families and reordering households. They also create untold financial stress. When a close friend's oldest son died suddenly in early 2019, he was her second child to die before the age of forty. Both children had died of cardiac arrest. Her son died in a frontier town outside the Northern Territory. His mother faced the impossible challenge of raising more than $10,000 to have his body released from the morgue and flown home—a preposterous proposition for a woman who struggles to get by week to week with barely enough money to feed the five grandchildren now in her permanent care.

When Robbins appeals to an "anthropology of the good," he directs our attention away from such grueling miseries to questions of what better ways of life might look like from the distinctive vantages of people living those lives.[39] Robbins reveals the hegemonic work performed by the suffering trope, yet his move in respect of "the good" can be read as simply enlisting an optimistic trope in place of a pessimistic one. In the process, he lightly oversteps entrenched structural orders that demand analysis. If anthropology is a medium of inspired cross-cultural storytelling, then there is logic to Robbins's argument. But if we want our work to intervene in the politics of the present, it needs to be more than that.

In the decade since publication of Sutton's *The Politics of Suffering*, the deployment of the suffering trope *has* taken on a dispersed life of its own. I find myself seeing suffering—chronic ill-health, the deep grief associated with premature deaths, hunger, economic hardship, and varying degrees of physical and existential brokenness—everywhere among Warlpiri friends. By contrast, it would not have been possible to imagine Nungarrayi's dislocation two decades ago. The kin-based, wider social and institutional relations that held her in place were relatively robust: a close-knit family unit, albeit troubled by her partner's sporadic bouts of drinking, nested within extended relations of care; a generation of elders who exercised firm authority through provision of guidance to younger kin and in ceremonial and community-based practice and politics; a community sector that called out the leadership of middle-aged biculturalists; and a public sphere centered on the "community meeting," through which issues that advanced to the status of "problem" were vigorously dealt with.

I ask myself: Is nostalgia at work in the way I conjure this long since past set of arrangements? It is a topic of discussion between Nungarrayi and me. We

FIGURE 1.1 Talking story, northwest Adelaide, June 2016 (photo by author)

both look back with considerable longing to the 1990s, as a space where various forms of order and optimistic possibility were tangibly present. Is this gloss an inevitable outcome of the mind's "settling" of past times? My anthropological memory is drawn to the certainty of recognizable arrangements, categories, and analyses I worked with, when emerging from fieldwork as a doctoral student. Certain persons who loomed large in orienting me to that time and place, many related to Nungarrayi and many now deceased, float as a series of spectral anchor points in my mind. Her memory produces a variety of narratives and perspectives, more or less dark or hopeful, depending on the day and her mood. But the basic arc of those memories does not change. In the period of her childhood, the 1970s, life was "really good." There were lengthy periods of carefree living at her father's outstation. There was much promise in the way the town functioned, in the division of responsibility for local precincts with tractors and associated resources for keeping the community clean and tidy, and in the operations of the Housing Association. But, I remind myself, Nungarrayi was a child in the 1970s. Could she really have had an eye on the workings of community development? What are the slippages of memory, the temporalities of nostalgia at work here? What other forms of security and insecurity do these memories index? How are the process of aging and its associated loss of innocence implicated? To what extent are we both longing for earlier manifestations of ourselves? Against a series of national images that celebrate the 1980s as the time of Aboriginal advancement, she recalls that time as marking the horrors of the explosion of petrol sniffing among kids.

The interplay between memory and nostalgia is an ever-present force in the interactions between us, as Nungarrayi works to settle her new situation into a coherent life narrative. She deploys nostalgic longing in terms that Svetlana Boym would describe as a "sentiment of loss and displacement."[40] Boym interprets nostalgia as a longing for a different time, but also for "the unrealized dreams of the past and visions of the future that have become obsolete."[41] Nostalgia is, she observes, "a romance with one's own fantasy."[42] More pointedly, nostalgia functions as "a defense mechanism in a time of accelerated rhythms of life and historical upheavals."[43] Nostalgia is a longing for a shrinking space of experience, the antithesis of an open, uncertain horizon of experience. It pulls in the opposite direction to globalism.[44] Destabilization would thus appear to unleash nostalgic thinking. Anthropologists Bruce Kapferer and Dimitrios Theodossopoulos point out that ethnographic practice *always* bears the mark of nostalgia and that anthropologists might embrace this as a critical faculty that enables one to reposition oneself "with respect to exteriority: to deterritorialize and detemporalize ethnographic practice" and, in the process, discover new meaning and unexpected perspectives.[45]

Friendship and Complicity

Like nostalgia, dislocation is a common feature of ethnographic experience. In classical accounts, long-term immersive "fieldwork" is often presented as a slow but steady shift in status from bumbling outsider/foreigner to accomplished known/knowing associate. But for white settler anthropologists working in Australia it is common for feelings of being out of place to endure well after fieldwork has ended. Dispersed anxiety is part and parcel of the position we occupy as researchers intervening in the circumstances of people whose structural displacement we are implicated in by our very presence, just as such anxiety is integral to the settler sensibility more broadly. George Marcus addresses this sensibility indirectly when he refutes the celebration of "rapport" as the ground of ethically guided ethnographic research. He suggests rather that complicity, with its complicated, ironic associations, is the more generative and appropriately morally ambiguous descriptor of the fieldwork relationship.[46] Marcus's exploration of complicity is an extension of his figuring of multisited fieldwork as the necessary ethnographic space of accelerated globalization. To commence with the realities of globalization is to read rapport as the impossible pursuit of "insider" status, the companion of a model of bounded culture. In what he describes as anthropology's shifting mise-en-scène, the destabilization of anthropological categories and associated ways of figuring places and relationships between places and persons demands a different attitude. "The sense of the object of study being 'here and there,'" he suggests, "has begun to wreak havoc on the 'being there' of classic ethnographic authority."[47] Complicity "does not posit the same faith in being able to probe the 'inside' of a culture (nor does it presuppose that the subject herself is even on the 'inside' of a culture, given that contemporary local knowledge is never only about being local). The idea of complicity forces the recognition of ethnographers as ever-present markers of 'outsideness.'"[48] In order to get at the new configurations of person, place, and time wrought by the large-scale transformations of late capitalism, Marcus suggests ethnographers seek not forms of local knowledge but understandings of a different kind of difference—a "difference that arises from the anxieties of knowing that one is somehow tied into what is happening elsewhere, but . . . without those connections being clear or precisely articulated through internal cultural models."[49] In terms of ethnographic relations, such a project only fully evolves when an outsider/anthropologist forms a relationship with a "subject also concerned with the outsideness of everyday life."[50]

Curiously, Marcus does not reflect upon complicity's primary definition: the involvement with others in an unlawful or wrongful act. I would argue that it is this meaning of the term that arguably gives complicity its most compelling force. If adopting an ethical stance in research requires me to stand alongside and become co-responsible with Nungarrayi and her kin, this includes coming to grips with criminality as a pervasive and intimate force in the lives of Warlpiri people. Ruth Gomberg-Muñoz writes with such power relations in mind when she advocates for anthropologists to become accomplices, not allies.[51] Allyship, she observes, confers innocence, including the innocence of settler nationalism. Accomplices by contrast are willing aiders and abettors of the criminalized who refuse to cooperate with racialized unjust laws. Yet there is also complex ground to be trod between assuming the rebellious, perhaps even romantic, disposition of accomplice and its enactment.

Three decades after Marcus penned his reflections on anthropology's changing mise-en-scène, the destabilizations against which he models a new approach have significantly accelerated. The local-global conjuncture has been further intensified, with pervasive forms of technological mediation now operating at the level of the mobile person, and impending environmental disaster figured at a planetary scale. In ethnographic and theoretical terms, anthropologists are chasing understandings of relationships between persons and places and larger processes that are shape-shifting before our eyes.[52] Grappling with the way persons figure relationships between a "here" and "elsewhere" is now a widespread concern of anthropological research. It is a logical progression of these developments that displacement and hypermobility give rise to anthropology on the move, investigations that are no longer place-centric, or even multisited, but person-centric, introducing new kinds of dynamisms and destabilizations into the anthropological endeavor.[53] But as I journey with Nungarrayi, I am constantly reminded of the place-based orientations at work in the way she lives life. Moving forward always involves a recursive loop of orientation: looking back remains a vital navigational resource.

Friendship on the Move

Research-related friendships arguably take shape as fragile composites of elements: some rapport, some complicity. It should be clear by now that in adopting friendship as a central prism for this book, I do so not in order to assume authority, nor to enlist, nor to ventriloquize my primary interlocutor as in harmonious agreement with my analyses. This is not a project of coauthorship. It is a project alert to the considerable risks to be navigated in framing anthropological research as a shared journey between two women, one Warlpiri and one sixth-generation white Australian, and equally aware of the vigorous critiques by Indigenous activists and feminist scholars of earlier related experiments and political campaigns.[54] Rather than deploy friendship to heroize anthropological authority, or to have it dissolve the tensions, miscommunications, and disagreements that inevitably color research relationships, in the pages that follow I embrace the inherently unstable character that makes friendship an ideal prism through which to ruminate directly on these matters. Further, in the context of Nungarrayi's new life in Adelaide, our friendship emerges as a potent space from which to glimpse what is at stake in her weighing up of the competing claims on her subjectivity. Friendship is not simply characterized by voluntarism and moral commitment. As Gadamer argues, friendships are not enacted between individuals; they are distinctively mediated by social and historical forces.[55] Friendships involve openness to the Other's point of view, and thus recognition of the limits of one's own perspective—and understanding—in the reciprocal flow of dialogue. Friendship instantiates open interaction not at the expense of each party's specificity but rather in the realization of mutual recognition. As such, genuine friendships can and should be transformative for both parties: "To reach an understanding in a dialogue is not merely a matter of putting oneself forward and successfully asserting one's own point of view, but being transformed into a communion in which we do not remain what we were."[56]

For the Stoic philosopher Hierocles, genuine friendship shares much ground with and indeed is premised upon kinship's foundational forms of acknowledgment and recognition of the specific character, skills, and experiences of persons, but is differentiated in its capacity to be realized across social distance and at a much larger social scale. Hierocles modeled *oikeiôsis* as a mode of self-other affective ties that begin with the self and immediate family, with the ability to be extended in ever-widening social circles.[57] Yet Hierocles had little to say on the implications of such stretching. Anthropologists have since debated the various ways in which kinship and friendship might be antithetical or closely related social forms.[58] In the pages that follow this debate is not easily settled.

One day in November 2017, Nungarrayi and I speak on the phone four times as she recounts her distress and fury over having discovered that her fortnightly Job Active payment had been canceled yet again, leaving her cashless and raising the prospect of power being cut to her transitional accommodations. As she wrestles against the sense of entrapment such circumstances inevitably give rise to and boards the bus to head down to Centrelink, Nungarrayi calls me on her mobile phone and says she wants to tell me a story, which goes like this: Once upon a time an old man had been drinking at a town camp in Alice Springs. He called out to all his adult sons and told them to accompany him to Centrelink, where he would collect a check and share his largesse among them. They arrived at Centrelink and waited their turn to see a case manager. The old man addressed the case manager, telling him, with the assistance of one of his sons acting as translator, that he was there to collect his check. The case manager consulted his database and told the old man his details were not in the system; he would need to register as unemployed before being eligible for any payments. He was asked to take a seat. The old man and his sons sat. They waited for a long time. The old man was a little bit drunk and began tapping his foot on the floor. His sons got in on the foot tapping and joked that they could enlist their father in their rock band. Finally, the old man was invited by the case manager to come forward. He approached the counter, again in the company of his interpreting son. The case manager told them that unfortunately there was a problem with the database and as a result they would not be able to register the old man that day. The case manager was apologetic, explaining that they needed to "wait for Otto to refresh." Alarmed and ready for a fight, the old man bristled and started yelling, "What about Otto? What's he doing getting mixed up in my private business?" The bewildered case manager tried to calm the old man. Otto was not a person, he told him; Otto was the computer database. The group left Centrelink with the father unsettled and the sons in uproarious laughter. The story quickly circulated among their kin.

This story unfolds a Warlpiri theory of government and an expectation from the earlier self-determination era, that government largesse is infinite and that governments have a moral obligation to provide help when help is required. Accordingly, a visit to Centrelink should deliver a bountiful check. The story also enacts a particular understanding of social causality: people—people wielding ancestral power or "black magic," not database systems and bureaucratic processes—are understood as actors in the world. Finally, as suggested by Nungarrayi's humorous recounting of this story to me in the midst of her own Centrelink-induced headache, there is a sense of transforming and transformative intergenerational familiarity with governmental practices and technologies and a sense that processes of change are themselves challenges to be faced in the nurturing company of kin. It is to such a setting of familiarity and nurture that Nungarrayi retreats when her cosmopolitan aspirations are blunted. As is clear, Nungarrayi is separated in time and place from the situation of dense sociality that her story turns upon. She attempts to settle herself by conjuring into being an instance of the kin-based social constellation from where she acquires her taken-for-granted sense of herself. Enduring the grueling entrapment of Centrelink's bureaucratic stranglehold becomes less painful when she can constitute such an experience as a familiar Warlpiri plight, regardless of location. The triangulation produced by my participation in her telling of the story, as the listener-friend who is able to recognize and interpret the features of the story and what is at stake in its telling and also recognize the existential stress she endures, is crucial to the process.[59]

My refashioning of Abu-Lughod's concept of tactical humanism through the prism of *journeying with* causes me to look to a larger intergenerational and wider social context to understand and de-exceptionalize Nungarrayi's displacement. It causes me to look to the proximate relationships that figure prominently in her daily life that are beyond the frames of anthropology's erstwhile concern with genealogy and kinship. The approach sketched here requires the examination of inheritances, in whatever form they might take. It requires an intimate focus on personality, aspiration, creativity, and vulnerability, as well as skepticism and self-doubt. Memory reveals life as distinctively recalled, storied, and reified. Memory is also a resource from which to draw creative strategies for dealing with the challenges of the present. In this sense, and as Edward Casey compellingly argues, memory is social process, as well as filter—a source of existential anchorage and emplacement.[60] Memory shares ground with, but is also to be distinguished from, nostalgia. Memory works vigorously in tandem with particular objects, particular songs, particular media. It is activated and stimulated by movement. The kinds of movement involved are both continuous *and* discontinuous with earlier chapters in a long history of Warlpiri mobility, as well as with forms of mobility that are identified as the cornerstone of modernity.

Precarious Affection

As we travel by tram one day through the city, Nungarrayi recounts for me, yet again, her Christmas Day run-in with the "Indian woman." I learn, for the first time, that the altercation occurred in Whitmore Square, where the fountain and water sculptures attract many visitors on hot days. December 25, 2016, was one such hot day. Nungarrayi was cooling herself off in the company of two female kin, splashing water onto her belly, half-charged and happy after a day of drinking, when she saw a woman looking at her. Nungarrayi called the woman out and made her declaration about being from this place, "a member of the oldest living culture." She lifted her shirt and proudly pointed to the bared black skin of her torso. In doing this, Nungarrayi mimetically performed what in Australia is a widely recognizable gesture drawn from the racialized ground of Australian Rules Football.[61] The offended woman, however, saw things differently and reported the incident to the police. The incident was caught on CCTV, and two blocks down the road, Nungarrayi was arrested for indecent exposure and public drunkenness.[62]

In two decades of friendship, I have never before known Nungarrayi to self-identify in this way. Her "oldest living culture" declaration is an identity claim called out by the distinctive duress of her metropolitan displacement, a plea to be recognized in terms other than those of individualized, anonymous marginality. Suspended between the terms of the nation's abstractions and her distinctive place-based identification as Warlpiri, her situation makes apparent the urgent, existential weight of exile. Her desperate appeal to the terms of autochthony and exceptional belonging invokes the state's own trade in images of essentialized ancient Aboriginal culture, as well as the dog whistle racist politics of competitive citizenship.[63] She calls out the Indian woman with an expectation of care—in a moment when she has no real expectation of such a response, but also no other moves to make, nor resources to draw on. This incident recalls Michael Herzfeld's insight that cultural intimacy is most intensively performed at the level of the body, in situations in which "state brutality leaves few private spaces uninvaded and so makes the self the only available refuge for any sense of intimacy."[64] It is in such moments that all the cosmopolitan attitude that Nungarrayi has worked so hard to foster, as well as its associated ethical horizon, dissolves, as she foresees and calls out her own dehumanized, criminalized entrapment.[65]

For now, I observe, Nungarrayi's cosmopolitan aspirations appear to have dissipated. They have been displaced in her reversion to the easy reverie of the kin-based drinking circle in the parklands. I am aware of my own discomfort and the judgmental urges that are becoming harder to contain as her daily life becomes more chaotic. Her retreat from cosmopolitan aspirations occurs in direct response to encounters such as the one with "the Indian woman," where she feels the weight of disapproval and negative judgment. But I am certain that there is something substantial to the dreams of self-transformation she energetically sketched for me during my first visit. At one level the conundrum seems both as simple and as complex as Fred Myers put it for the Pintupi neighbors of the Warlpiri thirty years ago—autonomy and relatedness, the two poles of subjective realization, continue to vigorously churn in the way desert people live.[66] Once transposed to the city, the instability of this interrelation is intensified, as is its transformative possibility.

Complicity entails irony and critical distance. As Nungarrayi enthusiastically adopts the role of research associate/ethnographic subject, she takes to narrating for my benefit her responses to all manner of stimuli. I have taken to reading drafts of ethnographic writing to her: a strange, self-conscious exercise that in turn produces new issues for us to negotiate. Money now regularly intrudes upon and shapes our interactions; my relative wealth and Nungarrayi's poverty constitute a blunt structural difference between us that will never be dislodged. This is a destabilizing force that I am becoming unhappily accustomed to. Kirsten Hastrup gets at something of the fragile ambiguity in our friendship when she writes of fieldwork as a generative space between those involved, but also simultaneously a space of inherent violence.[67] But this is not the end of it. Our newly reactivated friendship has also taken on a sentiment that Boym describes as "diasporic intimacy," which trades in stories and secrets, "thrives on unpredictable chance encounters, on hope for human understanding."[68]

"I miss you," Nungarrayi cries down the phone to me one evening in September 2019. She is drunk after a long day of "visiting family" in the parklands, stressed and hoarse from fighting with her boyfriend, and has just gotten off the phone with her son, who is happily ensconced with her aunties in the family camp in Alice Springs. It is in moments like these that she feels the emotional weight of her isolation most keenly. She is calling me to talk, not to ask for money. She has probably called several other relatives before she calls me. Diasporic intimacy, Boym writes, "is haunted by images of home and homeland, yet it also discloses some of the furtive pleasures of exile."[69] Renegotiating the terms of our friendship in this volatile space involves "precarious affection."

THROUGHOUT MY VISITS TO Adelaide, I have been struck by how my tendency to try and settle a predictable interpretive pattern across the new landscape of Nungarrayi's exilic existence gets continually upended by shifting circumstances. Just when I think I've got the shape of the thing, a relative settling of her situation, a new surprise, or tipping point, emerges. This is a story that started on my first visit with her vigorous performance of cosmopolitan aspirations. Yet, over time, her attention has lurched in the direction of intensified attenuated kinship, with its distinctive push and pull that provide anchorage *and* undermine life's possibilities, and which is cut across by the individualizing tendencies called out by her new city life. I set out to research and write what I subconsciously anticipated would be a relatively heroic tale of a woman struggling to remake herself as a new kind of person, a refugee pursuing the relative stability of respected migrant status in the face of near-impossible challenges. But as I've watched Nungarrayi wrestle with the terms of her imagined new life and the kin-based drinking circle that increasingly makes a strong claim upon her, I have had to confront my own desires, discriminations, and shifts in attitude. Where does one draw the line between the demands of writing close to life, the expectations of friendship, and the responsibility to intervene in life-changing situations? These are the kinds of unsettled and unsettling questions this journeying continues to generate.

2

Staking
New Ground

Reacquainting

Nungarrayi and I sit together on a mattress on her living room floor, surrounded by a jumble of clothing and blankets. When I arrived at her house an hour ago, she greeted me at the front door with a beaming smile. She had just washed the floor and asked if I would like some tea. She said she wanted to play me a song, whose lyrics she had earlier carefully transcribed in her notebook. Now she hands me the book and goes to a side room and wheels out what I guess to be the latest generation of boom box: a square black box with front-mounted large speaker and clear plastic dome on top. It plays songs she sends from her phone via Bluetooth. She flicks a switch, and the plastic dome showers the dark room with rainbow-colored rays of light—a portable disco in a box. She has some difficulty with the Bluetooth. After a couple of minutes of her fiddling around, I suggest she just play me the song from her phone. "No," she answers, adamant that we need to hear it through the large speaker. As she finally secures the connection and hits play, she tells me that when she was listening to this song she realized it was her story.

I've stood on the bank of a white raging river,
Trusting that I'd get across
And I'd made my way through some valleys and deserts
Believing that I'd never get lost . . .

Nungarrayi has pumped up the volume, and the bass reverberates through the room. Rolling colored lights dance across the walls and ceiling, splicing the darkness. The song, with its soaring chorus, and her performance of it, is an emotionally freighted narrative of survival. As she sings along, Nungarrayi's voice cracks with feeling. She reinforces the lyrics by narrating over the top of them, gospel style, making the song hers as she invokes her own life's struggles. She presses upon me the importance of our friendship over the years in helping her get by. She thanks God: *He's made me able to stand and survive, to come through alive when it sure looked like I couldn't win.* She invokes her newly individuated self: *Jesus is with me, so I'll take the victory, over and over again.*[1] It is a raw, impassioned performance on an intimate scale. By the song's end, she and I together have dissolved into tears.

Nungarrayi's tears mark a litany of losses. Most pressing is her forced dislocation, her separation from her hometown and close kin. The intensity with which she feels this rupture is expressed bodily, in an edgy disposition I have been struck by since I arrived the previous day on my first visit to her new home. This is the first time we have seen each other face-to-face in six years. I am equally rattled by the unfamiliar setting of our coming together and the stories Nungarrayi has been unloading in the last twenty-four hours. Her references to endurance and survival invoke several layers of trauma, but most pressingly the brutal assault she suffered six years ago at the hands of her ex-husband, Daniel. The assault was the culmination of a long, sporadic history of violence in that relationship. But he had never before hit her with such force. Her life-threatening head injuries required surgery, the implanting of a metal plate over part of her skull, and a lengthy convalescence. She now suffers from memory loss. The man responsible for this assault, the father of her two children, and once a close friend of mine, was sentenced to four years in

FIGURE 2.1 A disco in a box (photo by author)

prison and received a lifetime domestic violence order in South Australia that prevents him from approaching Nungarrayi in that jurisdiction. Her distress centers not so much on her bodily injuries as on her husband's betrayal and his destruction of their "little family" that had anchored her in the world and positioned them both confidently and prominently within their community. Meanwhile, as Nungarrayi contends with her new exilic existence, her beloved son, David, is incarcerated in Darwin prison. I am stunned to learn that David, who had served three years for his involvement in the altercations that led to the death that sparked The Troubles, has since returned to prison on domestic assault charges laid against him by the mother of their one-year-old son.

My tears are shed in shared grief for all of Nungarrayi's losses, which come enveloped in nostalgic longing for a time when our friendship, as well as the relationship between these two friends of mine, husband and wife, was differently located in time and space. I also cry from a sense of shame; contrary to Nungarrayi's insistence on the importance of my support, my own assessment of our friendship across distance—sustained by little more than sporadic phone calls and irregular transfers of small amounts of money to help her out in times of need—is that it could not have provided much comfort or made any noticeable impression on the situation she has endured. Our lives are not separated only geographically, but in so many other ways as well. The multiple stabilities and privileges of my white upper-middle-class existence are lodged between us as the most obvious stakes of a difference that will never be breached. When the desert town was the setting of our friendship, these differences mattered little. In the desert it was I who had to contend with my otherness. Warlpiri values and principles established the rhythms and contours of what mattered in life. We *kardiya*, whitefellas, were the people who would "come and go," as short-term enablers of the community sector, employees, managers of stores, researchers, friends to some, resources to be hustled, a presence begrudgingly endured by others. In such an environment of delicately balanced contingencies, research is an especially ambivalent space for friendship—one where fault lines of power, authority, and access to resources require constant negotiation.

Displacement introduces further disturbances into a once presumed order of relatedness. As soon as persons begin to move around beyond the parameters of a distinctively cultured sociability, dynamics change, at times with devastating consequences. It is in such movement that the gulf between commonplace expectations and experiences opens out widely. I come up against the limits of my capacity to empathize when I try to imagine myself being in some of the social spaces that structure Nungarrayi's life and influence the choices she makes. Never have I expected, nor would I, to find myself on the receiving end of the kind of treatment that is routine for Central Australian Aboriginal people—especially at the hands of the police and the justice system. German cartoonist Jan Bauer confirmed this entrenched gulf of discrimination, the different ways in which black and white bodies are registered and responded to on the streets of Northern Territory towns, when he set a test to try to get himself arrested while reenacting the last hours of the life of a Warlpiri friend who died in police custody in 2016. Kumunjayi Langdon, an extended brother of Nungarrayi, was arrested by police in Darwin for being drunk in a public place. He had a chronic medical condition requiring treatment, but this was overlooked by the police who processed his arrest and locked him in a prison cell where he was later found dead. Bauer drank until he was physically ill in the same stretch of parklands where Langdon was arrested. The only kind of attention he attracted, however, was from other Aboriginal drinkers concerned for his welfare.[2]

Competitive Citizenship and the Cultural Politics of Space

For two of the three years Nungarrayi has been living in Adelaide, she has shared her dwelling with a new Bhutanese partner, Ram, who along with his family of nine sisters, parents, and grandfather was granted asylum by the Australian government not long before the two met. Nungarrayi was allocated the modest two-bedroom house in which they are living by the South Australian government. The house is classed as transitional accommodations for victims of domestic violence. There are a number of similar transitional houses on the same street, and Nungarrayi has known numerous women who have cycled through these houses for short periods of time. None aside from her have stayed in these accommodations beyond a few months. She is anxious to move out of this stigmatized housing and into her "own" house and has been on the waiting list with the South Australian Housing Trust for more than a year.

Elizabeth, the suburb in which she is living, is identified as one of the most disadvantaged places in the country. It was planned and built in the early 1950s as a model industrial satellite town that would absorb thousands of newly arrived British migrants. Since the 1970s, the manufacturing sector that was to be the lifeblood of northwest Adelaide has been pummeled by the combined forces of automation, globalized trade, and transforming technologies. The iconic Holden car factory that once employed many hundreds of workers finally closed its doors in 2017. Rumors circulate locally that "the Chinese" are coming to run businesses out of the now empty vast, cavernous factory spaces. The area continues to absorb newly resettled migrants. Its shifting ethnic demographic is reflected in short strip shopping centers that host halal butchers, African salons, and Indian and Nepalese grocers. Shop fronts advertise competitive rates for international money transfers. Wide streets are lined with modest single-level brick houses. Weather-worn Australian flags fly from the television antennae of some of these houses, telltale markers of disaffected white nationalist sentiment. Along these streets, members of new and old marginalized communities—the postindustrial unemployed, retired, and working poor, single-parent households, and recently arrived migrants—find themselves living side by side, with varying degrees of toleration and friction. In the weeks leading up to the 2016 federal election, I watched on as a larger-than-life image of the anti-immigration populist politician and One Nation party leader Pauline Hanson slowly cruised these streets on the side of a truck, wooing voters.

The period of my visits to Adelaide has coincided with a time of great volatility in Australian electoral politics. In the ten years since 2008, the prime ministership of the country has changed eight times. This is a time of contradictory anxieties—conservative Liberal National Party politicians lend unwavering support to the coal industry and deny climate change, while stoking national sympathies for the great difficulties faced by farmers in the midst of severe prolonged drought and unpredictable weather patterns. Conservative commentary fuels antagonism over the supposed threats to social harmony and job security posed by migrants from non-European backgrounds. In late 2017, the High Court ruled a swath of federal politicians were ineligible to hold their seats after they were found to hold dual citizenship, in contravention of the Australian Constitution. The then deputy prime minister, Barnaby Joyce, leader of the conservative National Party, was caught in this net when it was revealed that he had not renounced the New Zealand citizenship he inherited from his father. The politics around dual citizenship unfolded in tandem with a media-fueled moral panic over threats to public safety posed by recently arrived South Sudanese youth, and an increasingly tough approach to asylum seekers arriving by boat being rerouted to offshore detention in Nauru and Manus Island. Shadowing similar developments in the United Kingdom, the Australian government established a new mega Department of Home Affairs in December 2017, incorporating federal law enforcement, national and transport security, criminal justice, emergency management, multicultural affairs, and immigration- and border-related functions and agencies. In the post-9/11 security environment, Australia has passed more legislation that impinges on civil liberties than the United States and the United Kingdom.[3] The minister for home affairs, Peter Dutton, has actively fanned public anxieties over asylum seekers, "home-grown terrorists," and African youth. He made an unsuccessful attempt to secure the prime ministership in August 2018 and continues to campaign vigorously for expanded powers for his portfolio.

Class and ethnic tensions also fuel paranoid nationalism and episodes in competitive citizenship at the level of local Adelaide electoral politics.[4] In a revealing face-off during a 2018 by-election, supporters of independent incumbent Rebekha Sharkie were accused of insulting her conservative Liberal Party competitor, Georgina Downer, daughter of Adelaide establishment figure Alexander Downer, who had led the party and later served as Australian high commissioner to the United Kingdom, and whose own father had served as immigration minister in the Menzies post–World War II government as well as high commissioner to the United Kingdom. Downer hit back, defending his daughter from what he described as the "horrible hate" of the campaign. "They must all be new arrivals," he was reported to have posted on Facebook. "Nation-building is in our [family's] blood." Sharkie quickly retorted that her father was a nation builder too, stating, "He built cars in a factory." Downer, she suggested, was "seriously out of touch."[5] Sharkie was reelected, but a year later the conservative Coalition was returned to power federally in an election it had been widely expected to lose.

Force of Circumstance

Adelaide has long been a destination for Aboriginal people from Central Australia. Faye Gale's classic study *Urban Aborigines* observed that migration out of the desert had been accelerating since the early 1950s.[6] Practices associated with the assimilation policy, introduced in 1954, aimed to absorb Aboriginal people from overcrowded government reserves and missions into "the general Australian community."[7] A decade later, further government policies were passed in support of Aboriginal urbanization, with special provisions made for the allocation of housing. Gale highlighted that many of the people who migrated to Adelaide continued to "belong" somewhere else. She observed that the movement of people from the Northern Territory was due to "force of circumstance" rather than voluntary migration, or reliance on kin.[8] This continues to be the case for significant numbers of patients with chronic health conditions transferred to Adelaide for treatment, for those imprisoned in Adelaide's jail, and for children sent south to attend boarding school. Yet others find reason to stay on for more or less lengthy periods after traveling to the city to purchase secondhand vehicles, to exhibit and sell art, to visit kin, or to seek respite from the stresses of home.

Nungarrayi's decision to stay was in part precipitated by her commencement of a domestic relationship with Ram. She draws great comfort from this relationship, but the trauma of exile and anger over missed opportunities of her earlier life weigh heavily on her. She and Ram share affinities through the small-scale places and communities from whence they come, as well as in their experience of socioeconomic and cultural marginalization in the city. For the entire period of my research on this project, Ram is caught in the vortex of perpetual training: to qualify for welfare payments, he must attend regular English-language lessons and a series of programs to enhance his "work readiness," with the promise of "real work" continually deferred. He and Nungarrayi both face a litany of bureaucratic and other hurdles if they are to transform their affective status from precariously placed "refugee" to settled "migrant."

Far removed from the intense forms of sociality that characterize day-to-day life in Central Australia, Nungarrayi spends many hours alone in a house that through the winter months is often dark and cold. After the deduction of rent and associated maintenance fees from government welfare payments, the couple have a modest $150 a fortnight to cover the cost of food and other basic needs. They call on friends and family to help them out when need be, but in winter the cost of heating can be beyond their means. During the day, while Ram is attending his mandatory job training program, Nungarrayi sits around listening to music on her phone. She keeps up with news and photographs of her dispersed family circulating on Facebook, she speaks to family, and most frequently to her son, who calls from Alice Springs prison.

Outside the house, as we walk the streets of her suburb together, Nungarrayi deploys images of her desert home to make this new place familiar. She insists on continuities and affinities between this place and the desert, pointing out resonances between the suburban streetscapes of Elizabeth and Alice Springs. Nungarrayi wills her new surroundings to affectively adopt recognized features of her beloved desert country, in a set of practices that strike me as a kind of gentle, decolonized reversal of the violent forms of placemaking practiced by imperial regimes that physically remake the lands they colonize.[9] The deep knowledge of her paternal ancestral country she acquired as a child is close to the surface, emotionally weighted, and easily recalled, as is a broader awareness of the seasonal transformations taking place in the desert during her absence. Relocated to Adelaide, Nungarrayi's memories of her early life in the desert are vivid, supercharged.

Her new situation is conducive to nostalgic longing. There are expansive parklands she can wander through and allow her imagination to transport her back to Central Australia; groves of eucalyptus and scrubby ti trees that remind her of the bounty of honey ants to be dug up and eaten at this time of year; and hilltops that allow glimpses of the snaking Stuart Highway that leads to the desert. She tells me she longs for a day when she and Ram will be allocated a Housing Trust house with a backyard in which she can light a fire and cook kangaroo tail and burn ashes for her chewing tobacco. Strikingly, her future-focused outlook does not sever connections with the past but rather enfolds them. There is something here of John Berger's idea of places being doubled, a here and an elsewhere held in fusion; a *here* inhabited with deep sentiments and ways of relating drawn from *there*, a *here* made bearable via this very process.[10] The presence of the highway also indicates the peculiar nature of Nungarrayi's exile, where here bleeds into there in myriad ways.

Rather than claustrophobia, confinement, and control, aesthetic and psychological forms commonly associated with exile, Nungarrayi describes her new situation in terms of openness, as peaceful and filled with optimistic future-focused possibilities.[11] Just as important as her deployment of images of her desert country to soothe the rupture of displacement are the contrasts she draws to elevate Adelaide as *more* desirable than the desert regional town of Alice Springs. Adelaide is quieter, friendlier, with "friendlier police," cheaper and better food, and "all these different people." So it is that a melancholic, desert-focused disposition coexists in tension with a more upbeat, enthusiastic embrace of the world-changing possibilities of life in Adelaide. On a good day, life in Adelaide is "free," "open." It is "relaxing" because of an absence of family pressure and the vitality of "all these different people" living side by side. Yet the same absence of extended kin hovers as a kind of dispersed rupture and puts serious existential and economic stress on the day-to-day challenges of getting by. Consumption is a vital element of successful accommodation to the terms of city life. Nungarrayi is well practiced in the arts of cosmopolitan consumption. When she has money, she shops with enthusiasm and vigor, piling her market shopping trolley high with what for desert dwellers is unusual bounty: loads of fresh oranges, leafy green vegetables, bags of red chilies, spices, cheap cuts of meat, and rice, the ingredients for the fragrant home-cooked curry meals on which she and Ram subsist. As she takes me around the market, Nungarrayi enthusiastically proclaims the health benefits of her new diet and describes the new domestic order established by Ram. He cleans her house. He has taught her to cook and eat differently. She has lost ten dress sizes since he moved in. To her delight, he has bestowed upon her a kind of gentle affection Warlpiri women do not commonly receive from Warlpiri men.

Outback's City

If exile presents itself as a series of tests, the first test Nungarrayi confronts is navigation, learning the geographic, bureaucratic, and social terms of life in the city.[12] On the second day of my first visit, Nungarrayi enthusiastically takes up my suggestion that she show me the Adelaide she knows. We leave her house and take a bus to a neighboring suburban shopping center. Along the way she points out several areas in parklands where Aboriginal people regularly congregate. We get off the bus and approach the cavernous Westfield shopping center. We immediately encounter three desert women leaving the center. Nungarrayi greets them as kin. They are related by marriage through her daughter's husband. One of them asks her for ashes for chewing tobacco.[13] We consume a meal of curry and rice in the food court and purchase some second-hand clothes before boarding another bus that will take us to the city center. We disembark at the hospital. As we enter the large foyer, Nungarrayi warmly greets two desert men she hails as brothers-in-law. She guides me up one floor to the Aboriginal liaison office. She wants to show me the place and people she has spoken about at length, a service provider she regards as doing a poor job of meeting the needs of the many patients from the desert who cycle through this hospital. Nungarrayi's idea of a dream job is to be employed as a translator/community liaison in this hospital. She confidently approaches the counter and asks the young woman if there are any people from Alice Springs in the hospital at the moment. As if to confirm Nungarrayi's criticism, she gives us a thin smile and responds, "I don't know." We make a quick pass through the hospital. This is familiar territory. She deftly guides me along a series of wings, engaging hospital staff with greetings and queries as she goes, asking after kin who have been recently admitted. We leave the hospital and head for the nearest bus stop.

We end up in a taxi on Nungarrayi's urging. She knows I can pay. It is already midafternoon, and she wants to get us to Hutt Street as quickly as possible. As we enter the confined space of the taxi, Nungarrayi's mood instantly shifts. She becomes aggressive and impatient. She asks our driver to drive faster. He responds coolly that we are passing through a forty-kilometer-per-hour speed-limited zone and he does not want to lose his license. Nungarrayi speaks loudly, gestures wildly, and swears more colorfully than usual. As we head down Hutt Street toward the parklands where desert drinkers congregate daily, she points out the offices that provide services to homeless people. Nungarrayi is looking for two sisters who came to Adelaide at the same time she did. She wants to introduce me to them. This is the third time in two days I have been taken aback at the sudden transformation in Nungarrayi's demeanor when she enters a taxi. Her default attitude toward drivers, especially if they are Indian men, is aggressive. I surmise that the weight of so many years of weathering discriminatory treatment in Alice Springs has brought out this response. She expects taxi drivers to be dishonest, that they are out to skin passengers for as much money as they can. She directs the taxi to drive another five hundred meters down the road and to pull over.

I pay the unhappy driver, and we leave the cab and head in the direction of a loosely assembled group. We come upon four men huddled against the back wall of a toilet block. One is seated on a broken plastic chair. Others stand or lean against the wall. Each of them drinks from a small plastic water bottle filled with bourbon and coke, and all of them look deeply grog soaked. The weather is bleak. The ground is muddy. It is early winter. Two of the men attempt to warm themselves by a thin, smoky fire. Another man dances in wild stumbling movements to music that thumps loudly from a boom box. We continue walking and come to a group of women sitting in a circle on a blanket, playing cards and drinking cask wine. As we approach, Nungarrayi erupts into a loud wailing cry.

She embraces one woman and then the woman sitting beside her. These two sisters are grieving the recent loss of a brother. Nungarrayi composes herself quickly and asks after the whereabouts of her sisters. She is given vague directions to a red building, "number six," to the west of the bottle shop. An arm is waved, "over there." We walk on and pass a final group of four men seated on the damp ground, all of whose hands we shake in acknowledgment of recent bereavements. I introduce myself. "Ah, you my right skin," says one of the men with a weak smile, indicating his and my relationship as potential spouses.

Leaving this setting of dense, fragile sociality, we cross the road and immediately return to the ordered tidiness of inner Adelaide's streets. We wander somewhat aimlessly for half an hour or so, before giving up our attempt to locate the flat where the sisters are said to be staying. As we walk, Nungarrayi offers her views on the immediate environment. She tells me forthrightly that she would not like to live in the city. She is disparaging of the heritage-listed gentrified bluestone terrace houses that line the inner-city streets—they have no room and no trees. "I'm a country girl," she tells me. Nungarrayi had visited me several years earlier in my suburban house in the national capital city, Canberra. My family and I had more recently moved interstate to inner-city Melbourne. I tell her that the house I now live in is just like these terraces; it has no yard or garden. I tell her I love the liveliness of the city. Our interaction puts me in mind of discussions with young Warlpiri men who left the desert for a period of city-based life after being drafted to play professional football in the Australian Rules Football League. A common explanation of those who return home before completing their contracts is that they couldn't stand life in the city because "the sky is too small."

Nungarrayi guides us to the bus stop from where we can catch the free city shuttle bus, and then ten minutes later we board another bus that will take us on a thirty-minute ride to the rehab center, where her extended sister Magda has been in residential care for six months. The most significant collapsing of the separation of the worlds of Central Australia and Adelaide occurs for Nungarrayi in her weekly visits to Magda, who is undergoing months of intensive treatment for a chronic spinal injury. Wheelchair bound, physically separated from her husband and family, Magda is also estranged from the dense company that characterizes life in the desert. I have known Magda as long as I have known Nungarrayi. She has always been a gregarious woman, always at the center of lively activity. When Nungarrayi first told me of Magda's situation, I was incredulous: How could Magda possibly cope with such prolonged isolation? Nungarrayi was dismissive of my concern, telling me, "She was upset when she first arrived, but now she's found Wapirra [God], she's really good."

As we arrive at the rehab center, I immediately sense a more complex scenario. It is four o'clock on a darkening winter's afternoon. The entrance foyer and wide corridor that leads to the interior of the building are quiet, with few signs of life. We meet Magda wheeling herself out of a doorway, wearing headphones, coming out of a physiotherapy session. It is a year since I last saw Magda in the desert. I am struck by how pale she looks and how much weight she has gained. She underwent surgery on a broken back nine months ago. Following that surgery, Nungarrayi tells me, Magda was immobilized in a hospital bed for two months before being moved to the rehabilitation center. Magda is visibly delighted to see us. Nungarrayi is her only close kin in the city at the moment, her only family visitor aside from the infrequent visits she receives from her husband and two other sisters. Magda was told by surgeons she would never walk again. But, Nungarrayi tells me before we enter the center's foyer, now that Magda has found God, she is happy, and she is recovering.

We follow Magda to her room. It is a comfortable space, reasonably well equipped for long-term residents, with a large window looking out to a garden. A wall-mounted television and spacious shelving alongside her headboard provide a glimpse of how Magda spends her days. Immediately Nungarrayi points to her mobile phone. "$600!" Magda tells me. Laptop, "$750!" and tablet, "$350," that have been recently gifted by "a friend"—a man who visits weekly. The women marvel as they reflect upon the retail price of each electronic device. I see that her friend has also equipped Magda with an array of reading materials that are strewn across a shelf—a copy of the Bible, a folder with pages that summarize teachings thematically, according to emotional need, and several pamphlets with titles such as "An Apple for the Road: Wisdom for Life."

In animated fashion, Magda opens the laptop and plays a series of short videos and songs for us from thumb drives that arrived recently in a package sent by her husband. Among the files is a video made by the desert media association that records a recent visit by two professional Aboriginal footballers, men who have grown up in the city without any substantive relationships to their Aboriginal communities. Magda's husband and several other Warlpiri men, including a celebrated Warlpiri football player who both Nungarrayi and Magda call grandson, appear on-screen, taking their guests on a tour of Warlpiri sacred places. The film ends with the two men, visibly moved, thanking their Warlpiri hosts for what has clearly been an emotional and transformative experience.

Magda pushes the laptop aside. Nungarrayi takes a USB stick out of her pocket and directs me to copy the contents of Magda's thumb drives so that she can share in this bounty: a fresh supply of music, recent recordings of desert rock bands, as well as popular music dubbed from other sources. Nungar-

FIGURE 2.2 Images from home (photo by author)

rayi returns our conversation to the Bible-touting, digital gift–bearing friend. He believes Magda will walk again. Magda smiles and nods. They have every reason to trust him, Nungarrayi continues in an especially upbeat mood, as Magda "felt something" in her left leg following his first visit. They dream that his prayers will be answered and that Magda will become the first Aboriginal woman to tour the outback with him in a small plane, bringing the word of God to all the bush communities. Nungarrayi continues excitedly, telling me that she too has a place in this dream. She told this man that she is a qualified interpreter. He told her he "will need her to come along as well."

We spend an hour sitting with Magda, trailing through all the family news. Magda asks after the young daughter of Nungarrayi's sister's son. This child of young parents who are drinkers and incapable of looking after her has been in and out of foster care and was recently admitted to the hospital following an accident in which she was burned. Nungarrayi takes an active interest in the girl's welfare, and the child's father lives intermittently with her. She participates in weekly supervised visits but to date has not made a move to apply for guardianship of the child. Talk then turns to a recent tragic car accident in Alice Springs that claimed the lives of a young woman and man. Two decades earlier, the three of us had danced together at the initiation ceremony for the deceased man. Both Nungarrayi and Magda speak of having received visits—signs of "something"—on the night of the car accident. Magda shows me a photo on her phone of the young woman who died. Magda tells us that American evangelist Billy Graham's son performed at Alice Springs Showgrounds two weeks ago. Their sister Amanda reportedly walked several kilometers from a town camp on the other side of town to attend. Amanda has recently had a successful kidney transplant, and Nungarrayi tells me with a smile, "Now she's everywhere."

Conversation with these women is an emotionally charged and heady mix of family news and proclamations on the power of God, the power of sorcery, love of country, and affirmations of care. Nungarrayi and Magda dream of better futures for themselves. Nungarrayi dreams of making enough money to buy a car, or even a house—she has heard it is possible to buy a house in Adelaide for "just $95,000." Her eyes sparkle as she tells us that Ram dreams of buying a camper van and taking her driving all around Australia. She dreams that the interpreter job she longs for will come about, and that she will be flown all over the country doing this important work. She dreams that she will end up in a job like me at a university, helping her people to learn. She dreams that her son will come out of prison and manage to stay out. She dreams that the woman in public office, her relative, who has been unfairly claiming her family's mining royalties will be exposed as a thief and publicly humiliated.

All of these dreams are premised upon an enhanced mobility, on life possibilities that are not tied to particular places, but nevertheless keep close in mind Warlpiri places and towns as well as the company of kin. Nungarrayi's dreams identify stark transformations, situations that are profoundly out of reach: private homeownership, travel for leisure, recognition and remuneration for her professional expertise, new kinds of stabilization in the life of her kin and their assumed ordering of the world. Magda's imagined future assumes no such thing as a return to a previous life, but rather seeks the achievement of an elevated status and a triumphal homecoming in a newly cosmopolitan guise, as an enlightened woman who would draw on the experience and knowledge gleaned during exile to deliver new goods to kin back home. But entangled with these imaginaries of self-alteration is an ethics of care grounded in concern for specific persons as well as the reproduction of a particular constellation of relationships. In her work drawing out the resonances between George Herbert Mead's relational self and the relational orientation of feminist philosophy, Heather Keith observes that practices of ethical caring prompt a moral compulsion—a sense of "I must"—in the self that turns upon "what is already felt in our relationships."[14] Together these women engage in a kind of empathetic magical thinking; there is something messianic in the future visions they conjure. They imagine themselves delivered into empowered situations in their own community as well as the world at large.

Exile's Encounters

The existential challenge Nungarrayi faces in her new metropolitan situation resonates with the circumstances of other displaced people. One perhaps surprising but striking set of resonances is to be found in Liisa Malkki's study of the situations of two differently located groups of exiled Hutu in Tanzania in the early 1990s, where she finds "two quite specific, locally situated liminalities that were intimately related to each other and yet irreconcilably opposed."[15] Residents of the Mishamo refugee camp narrate themselves as "a people" and distinguish themselves from those dwelling in the nearby town of Kigoma who adopt a more cosmopolitan and fluid set of identities "derived or 'borrowed' from the social context of the town."[16] Malkki observes how life in the camp is characterized by a "refusal to root," by a people awaiting a "millennia return," while for those living in the town the past "had simply passed," and they were eagerly focused on the work of assimilation.[17] Those in the camp see cosmopolitan life as dangerous, as representing "an absence of order and of categorical loyalties and rules."[18] For them, exile is a series of tests, a process of purification, requiring hard work. There is much at stake in reproducing this moral schema of exile and the practices it calls out; ultimately, it is thought, the deserving would be delivered back their homeland.[19] In Malkki's formulation these two groups stand for starkly opposed exilic identities and forms of personhood. The differences in these exilic situations turn upon the distinctive place-based structural circumstances each group navigates.

Nungarrayi's situation differs in several obvious respects, especially in the individualized nature of her displacement and in her unhindered mobility across differently ordered social spaces and situations. Her exile differs most markedly from the situation Malkki describes in that it is not constituted in a bounded separation between a here and a there. Yet, in other respects Nungarrayi's exile involves an *intensification* of processes described by Malkki, especially the reflexive identification of moral principles required to establish the terms of a livable life. What is striking is that Nungarrayi embodies and wrestles ceaselessly with the two expressive genres of "peoplehood" and "cosmopolitanism" identified by Malkki. These subjectivities coexist in tension in the one person, offering alternate possibilities and making contradictory demands upon a woman whose anxious, fast-paced demeanor bears little resemblance to the confident and steady person I befriended in the Central Desert two decades ago.

Nungarrayi's exile is both continuous with and to be distinguished from other earlier understandings of the exilic condition. Edward Said famously identified the key features of exile in terms of a "certainty of isolation" and loss of something left behind forever.[20] If exile historically involved a situation of physical and spatial separation, in the present many situations of displacement are overcome by digital communication. Nungarrayi might be physically separated from kin and country but can beam herself into those settings and participate in rapid-fire interactions in real time. In this contemporary reordering of time-space relationships, experiences of colliding sensory, spatial, and temporal orders are common, as is the feeling that nothing is stable.[21] Cosmopolitanism takes on new qualities and characteristics in an era in which the dualities that sustained interpretation in the previous era—global/local, national/international, us/them—have dissolved. Ulrich Beck and Natan Sznaider put it thus: "The nation-state is increasingly besieged and permeated by a planetary network of interdependencies, for example, by ecological, economic and terrorist risks, which connect the separate worlds of developed and underdeveloped countries. . . . a new historical reality arises, a 'cosmopolitan outlook' in which people view themselves simultaneously as part of a threatened world and part of their local situations and histories."[22] The simultaneity identified here resonates with Nungarrayi's wrestling between Warlpiri and cosmopolitan expressive genres. But I am uneasy about the dissolution of what might be distinctive to each that seems implied in Beck and Sznaider's "cosmopolitan outlook." As anthropologist Peter Geschiere has forcefully shown, manifestations of what he terms the "global conjuncture of belonging" often involve a return to highly localized preoccupations.[23] Geschiere also points out that these circumstances manifest an "increasing impatience with pluralism and cultural difference."[24] What comes through forcefully in Nungarrayi's back-and-forth between the terms and orientations of the desert and those of the city is her distinguishing between different forces, temporalities, relationships, and their relative orientations that she enters into and withdraws from as she moves around. The warm greeting of "Namaste" Nungarrayi exchanges with an elderly Nepalese man who lives on her block sits at odds with her studied disengagement with the aloof Indian shopkeeper who, sitting behind her counter, keeps a close eye on Nungarrayi as she browses racks of clothing. A further disjuncture appears in the aggressive disposition she herself adopts in the back seat of a taxi, as she anticipates the critical judgment of its Sub-Continental driver. In her encounters with ethnically marked strangers on Adelaide's streets, Nungarrayi unwittingly tussles between two subject positions the nation-state has established and calls her into: savagery and reverence, risk and redemption. Notably, the intensification of intolerance and her appeals to exceptional status occur in places and situations constituted in and through capital transactions.

My disquiet regarding the tendency of the concept of cosmopolitanism to dissolve agitation, unevenness, and disjuncture gains clarity in relation to David Harvey's work. For Harvey, cosmopolitanism ignores the way places and localized ways of living in places are "relationally constructed" by processes operating at "quite different spatiotemporal scales." Harvey draws attention to the way scholars of cosmopolitanism tend to "simply delight . . . in the conveniently disruptive metaphors of spatialities, cartographic metaphors, and the like," rather than confront "the banal problematics of materialist geographies."[25] The deployment of cosmopolitanism, Harvey argues, tends to undermine "the possibility of dealing with 'geographical difference itself.'"[26] He observes that a key dimension of neoliberal globalization is "a chronically unstable dialectics of space and place that brings geographical elements into the center of politics."[27] Most poignantly, Harvey observes, "*the way life gets lived in spaces, places, and environments, is . . . the beginning and end of political action*."[28] In approaching Nungarrayi's displacement, Harvey would, I think, urge us to look back across the transforming geographic production of settler colonial Australia and its subsequent capitalist expansion and, relatedly, to Warlpiri people's responses to their displacement and dispossession.

Looking back, it is possible to track the shifting terms of governance and associated edicts that declared Warlpiri and other desert-dwelling people would change their ways of life and residential practices in this or that way. In tandem, it is possible to glimpse the way Warlpiri deploy ex-hunter-gatherer pragmatics, ignoring certain state directives while remaining remarkably open to whatever useful new materials and methods might be brought before them in an expanding world of exchange. Such a process was at work in Warlpiri responses to early attempts to force them out of their bush shelters and into the first generation of "transitional" housing at the Hooker Creek settlement. The unlined, corrugated iron huts Warlpiri men were enlisted to erect and then occupy with their immediate families were for many their first exposure to the bizarre form of European structures that physically separate persons from each other and from their surrounding environment. Inadequate to desert conditions in almost every way, these "rubbish houses," as they came to be known, were freezing cold in winter and unbearably hot in summer, and they could blow over under the force of strong winds. They enabled no view of the surrounding environment and were too small to house a Warlpiri family. The sheets of corrugated iron that clad the huts, however, were quickly assessed by Warlpiri as a valuable addition to their bough shelters. In the months after people had been forcibly relocated to Hooker Creek, there was a vigorous contest over dwelling practices: just as quickly as bough shelters were demolished and tin huts erected under order by the superintendent, excess supplies of corrugated iron vanished and reappeared bolstering the walls of newly erected shelters.[29]

While the early experiment in remaking Warlpiri residential habits failed in the first instance, the broader cultural logic of government settlements worked in other ways toward a radical reconstruction of Warlpiri ways of living in, moving through, and relating to desert places. Once people's orientations to places were no longer distinctively shaped by hunter-gatherer imperatives and the seasonal quest for food on foot, places themselves would come to be known differently. Yet this was by no means a seamless transformation. Some Warlpiri pushed back against the logic of settlement with forceful acts of creative dissent. Their reorientation turned upon ritual exchanges with the Gurinji owners of the land on which the new settlement was based, as well as the creative dynamism of senior Warlpiri men who dreamed new cosmological-cartographic narratives into existence.[30] Hooker Creek was a setting of mass displacement, a tumultuous arrangement to which people were collectively subjected and would collectively respond. Nungarrayi finds herself displaced, by contrast, neither in the densely intimate company of kin nor in a place constituted through regional desert sociality. However, she has by no means left those associations behind. Nungarrayi's situation calls to mind Kwame Anthony Appiah's idea of "rooted cosmopolitans" who do not abandon their moral and emotional commitments to kin, but rather have multiple attachments.[31] But "multiplicity" is deceptively value-neutral, eschewing any concern for qualitative distinction or hierarchy of attachments. According to what pressures and needs does a person order their "multiple attachments"?

While the circumstances of Nungarrayi's and Magda's displacements differ, the closeness of their relationship, their shared endurance of The Troubles, and their shared experience living in Adelaide make them what anthropologist Basil Sansom would have called close consociates, or, in their own terms, "number one sisters."[32] Nungarrayi tells me she visits Magda weekly and has been active in her healing. She tells me Magda's weight gain is a result of fluid that has accumulated all through her body, inflicted by their sorcery-wielding enemies. Nungarrayi is aiding Magda's recovery by taking the toxic fluid into herself, taking it home, and sweating it out. But she impresses upon Magda that she must look to God. He is the only one who can really help her, not *ngankari*—a customary healer—like herself.

Drawing Lines of Belonging

As we sit together one day on a mattress in her lounge room, Nungarrayi draws a picture of the layout of the house where thirty of her close kin took refuge against the torrent of rage and violent retribution wielded by relatives of the deceased man the day following the death that sparked The Troubles. They were all crowded into the hallway of this one house, struggling to keep out of the rooms that had external windows. Their assailants had the house surrounded and had smashed all the windows. Nungarrayi's kin were stuck inside, under siege, for about ten hours. Finally, the police riot squad arrived from Alice Springs, just in the nick of time, as the brother of the deceased and his kin were about to start throwing handmade petrol bombs (drink cans filled with fuel) into the house. Everyone in the house could smell the petrol fumes. The police demanded that everyone outside the house put down whatever was in their hands. As the ringleader handed his can to the sergeant, Nungarrayi tells me, that fuel turned to water.

The police finally secured the area and escorted the families out of the house and into the women's safe house. Everyone was hungry and exhausted. A supportive store manager supplied them with food. Once they had eaten and the intensity of the situation had abated, everyone relaxed a little and started telling jokes. There had been some hilarious scenes amid the rising tensions inside that house. At the height of the chaos Magda had succumbed to fatigue and had quietly taken herself into the small bathroom, where she snuggled into a corner alongside the toilet, directly beneath a smashed window, and fell asleep. People were crouched in the hallway and watched on in amazement as Magda slept, oblivious to the rocks that were being hurled through the window and bouncing off her head. A man was standing in the hallway holding an ax. In a state of exhaustion, he slumped against a wall and kept nodding off, with his chin sliding down the ax blade. Nungarrayi was standing close by and growled at him to turn the blade around so he wouldn't slice himself.

Holed up in the house, people were watching Nungarrayi's Bible, which she had placed on the floor just inside the front door: its pages started to flutter. They were all praying to Wapirra, to the only power higher than the black magic that was being wielded upon them, and it appeared he was responding. After they were escorted out of the house by police, their assailants set it alight. Several cars were torched, including one owned by Nungarrayi. Her son turned himself in to the police, after which some semblance of calm was restored. But in the weeks that followed, the feud established new simmering spatial dynamics in the town. At one stage Nungarrayi and her husband were driving fifty kilometers down the road to the closest neighboring town to shop for food, rather than run the gauntlet of their own town square. The extended families clustered together in a makeshift fortress on the eastern edge of town, where upwards of a hundred people occupied three neighboring houses and a series of spontaneously erected tents. On a visit during this time, I found a surprisingly upbeat mood among the east-side campers. The dramatic intensity of the feud had charged the spirits of these people who historically identified themselves as Warlpiri warriors. The Troubles galvanized attention and reinvigorated a focus on kin-based honor and its related aesthetic forms, at a time when people's hold on the governance of their own community had been radically diminished by governmental fiat.

As winter darkness falls outside, we say farewell to Magda at her bedside and hail a bus. The route takes us around the edge of a hill that opens out to an expansive view of northwest Adelaide, as a vast plane of tiny radiant lights stretches out below us. Nungarrayi nudges me and points out the snaking highway that leads to Alice Springs. As she directs my attention, her voice catches with emotion. We are the only passengers, and shortly the driver advises us that the bus is about to terminate, and we need to get off. As we step onto the footpath on the edge of an unmarked arterial road, Nungarrayi becomes disoriented, no longer sure of the direction in which we need to look for our next ride. Cold and tired, I call us a taxi.

Notwithstanding her moments of disquiet, Nungarrayi refuses to succumb to the melancholy that often creeps up on me during the time of my first visit with her in Adelaide. I register that I am probably suffering from a low-grade state of shock. The situations I am being exposed to, the stories piling up, seem a world away from what I had been accustomed to in earlier times in Central Australia. She brushes aside my concern for Magda. She is OK—really good now that she has God. Across the turbulent circumstances of her recent life, Nungarrayi has mustered her faith in God as a vital, stable reference point, a pillar of strength in moments of loneliness and, along with tightly held memories of the "growing up" that shaped her as a person, an internalized locus of ontological anchorage. Christianity has been the primary source of solace and self-remaking for generations of Aboriginal people struggling to escape the ravages of alcohol, the related misery of family violence, and a more diffuse lack of control over life's circumstances.[33] Nungarrayi blames her ex-husband for "teaching her to drink," and in the present she turns to alcohol and marijuana as well as to music and God, to dull the pain of her multiple dislocations.

Displacement also sits at the heart of Nungarrayi and Ram's shared experience. But whereas she insists on continuities between her beloved desert and her new home in the city, Ram's experience of dislocation is more clear-cut.

He recalls for me the profound bodily displacement he experienced when he and his family first flew into Adelaide after their long flight from Nepal. He was struck by the absence of trees, the sealed roads, the strange houses, an environment without any noticeable features. Water tasted strange. Food had no taste. He felt unwell in the stomach. Everything was on edge, until he added chili. Once he added chili, everything started to get a little bit better, and his stomach settled down.

Ram was ambivalent about leaving Nepal. He had been in trouble with the police, he had spent time in prison on account of his involvement with armed gangs, and his parents insisted that he come and make a fresh start at life in a new country. In the months since arriving, he has progressively withdrawn from his family. This has been a vital part of the process of establishing himself as an independent person on a new trajectory.[34] His "marriage" to Nungarrayi is controversial in the eyes of his family. His parents have had some difficulty coming to terms with the relationship, primarily on account of the age difference between Ram and Nungarrayi but also for other reasons. Ram and Nungarrayi fight frequently. They have been full drunk and fought publicly in the presence of his family. One incident resulted in the police being called and Nungarrayi losing her license on account of drunk driving. She was sent to the police lockup to "cool off "after being charged with drunken and disorderly behavior.

Over the Horizon

Stuart Hall has observed that one of the outcomes of globalization is to enforce a "cosmopolitanism from below." Against the breathless celebration of the transnational mobility of the elite, he draws attention to the ways in which globalization

> bears down upon people who have no choice as to whether or not to become cosmopolitans. They have to learn to live in two countries, to speak a new language and make a life in a different place, not by choice but as a condition of survival. They have to acquire the same cosmopolitan skills of adaption and innovation which an entrepreneur requires—but from a different place . . . culturally, they are living "in translation" every day of their lives. . . . They are what, following the Jamaican anthropologist, David Scott, we should call "conscripts of global modernity."[35]

The social space Nungarrayi occupies in Adelaide demands her vigorous navigation of diverse and conflicting image-worlds, with considerable investment in fostering their points of connection. The world of exile is necessarily one in which the newly arrived person must, as a matter of survival, produce coherence for themselves. Out of this initial process of applying erstwhile ways of seeing and relating to new places, layers of familiarity, growing confidence, and attunement are slowly achieved. In existential terms, Nungarrayi's wrestling between the reference points of here and there establishes newly settled ground from which she tackles the ceaseless unfolding of new experiences and challenges. Berger conjures this existential back-and-forth as a paradigmatic dimension of the migrant experience.[36] Whereas Berger writes of the "unfreedom" of the migrant's working conditions, Nungarrayi yearns for what she imagines will be its transformative effects. Yet, in the postindustrial city there is little use for her labor. Berger, writing nearly five decades before the precarity of the present, is grim on the migrant worker's prospects: "The naturalness of his inferior status—the naturalness with which he is accorded his inferiority by people, by institutions, by the everyday etiquette of the metropolis, by ready-made phrases and argument—would never be so complete and unhesitating if his function, and the inferior status which it entailed, were new. He has been here from the beginning."[37]

In the shared marginalization that brought Nungarrayi and Ram together lies something of the visceral truth of Hall's and Berger's observations. But as our journey continues, another dimension will move to the fore. Anthropologist Henrik Vigh gets at what I have in mind in his retheorization of navigation as "motion squared," "the act of moving in an environment that is wavering and unsettling," or, more plainly, life lived "in the nervous shadow of uncertainty, poverty and conflict."[38] In Vigh's terms, journeying gives a doubled vantage on destabilization, not only on transforming social formations but also of Nungarrayi's own negotiation of those transforming social formations and her "constant attentiveness to change and movement."[39] When she says to me with a cheeky grin, "Hey, Nangala, see how we roll," she conjures a similar phenomenon to *dubriagem*, the term used by Vigh's interlocutors to gesture to their own dynamic navigation of the tumultuous circumstances of life on the streets of Bissau.

Yet in this situation of spontaneity and flux, traces of stability also feature in the Adelaide scene. In Nungarrayi's affectionate relationship with Ram, I see something of the open, steady disposition that initially brought the two of us together in intercultural friendship in her hometown. I also see glimpses of an attitude that can be traced through the intergenerational history of her family and longer settler colonial history of Warlpiri survivance, so many instances of remarkable openness and optimism in the face of their world being turned upside down.[40] I register my own pleasure in witnessing the love and care and genuine delight exchanged between these two newly associated people as they bring their moral horizons into alignment. Nungarrayi tells me proudly that Ram comes around to clean her house. I watch on as she gently corrects his use of English language and as they rehearse the similarities between the places where they were born, grew up, and still call home. Memories of these "beautiful places" are mustered into the shared space of their new city-based lives as points of ontological anchorage and comforting resources to deal with the present. Moments of great tenderness throw into relief the volatile outbursts that are part and parcel of shared life on the edge.

ONE OF THE MOST arresting selfies that Nungarrayi created and uploaded to Facebook in recent years is a triptych over which she has digitally washed rainbow colors. Three portrait photographs taken in quick succession, faces near-identically set: eyes downcast, slack-jawed, inwardly preoccupied. One day as we sit looking through photos on our mobile phones, she offers this to me as her favorite picture of herself. I am taken aback. I recall the first time I saw this image after she had posted it. I had not seen her in person for some time, and I was shaken by what struck me as her washed-out, desolate expression. I tell her that when I look at the photograph, I see a very sad face. She dismisses my reading. "Nah, I was just having fun!" She laughs. "It was my sister's birthday. She bought me a one-liter bottle of Jim Beam. It was a happy day." "Ah," I say. But I am reluctant to part with my original reading. On the morning of my departure, as I make ready to leave her house and head to the airport, Nungarrayi says she will catch a ride with me. She asks the cab to let her off a kilometer down the road at a hotel where she will spend the afternoon playing the poker machines. "It relaxes me," she tells me with a sparkle in her eye.

3

Between Here
and There

Running the Gauntlet

As Nungarrayi arrives off the flight I have organized to bring her from Adelaide, we embrace, and she is quick to tell me, with a beaming smile on her face, that "this is no longer my home. I don't feel like I am coming home." She already misses Adelaide and her man. If images of Central Australia are held close to the surface as Nungarrayi goes about life in Adelaide, as we journey around Central Australia together in October 2016 it is the emotional pull of Adelaide that asserts itself strongly. That emotional pull is, however, enfolded in a supercharged energy, an edgy engagement with our immediate surroundings, and an eagle eye, constantly alert, that scans public space looking for kin. We take our rental car and head for the hotel on Todd Mall where we are booked to stay. Nungarrayi's luggage consists of a single large striped plastic bag, bulging at the seams with recently acquired secondhand clothes, gifted, she tells me, by her domestic violence caseworker and purchased with money I deposited into her bank account a few days ago. As we settle into our room, she undertakes a series of costume changes in quick succession: trying on outfits, asking my opinion, until she is happy with an ensemble that will take her into Alice Springs public space for the first time in many months.

We walk across to the shopping center to buy something to eat and immediately run into a group of distant relatives. They are hovering not far from the bottle shop, keen to purchase grog. As out-of-towners, they are caught in the net of the local alcohol management plan, a mandatory "point of sale identification process" that requires all people purchasing alcohol to present identification at the shop counter. Profiled Aboriginal people are targeted and stopped before they enter the store. They must run the gauntlet of an iPad-wielding uniformed police officer, who will check their names against the Banned Drinker Register. This is a risky venture—the drinker register is networked via these iPads to a larger database, and it is not uncommon for people navigating the threshold of the bottle shop to be checked, charged, and arrested on the spot for outstanding warrants. Desert people are the primary targets of this regime, but in recent months prominent Aboriginal visitors to the town have lodged complaints after being racially targeted themselves.[1] On this occasion, emboldened with the new energy of arrival and stirred up by the noticeably expanded police presence since my last visit, I agree to help out. I take the fifteen dollars in crumpled notes handed to me by a man Nungarrayi introduces as her cousin and tell the group to meet me a couple of streets away. I walk into the shop, past the patrolling policewoman who ignores me, and purchase two bottles of Yellowtail brand white wine for fifteen dollars, as instructed. I register that the bottle label of the current drink of choice carries a dot-painted jumping kangaroo, mimicking the style of desert Aboriginal art. For a fleeting moment, as I leave the shopping center, I reflect upon the possible legal consequences of my grog-running actions, but I'm more affronted by the discriminatory regime of prohibition that is so blatantly being ramped up in this twenty-first-century frontier town.

After I have delivered the bottles of wine into waiting hands, Nungarrayi and I take our rental car and head south along the Stuart Highway toward the town camp where her aunties reside. As we approach the gap in the mountain range that separates the town from its hinterland, we spot Nungarrayi's Aunt Audrey and her husband ambling slowly along the footpath. They are heading home after some business that has drawn them into town on what will have been a ten-kilometer (more than six-mile) round trip. An emotional reunion follows. As the two women embrace, Audrey bursts into tears. Nungarrayi smiles. She tells me her aunty cries every time Nungarrayi goes away for a while. We help them into the car and drive to the town camp where Audrey and her sister Wilma, Nungarrayi's father's sisters, and their families have occupied two houses for several years. The core residents of the camp comprise Wilma, Audrey and her Arrernte husband, Wilma's two daughters, and the children of those daughters. Among those children are five-year-old twins, a boy and a girl, whose relatives call them "the Africans." Their father is a Sudanese man, a resettled asylum seeker who lived in the town several years ago. For four years he and the children's Warlpiri mother had a shared parenting arrangement, but he has recently relocated to Melbourne and is no longer actively involved in their lives.

Nungarrayi's Aunt Wilma is very unwell. She suffers from chronic diabetes and is currently beset by some other undiagnosed afflictions. When we arrive, we find her lying on a metal bed frame in an alcove on the porch of her house. The remains of a small fire smolder on the concrete slab between Wilma's bed and another that is piled high with blankets and clothing. Nungarrayi immediately sets about massaging the old woman's head and flings unseen substances into the fire. It becomes apparent that people are hungry. We make an expedition back into town to purchase a large family bucket of Kentucky Fried Chicken and distribute its contents among eager children and the other residents of the camp. The children's attention is focused on a litter of puppies. Two boys entertain themselves by trying to coax two of the puppies to fight each other. Later I watch as the young mother of one of the boys snuggles a puppy and feeds it small pieces of soft food.

As we drive back and forth between the house and the town, Nungarrayi and I catch up on each other's news. Our trip has come on the back of a tragic accident in Adelaide two weeks ago from which Nungarrayi and her Bhutanese partner, Ram, are still reeling. One of Ram's closest Nepalese friends was killed in a hit-and-run accident. Ram is devastated. As Nungarrayi recounts the story to me, she is deeply distressed that the death "wasn't even reported on the news" and outraged that "the forty-year-old white female driver" of the car has been "released without charge." Her response echoes an observation other Warlpiri are likely to make of their own plight: that across so many settings and situations their lives are treated as less valuable than the lives of white people. Ram's situation is existentially fragile; he is still trying to find his feet in Adelaide and is deeply frustrated by his inability to secure paid work. He is under considerable pressure at home. He is struggling to learn English. He and his Nepalese peers live with a sense that their presence in this new country is warily tolerated, an attitude falling well short of proper acknowledgment or care. They take comfort in the terms of affirmation they are able to offer each other, and in their shared consumption of marijuana. Nungarrayi is worried that her absence leaves Ram even more vulnerable than usual, and she calls him regularly, urging him to go and keep company with his family, not his friends.

We have several aims on this trip. Nungarrayi has promised to take me around Alice Springs to show me the town from her perspective. We then plan to travel to the small desert town where her brother lives and then travel with him on to their paternal estate in the desert. A more pressing concern for Nungarrayi is to locate her daughter-in-law and six-month-old grandson; she wants to check on the well-being of the child, whose father is still serving time in prison. One morning we visit houses in two town camps before finally being directed to a block of flats on the west side of town, where the mother has recently been allocated accommodations. We pull into the car park at the same time as another car driven by the case manager from a nongovernmental organization (NGO), who is also looking for her. He tells us he has received a briefing from police, who have a warrant out for the woman's arrest. She has been charged with drunk driving offenses, while driving with her three young children in the car, and also with stealing alcohol. A separate truancy charge hangs in the balance; her school-age child has not been attending school for some time. The case manager tells us it is likely that this young woman will lose her allocated flat on account of the list of charges against her. She was granted the flat after the domestic violence incident that resulted in Nungarrayi's son, David, going to prison. Nungarrayi tells the caseworker that the woman is probably in a small town to the north where her family live.

We climb back into the car and drive out to the Alice Springs cemetery to visit the graves of several recently deceased relatives. Visiting these graves is a moving experience for both of us, especially as we locate the final resting place of a young man who was Nungarrayi's son's closest friend-brother, the son of her close extended sister. As a child, the deceased man, along with his sister and their mother, Amanda, once spent Christmas with me and my family in Melbourne. After much searching, we find his grave, lovingly adorned with his treasured Melbourne Demons football club cap and two ceramic angels. The grave of this young man's grandmother, a much-respected ritual leader, is just a few meters away. An older extended sister of Nungarrayi who had spent several years in an Alice Springs nursing home and died just a month ago has also recently been buried nearby.

The cemetery is one of the most beautifully cultivated landscapes in the town. It is midspring, and recent heavy rains have made the lawns lush. The

FIGURE 3.1 Looking for family, Alice Springs cemetery (photo by author)

long arcing lines of burial plaques are bordered by carefully tended garden beds cascading with the vibrant color of native flowering shrubs. Here and there are graves of children, highly decorated with spinning plastic wheels and flowers. But this is not Warlpiri land. I reflect grimly that the turbulent displacements of the present extend all the way to death. Why are these Warlpiri buried here, rather than in close proximity to their kin back in the Big Town where these people lived? Or on their ancestral estates? At what point did the Alice Springs cemetery become a preferred place for Warlpiri burials? Everything comes back to The Troubles, whose effects can be bewildering. Alice Springs—the place where policing and governance and sickness and fighting bear down so hard on so many Warlpiri—has become the final resting place of choice for those concerned to avert further interference by enemies and sorcerers. This strikes me as the ultimate act through which Warlpiri participate in their own exile.

Circumstances dictate decisions taken by kin about where to bury a person. The sum of a life, which historically shaped considerations of funeral and burial arrangements, cannot in the present cut through the dispersed sensibility of fear; the idea that the desert is creepy and dangerous and that there are enemies to avoid now pervades the southern Warlpiri community. The senior Nampijinpa woman buried in Alice Springs was among a group of sisters I called aunty, who wielded significant authority in ceremonial and community matters in the mid-1990s. These women took enormous pride in their vigorous hunting and gathering skills, their knowledge of places, as well as the customary authority they commanded through an extensive repertoire of songs and dances. I observed this authority forcefully enacted on ceremonial grounds and in local politics, as well as at a regional gathering of Aboriginal women over several days in the winter of 1995. The Nampijinpa sisters loved nothing more than to be driven to their ancestral estate to camp in their own company. For days on end they would reminisce, sing, and hunt. They subsisted primarily on bush tucker, revitalizing themselves and their country. Arriving back in the Big Town after such a sojourn, they would parade their newly energized selves around the place, proudly displaying their shiny skin and desirably fattened-up bodies. The passing of this generation of women, with their confident knowledge of country and wielding of authority over the wider domain of community life, has left a profound vacuum. It is into this vacuum that the volatile chaos of The Troubles has swarmed.

New Magic

The pervasiveness of sorcery fears shadows the constancy of premature deaths. As she recounts the recent merging of what were once distinct categories of Warlpiri monsters, anthropologist Yasmine Musharbash observes that premature deaths have become a devastating fact of life that defies explanation from the perspective both of Warlpiri ontology and of the functioning of the wealthy Australian nation-state.[2] In making this connection, Musharbash implies that the catastrophic constancy of death dissolves an earlier set of certainties around the spatial distribution of fear. In the volatile present, distinctions between discrete monsters, and between monsters and humans, blur, as monsters take on many human qualities and human beings take on more monstrous ones.[3] Simultaneously, malevolent beings appear to have been disembedded from their earlier associations with particular regions and places—a geographic distribution that Mervyn Meggitt was able to report with remarkable detail for the desert in the 1950s.[4] Meggitt described elaborate ceremonies and practices of social containment that Warlpiri men mounted in their efforts to deal with and placate a pantheon of *jarnpa* spirit beings. He did not speculate on whether the traumatic experience of relocation to the new Hooker Creek settlement, just months before his arrival, had given rise to a spike in monster fear. However, some of Meggitt's observations, such as the belief that white people wielding guns were the only authorities with power great enough to ward off these dangerous creatures, indicate tight entanglements of colonial power and sorcery.

Today there appear to be no limits on where shape-shifting spirits, malevolent and otherwise, can travel. Such a relationship between deterritorialization, disempowerment, and sorcery beliefs has been widely observed everywhere colonial and capital domination have intervened in kin-based societies. Michael Taussig's classic study *The Devil and Commodity Fetishism in South America* elucidated the vigorous work undertaken by Indigenous miners and plantation workers in Bolivia and Colombia to apply their explanatory power of the devil to the turbulent transformations wrought by commodity extraction.[5] Taussig's work in South America, Peter Geschiere's intricate studies of witchcraft in Cameroon, Jean Comaroff and John Comaroff's analyses for South Africa, Lucas Bessire's shadowy caiman in the Chaco, and Dan Jorgensen's recent writings on Papua New Guinea, all direct attention to political and socioeconomic circumstances beyond the local, to the postcolonial politics of domination, hypermarginality, and containment as processes through which any exploration of sorcery must turn.[6] As Bruce Kapferer puts it, sorcery is never abstract. It is "a thoroughgoing force of the social and the political": "Sorcery encapsulates the violence of new politically and economically conditioned fears and struggles. Its monstrous symbolism and matching practices at once assume the phantom shape of the destructive, implacable and apparently irresolute forces of everyday life, and attempt to strike directly at them."[7]

Warlpiri sorcery accusations often intervene in transforming politics over the conduct of the rule of law, but also more broadly in the diffuse insecurities of life. So it is that one afternoon at the height of The Troubles rainbow serpents were observed circling the sky above the Alice Springs prison, casting judgment on inmates awaiting trial. A bout of torrential rain across Central Australia that same year was said to have been caused by an insufficiently sanctioned exchange between a drug dealer and a senior custodian of a sacred site. Sudden deaths by heart attack, shockingly prevalent among people in their twenties and thirties, always involve accusations of black magic, bone-pointing, or sightings of magic-wielding enemies entering homes under the cover of darkness. While sorcery powers were once understood as inherited or bestowed among kin, the current generation of sorcerers are said to acquire power outside of ceremonial contexts. At times sorcerers are self-taught. I am told they "copy things they learn from ninja films." More recent stories tell of the actions of a group of seven brothers with superhuman powers who travel at lightning speed wherever and whenever their services are needed. They are said to have faces that are too horrible to describe, but their willingness to intervene in situations on behalf of kin makes them true *marlpa*, kin-companions.

In the present, dislocation is no straightforward process of physical displacement. Accounts of the workings of black magic suggest a simultaneous shrinkage of the space in which people can act and effect change in their lives, as well as a radiating dispersal of destabilized power across space and time. The Troubles effect the stretching of kinship relations, putting those relations under heavy strain while keeping people caught in their grip. If displacement is ultimately a process of existential and social disembedding, The Troubles enact an especially devastating case of such cutting adrift, as sorcery acts are wielded against affinal kin—between those who historically intermarried and fulfilled reciprocal responsibilities for each other's places and people. The very ground of Warlpiri social organization is hijacked in these processes. Related fault lines of interpersonal violence and its ricocheting effects are everywhere. A daughter is "put in jail" by her biological mother following an incident of assault, ostensibly to "teach the daughter a lesson" on where authority lies. A young woman is medically evacuated to an Adelaide hospital after a brutal assault by her partner, leaving their one-year-old child to be taken into state care. Incidents such as these shadow the moral messaging of national politics that indicate remote-living Aboriginal people are incapable of looking after their own affairs, their own children, houses, and money. They need to be governed harder. A recent genre of mobile phone videos produced by young Aboriginal men in the north and uploaded to YouTube intervenes mimetically in their visibilized entrenchment as violent offenders: these men deploy into public space their own pictures of themselves as proud fighters.

Emplacement, Exclusion, Containment

If sorcery is "a thoroughgoing force of the social and the political," what are the tangible social and political forms that it responds to and feeds off on the ground in Alice Springs?[8] Here, I take up sociologist John Torpey's proposition that a cornerstone of modern state practices is the "expropriation of legitimate means of movement."[9] Torpey pinpoints the interrelationship between the production and governance of identity and authorization/exclusion of citizen-subjects' access to particular spaces, as vital to the workings of the state and production of a dependent citizenry. On the streets of Alice Springs, practices of policing and governance, on the one hand, and Aboriginal kinship and sorcery, on the other, operate as two ontologically opposed orders of identification and containment. Policing practices register transient Aboriginal bodies, singling out bush people in terms of heightened risk, as a category of moralized and criminalized people in need of monitoring, profiling, exclusion, and incarceration.[10] These policing practices pinpoint mobility itself as dangerous. People from the bush interact and transact in ways that pose a threat to the operations of capital—most pointedly because they do not straightforwardly obey its logic. By and large, they do not own private property and are not wage earners and are thus excluded from the "right to the city" and its commercial spaces.[11] Kin traveling together publicly perform their investment in values of a different kind; they practice their own forms of segregation in the manner in which they comport themselves, interact, and occupy and move through the town's spaces. For bush people, identity is variously assumed, given, and imposed by the town's exclusionary regimes.

From the perspective of settler colonial history, Alice Springs is relatedly a "space of competing meanings."[12] It is a place where Aboriginal people are both "loathed and desired," an intense microcosm of the continental situation that was established in 1788 when Europeans first arrived.[13] What followed, in psychological terms, suggests psychoanalyst Amanda Dowd, was "doubt, confusion and psychic pain," and ultimately, structurally, "a psychological act of obliteration" that would later be enshrined in the doctrine of terra nullius, the idea that Australia was, when the Europeans arrived, land belonging to no one.[14] The ongoing failure of successive Australian governments and the polity at large to squarely face the traumatic circumstances of rupture and loss on which the nation is founded has led to Australian settler society being described as "elusive," with a quality of being "neither here nor there," what Ken Gelder and Jane Jacobs describe as the anxiety of the uncanny.[15] In Dowd's reading this anxiety of the uncanny is an anxiety of belonging, a displacement anxiety that arises out of existential doubt about "having a place to be" and "having a place in the scheme of things."[16]

It is not necessary to adopt Dowd's psychoanalytic framework in order to be compelled by her argument. We might equally enlist the concept of emplacement in making the same argument. Emplacement and the idea of *being securely held in place* that it connotes are vital dimensions of subjectivity and person-place interrelationships.[17] It is only through emplacement that a person has a point of view and experiences legitimacy. Digging more deeply into the specific terms of the production of Central Desert personhood, Fred Myers describes the intersubjective relations through which persons "hold" country, and in the process are produced and known as particular, distinctively related persons.[18] The threat of disruption to this matrix of emplacement is a threat at the level of security, ontological safety, and identity. This is the threat of literally being out of place. Alice Springs is a space in which emplacement's meaningful containment of identity is ruptured for all Aboriginal people, including its "traditional owners," and relatedly for those who came after, with many frictions and vulnerabilities to be navigated. Settler vulnerabilities take on a heightened form in a town where the violence of dispossession is apparent in so many self-other transactions. Yet, such anxiety is by no means equally shared by all Alice Springs residents. As Åse Ottosson points out, division and difference are produced unevenly across experience, with the highly educated, white, antiracist employees in the Indigenous sector acquiring a markedly different set of attitudes and sense of belonging than manual workers.[19] For Nungarrayi, Alice Springs is in the present an intensely liminal place, one in which her own ambivalent status—as here but not here—is amplified.

Traveling around town with Nungarrayi, I gain a new sobering vantage on the fracturing of emplacement and relatedly on what I have come to think of as the conjuncture of postcolonial exclusions, the old and new forms of securitized containment that are brought to bear upon Aboriginal people from the bush. A series of roadside markers memorialize Warlpiri killed in car accidents, including one very recent incident that claimed the lives of a young couple in their thirties. Another memorial on the Stuart Highway marks the site where the two-year-old grandson of Nungarrayi's husband died after he ran onto the road directly in front of an oncoming tourist vehicle towing a caravan. These memorials are like satellites for the growing number of Warlpiri graves in the Alice Springs cemetery. Then there are all the places that instantiate Aboriginal people's exceptional status in this town: the hotels renowned for racist managers; the shops where uniformed police stand guard watching over the movements of Aboriginal customers; and one particular establishment that people are especially affronted by, where a sign is placed in the front window during the summer season of initiation ceremonies, stating baldly that people covered in red ocher are not permitted to handle shop goods. There are the art galleries that line the town's main promenades, selling Aboriginal art to tourists. There are the cafés next to these galleries where staff chase away Aboriginal beggars. There are supermarkets where customers from "prescribed communities"—those small towns identified by the federal government as subject to the "emergency response"—must shop with a government-issued Basics-Card in order to access their "quarantined" welfare payments. There are the car yards known to benefit greatly from Aboriginal money. There are the large offices of the Central Land Council, the powerful regional organization that has become the focus of various forms of dissatisfaction. There is the Todd riverbed and other public spaces where bush people congregate, that are heavily patrolled by police. There is the new multistory, multi-million-dollar supreme court building that towers above all other buildings, asserting the town's core business as the enforcement of the rule of European law. There is the new prison twenty kilometers (twelve miles) south of the town, well out of sight, where more than 90 percent of inmates are Aboriginal.[20]

Alice Springs only comes fully into view as a distinct kind of place from a Warlpiri perspective when seen through the vantage of relational geography. A longer historical perspective would trace the various forms of marginalization that have been imposed on visitors from the bush since the town's inception.[21] The most recent geopolitical developments and related expropriation of the legitimate means of movement are enshrined in legislation passed by federal and Northern Territory governments since the 2007 Northern Territory Emergency Response.[22] Seventy-two bush towns were subject to new land tenure arrangements as the federal government compulsorily acquired land that had until then been subject to the local Aboriginal authority under the terms of the Aboriginal Land Rights Act (Northern Territory), ostensibly to enable streamlined and intensified government service delivery and provision of new housing. Large blue painted signs were erected on public roads leading into these towns, much to the shame and anger of local residents, declaring them to be areas into which it was illegal to bring alcohol and pornography, implying by their very presence that such trafficking was widespread. In such ways, as Daniel Fisher observes, the Australian government conjures "the very violence it seeks to govern."[23] Simultaneous with these new stigmatizations of places and their residents, a new income management regime was introduced that sequestered expenditure of social security income, prohibiting bush people from purchasing alcohol and forcing them to shop at commercial outlets licensed to deal with the card. In the early period of the operation of the BasicsCard, residents of some towns were forced to travel hundreds of kilometers at their own cost to access shops in regional centers with the technological capability to process transactions with these cards.[24] The declaration of the Northern Territory Intervention triggered generalized anxieties among Aboriginal people and precipitated a swelling of numbers of bush visitors to Alice Springs.[25] Their increased presence stirred tensions across many levels of Alice Springs society, not least with local Arrernte Aboriginal traditional owners. In 2011, as part of the "Alice Springs Transformation Plan," the Commonwealth government funded facilities at a new "visitor park" to be run as an Aboriginal hostel, offering the cheapest accommodations in town. The "park," encased by a high fence with a security entrance that is locked from 9:00 p.m. to 6:00 a.m., is promoted as safe, and drug and alcohol free. It is segregated from the commercial precinct on the outskirts of town.

The fusing of mobility with criminalization has been a widely observed dimension of modern governance, yet recent approaches to policing the movement of people from the bush fuse criminalization with mobility *and* emplacement.[26] It is by virtue of their identification *with* particular places, and their mobility *from* those places, that bush people come to be marked in terms of heightened risk. Alice Springs already boasts three times the national average of police officers per head of population. The Northern Territory government predicts it will double its current number of police to fifteen hundred by mid-2020. An additional seventy-five "police auxiliary liquor inspectors" are in the process of being trained to meet the expanding demands of the point-of-sale identity checks, which are currently funded to the tune of $11 million per annum. Yet, as is the case in other parts of the world, this expansion of policing occurs at a time when incidents of criminal activity, including assaults involving alcohol and domestic violence, are reportedly at their lowest rates in ten years.[27] Such a disconnect confirms the logic of securitization as an encroaching culture of governance that turns upon the intensification of containment.[28] The same logic is at work in the Australian government's offshore detention of asylum seekers in prison camps in Papua New Guinea, where 75 percent of the 271 men still detained in 2019 had been determined by the government to be genuine refugees.[29] Such is the transit of empire, as Jodi Byrd argues, the trajectory that conjoins settler colonial dispossession and the post-9/11 security order.[30]

But these are not the lenses through which most Warlpiri understand their place in Alice Springs. For some, the town is not only a place to visit but also a rightful place of long-term residence, and sometimes home. Attachments to place are multilayered. Hundreds of Warlpiri were born in the Alice Springs hospital. Some have married and produced families with Alice Springs Arrernte traditional owners. There are the dozens of Warlpiri houses of intergenerational residence scattered through the town camps as well as other town-based rental accommodations. Nungarrayi's first experience living in Alice Springs came in 1990 when one of her extended fathers took up employment with a petrol-sniffing prevention program and was allocated a house in a town camp. Also participating in this relocation were her grandfather, who was a significant ceremonial leader, three of his sons, and as many as ten grandchildren who had previously lived between the Big Town and their outstation. Two aunts and their daughters, as well as one of Nungarrayi's sisters, would go on to be more or less permanent Alice Springs residents. Nungarrayi sent her own children to attend boarding school here, and she takes prides in recalling her employment during those years as a translator at the local hospital. Other relatives continue to move sporadically between larger regional and smaller desert towns spread across the vast intersecting regions that span the Central and Western Deserts.

This history of family movement is close to the surface for Nungarrayi as we drive around town. But her agitated and determined pursuit of recognition among kin, close and extended, registers her current mobility in the terms of rupture much more strongly than continuity. Over the days we roam Alice Springs streets, bars, Aboriginal agencies, and hospital, Nungarrayi is highly animated and pursues the reactivation of extended kin relationships with irrepressible energy. She is aware that in her relocation to Adelaide she has acquired transformed status among her relatives. She is self-conscious about their responses to her newly slimmed-down body. As we travel around, she insists that we eat "junk food" and talks of asking one of her aunts to make her special tea that encourages weight gain. She takes every opportunity to diminish the social distance that is an inevitable outcome of her exile.

As we drive around one morning, Nungarrayi mentions in an offhand way that two weeks ago she had her Northern Territory driver's license confiscated for twelve months, after being arrested by Adelaide police for drunk driving and disorderly behavior in a public place. As a consequence, she is without any formal identification. She asks if we can visit the Motor Registry office, where she expects to be issued an interim ID card. The woman across the counter greets Nungarrayi and asks for her address. Nungarrayi tells her she is living in Adelaide "at the moment," and the woman immediately responds that she cannot issue identification for persons who reside outside the Northern Territory. Nungarrayi seems nonplussed, tells the woman, "OK, thanks," and we leave. Back in the car, she suggests we go and get a copy of her birth certificate, and we drive directly to the Registry of Births, Deaths and Marriages. After some easy joking interaction with the female employee who is attending the desk, Nungarrayi's mood instantly shifts when the woman suggests there might be a complication in issuing the certificate. Communication across the counter becomes a little unclear. As if a switch has been flicked, Nungarrayi goes off, aggressively accusing the woman of deliberately withholding the certificate. The woman's friendly attitude instantly dissolves as she retreats behind a reserved disposition and reduces the scope of her communication with us. Looking to defuse the situation, I lightheartedly pose some questions: Is the holdup a result of a computer glitch or the relocation of services between offices, or does it have to do with the confounding variety of spellings of names in the registration of Aboriginal births? No reply. Finally, the woman, with assistance from a colleague, successfully navigates the computerized database, locates the correct record, and prints the certificate. She hands it to Nungarrayi without making eye contact. I pay the thirty-dollar processing fee. As we leave the office, Nungarrayi hands the paper to me and asks me to look after it.

Later the same day, again on Nungarrayi's urging, we visit the office of Northern Territory Translation Services, with which she was registered and employed for several years in work for the Alice Springs hospital and court system. It is a Thursday afternoon, and the office is quiet. Two young female employees are killing time, chatting in the waiting room. One of them has recently applied a white clay mask to her face. Nungarrayi and the women acknowledge each other. She asks after the manager, her former boss, who emerges from a back office to greet us. Nungarrayi explains that she has recently moved to Adelaide and asks for a letter of recommendation so that she might pursue translation work in South Australia. The manager goes to consult a file and returns to advise Nungarrayi that she would need to complete a "refresher course" in order to qualify for accreditation. She offers Nungarrayi a place in a course the following week. "Sorry," Nungarrayi replies in frustration, "I'll be going home to Adelaide by then."

As suggested across these scenes, Nungarrayi's identification is multiply attenuated—in her newly distanced relations with kin who register her as having moved away; in her status as unemployed, which keeps her tightly hitched to the grueling dead-end requirements of Centrelink; and in her recent criminalized punishment that leaves her without a driver's license. All of these interactions confirm the liminality of her situation. In Alice Springs she cannot help but have a heightened sense of being precariously placed, inside and outside the world she occupies. The uncertainty of each of these encounters might appear relatively banal—and arguably muted as such by my presence—but as Nungarrayi's triggered response over her birth certificate indicates, there is much at stake. Here is a glimpse of her awareness of a terrifying possibility, a situation in which, as Victor Turner would put it, she is "no longer classified and not yet classified."[31]

Our journeying around Alice Springs also reveals what in another context Roberto Benaduce describes as distinctive "cartographies of pain and anxiety."[32] Writing of the epistemological violence of "the national order of things" that reduces the experiences of displaced people to the categories of "refugees," "victims of trafficking," "asylum seekers," "sans papiers," "illegal immigrants," Benaduce observes that the lived experience of actual displaced people is irreducible to consistent narrative reconstruction and its neat resolutions.[33] He pushes further, arguing that ethnography provides a rare mechanism by which "we" observers of distant suffering are forced into a differently structured relation to the displaced other as we are made to "stand by the pain and confusion" and stories of inhumane violence.[34] This repositioning occurs when we confront the "political fact" of displacement, the "violence of the contemporary moral and economic horizon" through which displaced persons are forced to navigate the interstices of social being and nonbeing.[35] In the settler colonial setting of Alice Springs, it is not only the "complex political and human dimensions" of Nungarrayi's experience that are revealed but "also the density of an unspeakable, *repressed* collective past, still waiting to be redeemed."[36]

Stirring Anxieties

Nungarrayi says she has not slept well since leaving Adelaide. She finds it hard to sleep since a *ngankari* healer bestowed that power in her belly. It keeps her aware/awake even when she is sleeping. The writhing nature of that newly acquired power is one kind of compelling explanation for her supercharged, hyped-up dynamic, the force she has become. It is as if in the midst of The Troubles Nungarrayi faced a choice: to die or stay alive. In choosing to stay alive, she has committed herself to a state of hypercharged aliveness—not able to rest, always on alert, always aware she is somewhere other than where she should be. She ceaselessly interrogates memories for a sense of how her situation has come about. Places and situations of true, unconscious belonging are now beyond reach. Maybe they always were? Separation, longing, and recognition are ever-present in the emotional energy she applies to the work of creating relationships, of trying to anchor herself in Warlpiri *and* administrative space.[37] Identification rarely has cause to establish itself as a genuine concern for Warlpiri living in bush towns. Paper-based identification emerges as a pressing issue only when one can no longer take for granted densely situated social standing with kin. Across the mutually exclusive identifications of kinship and citizenship, Nungarrayi is aware of her destabilized status. She is neither here nor there; neither local, nor cosmopolitan. Axel Honneth captures something of the fragility of Nungarrayi's situation when he writes that as consciousness of one's individuality grows, a person comes "to depend on the conditions of recognition they are afforded by the life-world of their social environment."[38]

During our time in Alice Springs, I am becoming more aware of Nungarrayi invoking our friendship as a liminal space of care. It is a distinctive element of our research-as-sisterhood that "we" effectively mediate between and attend to these two social formations of belonging: kinship and abstract documented identity. Nungarrayi turns to me as someone who has known her and her family on either side of her upheaval, but perhaps also because our interactions have always been driven by reflexive exploration of life's possibilities. But this is no leveling exercise. It is a paradox of this journeying-together-research that the more fragile Nungarrayi's situation appears, the more stable my own feels. Perhaps it is the very setting of Alice Springs that delivers this unequal conjuncture. When we part company, our default positions are antithetical to each other: hers, into the intense swirl of hypermobile kinship; mine, into capital-enabled individualized seclusion—café, bar, hotel room. Despite best intentions, at times I have a sinking feeling of dread that in this research I am simply replicating anthropology's erstwhile use of the other—the crisis of my own privileged existence neatly deflected in Nungarrayi's more absorbing, more tangible crisis.

Nungarrayi often turns our conversation to her ex-husband, Daniel. I have been friends with Daniel as long as I have known Nungarrayi, but only now in the context of this research am I learning some crucial elements of his life story. Daniel's mother died when he was very young, about four years old, in circumstances that probably involved a ritual killing. How to comprehend the mark left on a small boy by such a sudden, devastating loss? Through the nearly twenty years of their marriage, Nungarrayi tells me, she tried from time to time to get him to talk about what she recognized as a deep pain inside him, a pain that registered in night terrors and inexplicable eruptions of violence. I am shocked at my own ignorance as our discussions explore the childhood situations of other peers, which cumulatively open out as a normalized, intergenerational plane of rupture. Previously I had little sense of how widespread alcoholism had been in the generation of Nungarrayi's parents. I did not know that many of my friends had grown up in the absence of one or both biological parents, who left them behind to go to town drinking, or to flee violent relationships. This was the case for Nungarrayi's mother, who left for Darwin when Nungarrayi was about ten years old. Was my lack of knowledge the result of friends' silences, or my own failure to register such sensitive matters? Could it be that the web of extended kinship I observe Nungarrayi vigorously reactivating now as we journey around town by foot and by car is itself an outcome of such widespread fracturing of smaller intimate family units? The loss of a parent is counteracted by the seemingly infinite capacity of other close relatives or assemblies of kin to assume responsibilities to "look after" or "grow up" displaced children. Hyperkinship, however, at times appears to perpetuate its own feedback loop; it is part and parcel of precarious Aboriginal life, a visceral, existential response to the fracturing of intimate parental bonds, to the near constancy of bereavement, to rejection by stranger-others, a mechanism for spreading emotional and existential attachments among a wider web of relatives. Stretched across space and time, as Nungarrayi's cosmopolitan aspirations and emergent subjectivity falter, acknowledgment and affirmation of extended kin take on a newly weighted urgency and necessity.

As I sit in an Alice Springs café punching the keys of my laptop, writing notes on observations of recent days, Nungarrayi is ensconced in her family camp, rubbing the body of her very ill aunt who is telling her stories her family history, inspired to do so by our research-related visit. Nungarrayi is declaring loudly to all who will listen her love of family, her commitment to look after her family. She presents me with a rapid-fire version of the stories her aunt has told her, as I drive into the camp on her request to give her money so she can buy some dinner. What transpires is a return trip to the bottle shop. Nungarrayi is already charged—not full drunk but speedy and highly animated as she tells me of these new family discoveries. The narrative turns upon a *jilkija* initiation journey across the desert into Western Australia involving her father and grandfather, sometime in the 1960s, before Nungarrayi was born. The two men are said to have stayed on for some time in a small Aboriginal settlement where they both married and started families. Nungarrayi may have siblings she did not previously know of. She tells me that an airstrip was named after her father in recognition of the hard work he did while he was there. Nungarrayi says that Aunty Wilma "wants to get her stories down before she goes." We should go back to see her tomorrow with my tape recorder. Nungarrayi is high on our project, on attention to her life, on affirmation of her importance, on being in the company of close kin. I am reminded of Basil Sansom's observation that an Aboriginal person's movement between places is regularly described by others in ways that are morally inflected.[39] To move, to leave the company of kin, and to enter the company of others are morally weighted decisions. To broadcast one's intentions and commitments is to intervene in the collective formation of assessments and judgments. To leave an assembly of kin on one's own rather than through the more common means of kinship riding places one in a highly vulnerable position in relation to such assessments.

As I pull into the small supermarket car park, I make clear my displeasure at being misled and lured across town after dark on what amounts to a grog-running expedition. I am astonished when Nungarrayi dissolves into tears and then apologizes profusely. Such emotional fragility is completely out of character. I deposit her and her nieces who have come along for the ride in the car park while I drive around the corner to the bottle shop, where police are on duty checking IDs. I make a quick and seamless purchase of a bottle of rum and one liter of Coca-Cola. I deliver Nungarrayi, her kin, and the purchases back to camp, a setting where the consumption of alcohol is prohibited.

In the perilous movement of people through time and space, both places and kin are made and remade. A primary driver of movement is the opportunistic pursuit of resources: a meal, an adventurous ride, the numbing release of alcohol or ganja, the conviviality of assembled kin, a relatively safe place to stay. There are larger possibilities of movement at another scale enabled by receipt of mining royalties, or largesse from some new government policy. All of these forms of Warlpiri movement, no matter their diversity, never seem to be in search of a destination per se. The near-pristine abandoned houses at one of the outstations on Nungarrayi's ancestral estate attest to this; the houses stand as a kind of melancholy memorial to the collapsed outstation movement more generally and the bewildering history of the disconnect between government imaginaries and Aboriginal ways of living.[40] Warlpiri rarely look to *settle* in the conventional Western sense; they do not arrive at a destination. They keep moving, always on the lookout for what is coming next. But this movement is no pure nomadism, no movement for movement's sake, no universal wayfaring.[41] Rather, it is movement governed by particular constraints. Places may be dreamed or desired into being, but the *process* of placemaking is constant and contingent and always influenced by forces beyond one's control, most profoundly the demands of kin, but also by whatever governmental imaginaries are in play. Immediacy is always a driving force.[42] Nungarrayi's displacement causes her to elicit the demands of kinship. She puts herself in the social spaces that call out such demands. She *needs* to be demanded of, needs to be recognized as *walalja*—a countrywoman, sister, niece, mother. It is only in being drawn into such an emplaced order of relatedness and the attendant issues that arise that her focus is diverted from the alienating world at large. These primary social relations establish moral particularism, to invoke terms that both Honneth and Hans-Georg Gadamer deal in. Emplacement is the primary relationship, the social setting in which one's distinctive abilities and contributions are recognized. This form of recognition is foundational if persons are to achieve status as morally accountable active subjects.[43] Kinship has none of the conditional or contingent dimensions of citizenship as experienced by Warlpiri. Or does it?

On the night of our lightning visit to her hometown in October 2016, the three-hour drive in darkness into Alice Springs stimulated much memory work and storytelling. Nungarrayi recalled several episodes from years long past, journeys made along that road, driving home in the company of her drunk husband who was threatening to beat her. She described one incident in which she pulled the car off the road and made a run for it with her daughter and another small child who was traveling with them. They stumbled around in the dark until they found the cattle station fence line and then followed it in the direction of a roadhouse. By luck or design, they were not far from the roadhouse, the only place to raise an alarm for help along a 300-kilometer (186-mile) stretch of road. In her stressed state, Nungarrayi got disoriented and separated from the children. Her daughter ran the remaining distance to the roadhouse and alerted the managers. Someone came and found Nungarrayi. The police were called. Her husband was arrested on a charge of assault as well as on outstanding warrants and was taken away in the back of a police van. In a separate incident when Nungarrayi was driving the family back from town, her husband started a fight, making jealous accusations against her. Nungarrayi stopped the car and ran off. She remembers the kids watching on and laughing as he chased her through the scrub. She laughs too as she recalls the scene. She also remembers her husband was always without a driver's license, having had it canceled for drunk driving.

Alter-security

In the in-between space of Alice Springs, a vitriolic critique that I have become accustomed to hearing, one that has been obsessively worked at a distance, dissolves in the face of kinly intimacy. The woman who elsewhere Nungarrayi dismisses as "not entitled" is embraced face-to-face as a loving sister. Relatedness in the here and now is worth much more than the tens of thousands of dollars the woman is said to have unjustly claimed in mining royalty payments that have been allocated for distribution among Nungarrayi's paternal family. This sister has lived in Alice Springs for many years. She has a prominent public profile, a white husband, and a daughter who sits on the Alice Springs Council. All three have been highly vocal on the problem of domestic violence in desert communities and attribute that violence to the structures of traditional culture. The husband is infuriated with the line of liberal critique that "blames white culture every time an Aboriginal man kills or beats his wife." As we sit on cane chairs on his porch, he talks at me—on and on through incident after incident—like a man possessed. He did not want his grandson to be initiated and was "so proud" of his wife when "she told senior men to their faces that she did not want the boy to go through business." Male initiation has been corrupted, he tells me—"the cutting can be done by someone who has been in prison and knows hardly anything or is drunk and can mutilate the boy." Initiation is the context in which men learn it is acceptable, a sanctioned part of being an Aboriginal man, to be violent toward women. He sees himself as being on a mission to expose the truth of this corrupted culture.

This is a distillation of one side of a vigorously argued debate in Australia. The day after my interaction with this man, prominent Aboriginal woman and recently elected New South Wales parliamentarian Linda Burney published an opinion piece in the *Australian* that articulates the other side: "Cuts can lead to bruises and far worse for women."[44] The dozens of comments posted online in response to Burney's piece—all by men—unanimously dismiss her appeal to recognize the structural issues at play in the violence that pervades Indigenous communities, including the government's slashing of funding in support of family violence programs. These correspondents, like Nungarrayi's sister and her white brother-in-law, criticize the secrecy of Aboriginal culture and invoke the responsibility paradigm. They are advocates of boarding school for Aboriginal teenagers, of private homeownership, of aspects of customary law being criminalized, and of the reform of Northern Territory land rights legislation that enshrines forms of inalienable communal landownership to allow individualized title.

One morning the police turn up early at the family camp and arrest the teenage boyfriend of Wilma's granddaughter Julie and take him away in handcuffs. Nungarrayi tells me no one knows why. Two days later we are sitting in camp as an NGO caseworker drives in to check on Julie. Julie is fourteen or fifteen, and the caseworker tells me the organization she works for is trying to "get her into a good school situation" and to help "get her on track" to being able to do some kind of "meaningful work." Nungarrayi reminds the caseworker about the recent public revelations of maltreatment of Aboriginal children in Darwin's Don Dale youth detention center. Two months before our visit, the Australian Broadcasting Commission's investigative program *Four Corners* had detailed shocking accounts of the workings of the detention center, including the stripping of inmates and the use of tear gas and mechanical restraints.[45] In an image that would become iconic and trigger the calling of a Royal Commission, the program included chilling footage of a youth whose arms and legs were manacled to a chair, his head covered in a "spit hood" that was secured around his neck. The Don Dale images echo the degrading photographs that depicted the post-9/11 US imprisonment at Abu Ghraib of men accused of terrorism and detained without trial. The Australian images are of children. I know from Warlpiri friends how widely this program was watched and how distressed people have been by its revelations. Everyone has a relative who has spent time in Don Dale, whose inmate population is 100 percent Aboriginal. When I visited him in jail, Nungarrayi's ex-husband told me of prison inmates, some of whom had spent time at Don Dale when they were children, climbing onto the roof of a prison building in anguish and protest after the program was broadcast. Nungarrayi urges me to watch that program "all the way through." She pleads with the caseworker, asking her and her colleagues to "keep a close eye on what is going on in those detention places with young kids." Her implication: go and do your work where it is actually needed.

The hearings of the Royal Commission triggered by the Don Dale revelations commence while we are in Alice Springs. On the opening day, counsel assisting Peter Callaghan sets the scene: As of 2015 the Aboriginal population of the Northern Territory stands at 30 percent. Of those in juvenile detention, 95 percent are Aboriginal (a rate that plateaus at 100 percent just weeks after these remarks are made). Eighty-six percent of children subject to care and protection orders are Indigenous. Callaghan also observes that fifty reports with relevance to the proceedings have been produced in the last ten years, suggesting that the circumstances under inquiry are not exceptional, but rather indicate "persistent failure." He asks, "Do we need to confront some sort of inquiry mentality in which investigation is allowed as a substitution for action and reporting is accepted as a replacement for results?"[46] Pat Anderson, an Aboriginal woman and coauthor of the report on Aboriginal child abuse that the federal government cited as its touchstone in declaring a "national emergency" in 2007, told the Royal Commission that the Intervention "brought Aboriginal communities to their knees." The last ten years, she said, "have been just appalling."

See How We Roll

I often think the scenes I witness in Central Australia are more conducive to being captured on film than in words. This afternoon, as we drive into the town camp, I glimpse a group of kids playing at the end of the road adjacent to the railway line, throwing stones and larking about, while being watched over from a distance by a senior woman leaning heavily on a walking stick. Hours earlier the aunties scolded these same kids for roaming the camp with a heavily pregnant desert lizard they had caught and were carrying around by the tail. They should be at school. Their grandmothers express this view but do not enforce it. Movement catches my eye, and I turn to watch a lone drunken man stumbling about, swinging his arms, engaged trancelike in an imaginary fight or a dance. Last night as I was heading back to my hotel, I passed a police car and ambulance coming in. This morning, I watch as a steady line of shiny white government cars whizz by to monitor the inhabitants of houses across this tiny community, checking on children's welfare and school attendance under a raft of recently expanded government and nongovernment programs. Nungarrayi's Aunt Wilma was collected by health workers earlier for dialysis treatment. She has been largely bedridden since Nungarrayi and I arrived in town. Nungarrayi has spent the last two nights camping with her aunt, rubbing her aching head and limbs, cooking her food, ensuring that she has everything she needs. Yesterday, at Wilma's request, we visited the Arrernte healing center and acquired several pots of bush rubbing medicine on her instruction. Later the same evening Wilma asks me to go looking for a different kind of rubbing medicine at the supermarket. Her resident daughters are passively dependent, not reliable carers. They are alarmingly overweight and unemployed and spend most of the day lying around, waiting for action to come and sweep them up. Kids, meanwhile, have been telling their elders that clowns are coming to murder people. They picked up the news on social media of a series of scary clown incidents in Perth, Western Australia, and are convinced the clowns are now making their way across the desert. The aunties described an unusually quiet night across the camp as children were uncharacteristically demure, on alert lest they attract the attention of clowns. In a reversal of the usual nighttime dynamic, kids pleaded with their mothers and grandmothers to come into the house to sleep. Abandoning their usual practice of roaming around until late, the kids stayed in camp. Cheeky scary clowns have joined the pantheon of monsters that preside over this unsettled landscape.

This afternoon we have spent two hours driving around town in our rental car, trying to find Nungarrayi's close extended sister Amanda. I was friends with this woman in the mid-1990s and knew her as a gifted artist and a very capable worker and adviser at the community art center. Grief-stricken in the wake of the death of her much-loved son, Amanda fled her hometown for the drinking circles of Alice Springs. She was subsequently diagnosed with chronic renal failure and last year underwent a successful kidney transplant. I have not seen her for years and am keen to do so. We drive to the block of flats where we are reliably told Amanda is living with her sometime partner, a man from Tennant Creek, and his mother. The flat was allocated by an NGO to Amanda while she waited for the kidney transplant and for the duration of her postoperative recovery. There is no response to our knocking, but when I return to put my university business card with my mobile number under the front door, I hear the voice of an elderly woman inside. She opens the door in response to my loud knocking and tells me she is deaf, and a shambolic interaction follows. Nungarrayi makes the woman understand that the card is for Amanda. We cruise to the Todd Tavern, a favored Aboriginal drinking spot, and run into several of Nungarrayi's family, including a brother from a small desert town to the southwest who is delighted to see her. But no Amanda. Our next stop is the Memorial Club, which has recently become a popular gathering place since new managers have aggressively promoted the venue to Aboriginal clientele. Two days earlier we had found this place pumping with people. This afternoon the large central room is empty but for two tables of quiet drinkers. A slight woman with a bandaged arm looks up as we enter and cries out; she is another of Nungarrayi's extended sisters. The grog-soaked woman bursts into tears as the two embrace each other. While Nungarrayi is caught up in this reunion, I am entranced by her sister's drinking partner: a black, aging Rod Stewart, dressed in a shiny purple running top. A yellow headband is wrapped around his abundant, recently dyed, curly black hair that frames a face with sparkling eyes set in wonder. He does not speak. A cloth lanyard around his neck declares him to be SUPER HERO. The jukebox is playing a throbbing number. I cannot identify the song, but whatever it is, it is an ideal soundtrack to this scene.

Later that evening we make a return visit to Amanda's flat. She had phoned me in the afternoon, after arriving back from her hometown where she had attended a much-anticipated "community lease money" meeting with land council staff. Contrary to a fevered rumor mill that had been running hot in recent days, attendees at the meeting were advised there would be no distribution of moneys until the next year. The sun has set, and darkness is falling by the time we arrive at her flat. At the door we are confronted by her partner, wildly drunk and yelling out to us to come inside. I grab Nungarrayi by the arm and tell Amanda we are leaving. She looks at me pleadingly and says, "Call the police." As we leave, Nungarrayi tells me Amanda's partner is a *kuku* (magic man) so we can't call the police. We mull over the situation as we slowly drive down the road to the flat where Nungarrayi's close brother-in-law Evan is staying. While I wait in the car, Nungarrayi walks in on another drunken scene. I register that I am an idiot: today is of course payday for unemployed welfare recipients. A woman I have not met before comes outside and introduces herself to me. She asks if she can come driving around with us. In the midst of this exchange, Amanda calls my phone and in a whispered voice asks me to come and get her. She is running out of her house now. She tells me where to pick her up. Nungarrayi, her brother-in-law, and this other woman climb into the car at my urging, and we take off in search of Amanda. Along the way Nungarrayi becomes increasingly agitated by the interventions of our spontaneous kinship rider, who I now see is drunk and demanding smokes, sweaters, and anything else she can think of. We meet Amanda at the planned rendezvous point. She emerges from bushes on the side of the highway not far from the old telegraph station, wearing a woolen beanie pulled down firmly over her head. We drop off the troublemaker at a town camp, but not before the woman provokes Nungarrayi to the point where she jumps out of the car and threatens to punch her.

By this time all of us are pretty worked up. I suggest we find a quiet place to sit down and relax. Yet the reality of bush people's lives in Alice Springs is that there is no neutral place, no place of comfort without complication, so I drive to a roadside stop on the verge of the Todd River on the outskirts of town and we sit in the car. Evan, in the back seat, happily settles into story-telling mode, taking no small amount of pleasure recounting for me the various events leading up to his acquiring the astonishingly large indentation that graces the front of his forehead. He is so physically transformed that I didn't recognize him when he first came out to the car. He must have lost a third of the body weight he was carrying last time I saw him. But he is still his charming, highly articulate self, with a hilarious sense of humor. The story goes that his partner—he confirms she is still his partner—hit him over the head during a drunken argument just over a year ago. He thought nothing of it at the time, but two weeks later he collapsed. He was taken to the hospital and underwent some testing before being medically evacuated to Adelaide. Scans revealed an infection that was eating away at his skull. Surgeons told him that if the situation had been left untreated for another week the infection would have spread to his brain and he would have died. He had been fasting since being admitted to Alice Springs hospital and was absolutely starving, weak with hunger. The doctors told him to take two days to eat as much as he liked and then they operated, sawing through his skull to remove the infected section. Two days after surgery he flipped out in the intensive care unit and started throwing plates around. He received another MRI scan, and the doctors told him they had to operate again; it was a matter of life and death. The second operation was a success, and Evan spent two months in Adelaide recovering. He is supposed to wear a special helmet to protect his brain—if he were hit in the place where the skull has been removed, he would die. But he tells me, nonplussed, that he left the helmet in a house in his hometown a couple of days ago. He is waiting for an assessment with his surgeons next month and expects to have two more surgeries, the first to fit a metal plate over the hole and the second to reconstruct his skull using cartilage or bone from his leg. He tells this story as a raconteur, taking much pleasure in the telling, and narrating it with a great deal more humor than I have recounted it here.

While Evan is regaling us with tales of his recent life and near-death experience, of journeys across to the Western Australian coast and farther afield, Amanda sits beside him looking anxious, cold, tired, and unhappy. She herself was only discharged from hospital the previous day. Her new kidney is working OK, but she had an infection in her side that she says kept her in the hospital on intravenous antibiotics for two weeks. Her alcoholic partner has been mistreating her ever since she came home, and she is badly in need of sleep. She tells me her oldest son has been in prison since the beginning of the year. When I inquire what he went in for, she tells me it was for not wearing a seat belt. I speculate that this must have been the final charge in a longer list of warrants. Her daughter faced bush court today and is in the police lockup overnight pending a reappearance tomorrow; she was charged with assault following a fight defending the honor of a young female relative. Last week Nungarrayi and I visited the grave of Amanda's mother and her youngest son. With the prospect of her daughter going to jail, Amanda is now worrying for her young grandson, but she has no capacity to care for him herself.

Contemplating these layers of tragedy, misery, and stress, I am struck by our scene. Here we are, the four of us, sitting in a rental car in the dark on the edge of town. Each of my three old friends has suffered life-threatening assaults by domestic partners in recent years. Two are still living with those partners, but they enthusiastically talk of imagined futures in other places. Every Warlpiri friend I can think of is living with multiple forms of dislocation and brokenness. All have lost close relatives prematurely. All have close relatives, often their children, in prison. Many have chronic health problems that require regular ongoing treatment if they are to live on for any period of time. These three talk of differently ordered futures, but the tight lure of kin-based misadventure consistently undermines any prospects of change. Amanda says she wants to go somewhere else but is worrying for her son while he is in prison. Evan says he might leave his partner and go to Adelaide. Work does not feature in their imaginaries. Dreams of different lives are all about travel, journeying to new places, keeping up with or getting away from kin. The force of movement, spontaneous promises of excitement, not planning or reflexive consideration, are what dictates practice. So it is that Evan finds himself in Alice Springs while his mobile phone and the protective headgear he should be wearing to shield his skull-less forehead—the accoutrements of specific, individualized need—have been left behind in the spontaneous rush to join a family excursion. Eighteen months after this gathering, Evan undergoes further surgery. Amanda never recovers from the compounding effects of grief, stress, and bodily ravages of end-stage renal failure. At the age of fifty-four, she succumbs to the inevitable consequences of her life's entanglements. She spends her final days in the Alice Springs hospital intensive care unit, lovingly watched over by her heavily pregnant daughter.

AS I JOURNEY AROUND Alice Springs with Nungarrayi, kinship unfolds as an infinite mosaic of relatedness. It is impossible to find the edges of these extensive networks that appear to gather up just about every Aboriginal person we cross paths with. The constant, energetic work that goes into keeping up with kin—close family and extended relatives alike—is where the moral basis of life is established and vigorously sustained. Honor, social recognition, and responsibilities to others are the very ground of personhood and what is at stake in these relationships and the forms of acknowledgment they engender. This is why young women will put themselves willingly in mortal danger, standing side by side, sister by sister, facing carefully choreographed customary punishment or more chaotic attacks of enemies in a jealousy-fueled fight. There is no question of not standing side by side. To not stand by is to reject relatedness, or conversely to absolve oneself of identification, one's very status as a person. But somewhere along the line these matters of honor and social standing, responsibility and care for kin, have become embroiled in counterposing forces. The insidious mix sometimes feels like a suffocating vortex. All that enables *and* undercuts life lives in its currents.

While the entwined processes of hyperkinship and sorcery can appear all-encompassing, our journeying around Alice Springs has revealed multiple techniques, biopolitical and otherwise, that fuel and impede their workings. Elizabeth Povinelli has described the governance of Aboriginal exclusion in terms of an "economy of abandonment," a technique for managing the crisis of liberal legitimacy. In the politics of representation that accompany this mode of governance, Aboriginality has undergone a stark inversion. "Culture," once apprehended positively in terms of the "agency of care" as in multicultural recognition, is now the "cause of crisis" for the security state.[47] The "value" of Aboriginal culture as figured by the multicultural nation has significantly diminished. The numerous vacant shop fronts in the town's Todd Mall that once thrived with tourist traffic seem to confirm such a waning of effect. The imminent critique Povinelli brings to bear on this shift is all future-focused, directed to projects that imagine life beyond entrenched battles over land and identity and the coercive imaginaries they reproduce. From my vantage, traveling with Nungarrayi, it is difficult to envisage such a break. Povinelli's insistence on the cosubstantial implications of abandonment, however, draws us back to the crisis of emplacement as one that is shared. Any serious apprehension of Nungarrayi's dislocation and the slow, violent processes through which it unfolds cannot occur without disrupting the national order of things.

4

Ties
That Bind

Don't Say Goodbye

Nungarrayi opens her front door and comes out to greet me as my taxi pulls into her driveway. She has been repeatedly texting my phone all morning, anxious to know when I will arrive. She is switched on, upbeat, and tells me as I enter the house that she has to play me a song. A strong reggae beat belts from a boom box perched on her kitchen bench: "Don't Say Goodbye," a country/gospel song with soaring chorus.[1] Yesterday, as I was preparing to leave Melbourne, Nungarrayi told me on the phone that my visit would coincide with the transfer from Alice Springs to the Adelaide hospital of her ex-husband's brother, the dearly loved Alan. He has been chronically ill with diabetes for some time, and indeed I have known him as unwell for ten years. Family photos posted to Facebook over that period reveal the telltale signs of escalating kidney disease: a once-vigorous and handsome man increasingly stripped of weight, his face cruelly transformed from beaming openness to preoccupied introspection wrought by chronic pain. Now he lies in a coma on life support in the intensive care unit. His father, who is a prominent ceremonial leader, his stepmother, three sons, their associated partners, and grandchildren have all converged on Adelaide. I ask Nungarrayi if there have been any signs of improvement since his admission to the Adelaide hospital. She thinks, then tells me that yesterday he coughed. That was read as a sign of hope.

Nungarrayi, her sister's son Nathan, who is currently living with her, and I leave the house promptly. We catch a bus and then a train to the city, an hour-long journey. As has become customary when we travel into town, we head for the food court beneath the Rundle Mall and eat a quick meal of chicken curry and rice, and then head along North Terrace toward the hospital. Our travel by foot is unexpectedly impeded by a torrential downpour of rain that seems to have come out of nowhere. Nungarrayi accuses me of having brought the rain; my adoptive subsection Nangala places me in a lineage of *ngapa* (water) custodians, inheritors of the power to summon rain. At one stage, soaking wet, we take refuge with city workers and students in the grand balustraded entrance to a building that is part of the University of Adelaide. Nungarrayi musters her *ngankari* powers and flings substances from her armpit into the sky in an attempt to send the rain away, while those with whom we share the shelter watch on in curiosity.

On arrival at the hospital we head for the women's toilets and use the hand dryers to take the edge off our sodden hair and clothes. Then we make our way to the intensive care unit. Turning a corner in the hallway, we come face-to-face with a tight-knit posse: Alan's father, stepmother, three grown sons, first wife, and two grandchildren are on their way out. I'm unprepared for the emotional impact of this collective assembly of heartbreak: all adult faces identically set, overcome, shattered. The news is grim. Alan has not responded to medication, and the family have been advised by medical staff that nothing further can be done. We each embrace, one by one, as we pass in opposite directions along the hallway. At the intensive care information desk Nungarrayi and I are told we will need to wait a few minutes as medical staff are attending to Alan. "Come on," Nungarrayi says. We go looking for her Aunt Wilma, who was flown in from Alice Springs last week and admitted for X-rays and related tests. A search along a wing of rooms fails to reveal her presence. A nurse pops her head out of an alcove to ask who we are looking for and advises that Wilma was sent home this morning. Nungarrayi is pleased with this news. We return to the intensive care unit. I register the large sign on the wall that declares this to be strictly a space for immediate family only. But the kindly elderly woman at reception raises no questions when Nungarrayi and I present ourselves together as kin for Alan.

I have had the good fortune not to have visited an intensive care unit before, and I am not prepared for the shock of seeing Alan in his comatose, technologically governed state of aliveness. Tubes protrude from several parts of his head and neck. A clip that glows bright red is clamped to his ear. He is being kept alive by what Warlpiri call "the breathing machine," which pumps his chest unnaturally high at regular intervals. He looks utterly ravaged, like an old man whose body is worn out. Nungarrayi and I are at his bedside along with two of his sons. Standing close together on both sides of the bed, we place our hands on his arms and legs. We talk to him, tell him who we are, give him messages of love and strength. It is an intense and moving experience. As we prepare to leave, Nungarrayi steps to one side and sternly addresses her nephews, "You must not let fear and doubt come into your hearts. You must keep praying. Miracles can happen." We bid our farewells to Alan and leave his sons to their intimate grieving.

The Devil and Diabetes

Diabetes and end-stage kidney disease are shockingly widespread among desert people, with a 2012–13 study identifying nearly 30 percent of the Northern Territory adult Aboriginal population as diagnosed with diabetes and 40 percent with chronic kidney disease. The rate of end-stage kidney disease for remote-living Aboriginal people is twenty-six times higher than for non-Indigenous Australians.[2] Mortality rates resulting from these diseases are nine times higher for Aboriginal people from the Northern Territory than for non-Indigenous Australians. This is an escalating situation, with the incidence of end-stage kidney failure having increased by nearly 70 percent in the period between 1996 and 2014.[3] Being diagnosed with kidney disease has serious consequences for the capacity of people to pursue satisfying lives, most particularly because it profoundly impacts their ability to move around. Patients who require regular dialysis need to be proximate to well-equipped treatment facilities. For many, a diagnosis of chronic kidney disease ultimately results in relocation from desert towns, away from the dense company of kin to allocated accommodations or rough town camp conditions in a regional center where, for those who do conform to a prescribed biomedical regime, daily life becomes ordered around individualized treatment schedules. To identify oneself as sick is to risk social marginalization and "untenable exclusion."[4] In this way, as Françoise Dussart observes, kidney disease is "a neo-colonial condition that undermines both personal autonomy and social connectedness and adds unbearable 'social suffering' to lifelong physical distress."[5] The compulsion to be among kin, to "look after" family, and to have the capacity to do so while preserving one's personal autonomy consistently takes precedence over attending to one's physical well-being. So it is that festering wounds, chronic pain, and life-threatening symptoms commonly go untreated, and vital medication is left behind as individuals drop everything in order to join relatives on spontaneous excursions.

The most robust Aboriginal-controlled health agencies are innovative and determined in their pursuit of chronically ill mobile countrymen and countrywomen. Since the year 2000, the organization that has come to be known as Purple House has expanded to run sixteen remote clinics, a mobile unit, as well as a permanent Alice Springs unit.[6] The expansion of this organization across space indicates not only the scale of illness among people from the desert but also the constancy of movement as an organizing force in Aboriginal life. While the rhythms of ex-hunter-gatherer hypermobility are directly at odds with the strict temporalized schedules of biomedical regimes, the prevalence of the disease means that newly diagnosed patients who do relocate for medical treatment are increasingly likely to find themselves in the company of equally sick kin.

Pervasive chronic illness and premature death make Aboriginal family life a setting of "trauma" as well as "succour."[7] Sorrow associated with the death of a loved one is commonly compounded and stretched by fear—fear that comes from the knowledge that deaths are rarely naturally caused and that any death by ensorcellment carries potential further danger and dispersed effects for relatives of the deceased. Death is rarely experienced as a singular event. The fear created by sorcery contributes directly, as Victoria Burbank argues, to the stress of daily life and indirectly to premature mortality and morbidity.[8] The causal interpretations circle around, as Burbank casts a group of chronic illnesses—high blood pressure, obesity, diabetes, coronary heart disease, kidney failure, and depression—as diseases born of the legacy of extreme stress, loss of autonomy, and the lack of predictability and control over the terms of life.[9]

Navigating the National Order of Things

We leave the hospital and join the small gathering of smokers huddling away from the damp, melancholy weather under a balcony. The wives of Alan's sons, his grandchildren, and other cigarette-smoking hospital visitors share the space. We walk off in search of Alan's parents, who we are told have gone to "get money," no doubt via a postal order from a sponsor back home. We find them at a café opposite Victoria Square, the place where Aboriginal people used to congregate before the square was redeveloped and they were moved on. Alan's father looks utterly bereft. We sit quietly while others order and consume food. Emily, another of Nungarrayi's sisters, is among the group, and her characteristic cheeky humor brings some light relief to those of us perched on the edges of this somber gathering.

There is family business to attend to, and so we all move on and catch the free city loop bus, heading for the parklands. We accidentally catch it going in the wrong direction and are taken on an extremely long, meandering tour of the inner suburbs. Tired and emotionally absorbed, people seem relieved to give themselves over to the journeying of the bus. Some sit quietly and take in glimpses of the country through which we travel. Others huddle in animated conversation. Riding public transport can be pleasurable. Movement itself is stimulating, as is visual engagement with passing environments. Transportation stirs anticipation of the events that will unfold at journey's end. Riding the train to the city one day, Nungarrayi tells me the story of a young relative who once walked all through the night along the train line, all the way back to the western suburbs from the city after the trains had stopped running. The meandering pace of suburban buses is conducive to reverie and memory work. But trains and buses are equally spaces of tension, of unpredictable mobile encounters. Public transport affords a special kind of contained public space that can elicit wellworn expectations and forms of recognition, where the national order of things and its hierarchies of citizenship are called out and performed, just as chance encounters may give rise to interactions that break with such convention.[10]

The difference between our party and other passengers is multiply marked not just by skin color but by the loud, expressive talking that goes on in the Warlpiri language. Warlpiri ways of calling to each other register as an affront to the quiet, inwardly absorbed etiquette that marks the cultivated disposition of metropolitan comportment. Warlpiri travelers stimulate responses that range from the curious, to the fearful, to the outright hostile. Some passengers register their disapproval in the stern looks they throw our way. Lurking close to the surface of these responses lie judgments and presumptions of normality and criminality. Warlpiri alterity appears at its starkest among the smartly dressed, disciplined laboring bodies of city-based commuters. Such differences are diminished in the outer suburbs. At times suburban public transport can feel like a volatile pressure cooker of diverse marginality. When Nungarrayi and I board a bus or train in the outer northwest, we commonly form company with an assembly of the aged, the physically disabled, the mentally ill, the unemployed, and newly arrived migrants. In these spaces it is age, not ethnicity, that often strikes me as the strongest outward marker of difference. Young people's faces by and large remain open, hopeful. Older people wear the misery of life's cumulative disappointments, the ravages of alcoholism, the stress of poverty, and disfigurements of injury and obesity on their bodies and faces. It is this same demographic that frequents the large shopping centers we visit. In Central Australia, Warlpiri are accustomed to being marked by their difference from white workers and tourists. In Adelaide's northwestern suburbs that difference still registers, but it is cut across by class, by the socioeconomic marginality they share with others, a status that produces affinities as well as tensions across racialized registers of difference.[11]

As our group tours the city on our circuitous route, we join company with a desert man sleeping across a bench toward the back of the bus. The bus driver keeps an anxious eye on the man in his rearview mirror. At one point he idles the bus at a stop and comes down the aisle to check on the sleeper. Farther down the road the driver stops the bus again and addresses the dozing man loudly from the driver's seat, "Where do you want to get off?" Sitting next to Nungarrayi, I sense her immediately stiffen. "He's all right, he's getting off at the next stop. He's with us," she calls out. As we all make to leave the bus, she hauls the disoriented man to his feet. The moment of the bus driver's focus is one of heightened tension. It exposes the gulf between Warlpiri forms of care and the regime of public order. Nungarrayi's intervention anticipates the weight of heavily sedimented attitudes and the expectation that consequential action could follow. Not long after this interaction, Tanya Day, an Aboriginal woman who had fallen asleep on a train in rural Victoria, was removed from the train by police and arrested for public drunkenness. She was locked in a cell in a regional police station. She fell heavily several times in that cell and died after sustaining fatal head injuries.[12]

It is a relief to step out of the bus and into the fresh air and open space of the parklands. We happen upon a good-humored scene of desert drinkers. I chat with a couple who tell me cheerfully how much they prefer living in Adelaide to Alice Springs. They are both diabetics. The husband tells me there are much better medical services and ways of looking after people here. He tells me his wife is deaf and he has had a boil on this foot that has been there for seven years and will not heal. He tells me that they both drink grog every day. Nungarrayi and I leave the group. She has met her responsibilities as local escort. She tells Nathan to stay and drink with his countrymen, it will be good for him to have their company. On my suggestion and out of self-interest, I suggest we travel home by taxi via a city supermarket. I know that if we don't shop for food now, there is a fair chance we will not eat tonight. Ram is at home when we arrive, and I volunteer to cook a curry meal. I drink wine, and Nungarrayi drinks bourbon and coke. She plays music from her phone through a portable wireless speaker. Ram brings out a small bag of marijuana, and the two of them smoke from a well-worn Coke-bottle bong. Ram talks to me about his family and his life in Nepal. He tells me that his father's father had seven wives, and his mother's father was a man who worked with elephants. I ask him, not for the first time, why they left Nepal. It had to do with the war, he tells me in his broken English. It had to do with his father having been a commander in the army. Ram's English is much improved since my last visit, but notwithstanding his keenness to communicate and the warmth between us, there remains much that gets lost in our interactions.

Nungarrayi is at her most animated and sharply focused when she has family in town and related purposeful business to attend to. She is affirmed in her interactions with kin. She is looked up to as a knowledgeable person with valuable local expertise. The verve with which she applies herself to the work of escort, navigator, host, and translator indicates the craving for affirmation that accompanies her prolonged periods of alienation and loneliness in the city. Her very ability to act in the world as a person with a positive sense of herself turns upon this recognition.[13] As Axel Honneth observes, there is a moral particularism to primary social relations. Kinship not only constitutes the primary source of unconditional love but also affirms a person in their lived relations to others, in their abilities, dignity, and integrity. In the company of kin, Nungarrayi is affirmed as a person with a history and her own coherent story. More than this, the coming together of countrymen and countrywomen reactivates a moral universe, a shared purpose, and co-responsibilities. Transposed to a metropolitan setting of diversely constituted distanced relationships and pressures, the bonds of kinship are stretched but also strengthened. Where positive recognition in the public sphere of self-other interactions fails to register one's worth and fellow humanness, the affirmation of kin takes on a reactive, heightened importance.[14]

Throughout these intense episodes involving visiting kin, I am reminded of the unusual nature of Nungarrayi's exile. Her agitated situation betwixt and between the affective associations of Adelaide and the desert bears no resemblance to the heroic, linear tales of transformation narrated by Michael Jackson as he tracks the personal achievements of young migrants who make good on the other side of displacement.[15] Nor, at least for now, does her situation echo the doubly compounded trauma suffered by African women who have been resettled in Australia, only to be subjected to new horrific forms of governmental violence, as described by Georgina Ramsay.[16] As Nungarrayi navigates the unstable terms of her new life, the hypermobility of her desert-dwelling kin and her own vigorous pursuit of family living in Adelaide provide the mechanisms by which she can tap into desperately needed sources of affirmation. Correspondingly, the more deeply immersed she becomes in the inwardly turned world of Warlpiri sociality, the thinner her engagement with Adelaide's cosmopolitan possibilities.

Assent to the Powers of *Marlpa*

On the second morning of my visit, I read out loud to Nungarrayi some sections of writing I have recently composed. I need to get a clear sense of how she will respond to my attempt to ethnographically distill the events at the heart of her displacement. I had drafted a description of circumstances of the past few years as I had heard these variously recounted by her and by others. I am nervous and unsure how she will respond. We sit in the small bedroom, her on the single bed, me on a chair. As I begin reading, she lies down. She asks me to close the door so that the noise of the television is filtered out and others in the house cannot hear us. As I continue to read, I am aware that she is becoming agitated. At a certain point she starts rocking back and forth. I pause and look up. "Can you just stop? Can you just take out all of that bit about people and what happened?" In this succinct response Nungarrayi neatly throws into ethical doubt an entire coherent approach to ethnographic writing as explanation. I feel like I have been punched. But I also find I recover quickly. I register that I am not surprised by her response; in fact I probably expected it. The vulnerabilities that give affective shape to our time together are constitutive of everything. Instability is the ground we tread. I feel chastened and ashamed by what to Nungarrayi's ears must have come across as a set of inelegant, vulgar transgressions. In the section of writing I read aloud, I had not named individuals directly. But I had described an unfolding series of events that ricocheted around the death of a much-loved relative. Witnessing the bodily effects of my words is sobering and confronting—a firsthand experience in doing violence by re-presentation. Clearly, I need to think some more on how to go about writing this book.

Nungarrayi's response indicates something of the way forms of storytelling are distinctively cultured. I tend to think of the process of writing ethnography as involving a gathering up of stories heard and scenes observed, assembling strands of these into a narrative form that does aesthetic and ethical justice to the contexts from which the strands are drawn. Yet the very process of assembling a narrative in this way—even when the persons whose stories are gathered give consent—is at odds with Warlpiri aesthetics and ethics of storytelling. Who speaks, how they speak, who listens, and the wider circumstances of a telling are fundamental factors at play in the complex dynamics of Warlpiri interchange and performance. Ethnographic writing, like any other kind of recording technique, collapses time and space, the specificity and dynamism of intercourse, the nuanced flow of words and gestures exchanged through direct and indirect forms of communication and identification, into something set flatly on the page. The permanency of the printed word is also a structural affront to the various contingencies of a person's right to speak—the relational constraints that establish authority for public testimony in respect of a particular topic, as opposed to more private contexts in which gossip might run on in any direction. People make forceful statements along a particular line of argument in one setting that they may disregard or contradict in another. Fred Myers writes of the fragility of the polity that assents to a particular decision taken in a public meeting.[17] But Nungarrayi's response to my writing gets at something even more basic in terms of the volatilities of the present: words spoken out of turn, especially the naming of persons presumed to be responsible for certain actions, or around whom unresolved matters continue to swirl, can be dangerous. Writing does not pass comment on life, it is part of life. At times and indeed throughout recent Warlpiri history, episodes in published writing and speaking have intervened in life and agitated preexisting tensions with dramatic consequences. In a context of dispersed worry and stress, there is endless potential for misrepresentation and for the incitement of fury.

We talk back and forth over some minor details. Nungarrayi gets up from the bed and makes for the door. This conversation is over for now. There are more pressing issues to attend to. We leave the house and catch a bus to go visit Magda. Since I had last seen her in rehab several months earlier, Magda had been transferred into community housing. This sounds like a major development, but she remains wheelchair-bound and is currently receiving daily care from health workers and her biological mother, who has come to stay. This older woman, whom I have never met before, seems dazed and does not register our arrival by eye contact, word, or gesture. She does not speak through the entirety of our visit. Nungarrayi tells me later that Magda's mother is mute; she went away to town drinking with her husband when Magda and her siblings were children. Also staying with Magda is a sister who tells me she came to visit on Christmas Day, two months ago—and volunteers with a slightly crazed smile that she can't wait to get back home—and three of Magda's grandchildren who were deposited at the house that morning by their mother, who has gone to town drinking. An official notice taped to the door of the refrigerator declares the rules of the house, specifying that care and cleaning are only offered in support of the patient, not extended family. Magda and her mother sit at a table in the kitchen eating two-minute noodles, boiled chicken legs, and white bread. Two young children have been playing with water in the bathroom, and the floor is covered with a mess of sodden clothing and discarded food.

Magda continues to command significant authority from her much-restricted position in a wheelchair. It was she who received the call earlier that morning that summoned the family to the hospital to authorize and oversee the turning off of Alan's life-support machine. A demure mood and quiet sense of shock and sadness pervade our group. Nungarrayi, Nathan, and I head off in search of a shop to purchase some takeout lunch. We return with a large package of fish and chips and arrange the food picnic style on a rug in the front yard. Somehow the salad we ordered gets left behind in the shop, much to Nungarrayi's irritation. Magda wheels herself out of the house to join us in a second lunch. Her sister takes up a hose and sprays a forceful torrent of water to shift detritus from the front porch and down the stairs, clearing the entrance to the house. Discussion turns to the cause of Alan's death. Planning is already underway for the return of the family to Alice Springs. They will leave by bus tomorrow night. The extended family will conduct the funerary rights of "sorry business" at a neighboring desert town to avoid grieving kin becoming embroiled in further fighting or sorcery.

Among the dispersed and incoherent forces that are identified as at work in Alan's death, Nungarrayi tells me, "You know, when you get admitted to the intensive care unit you get a choice of which machine to go on." Patients are asked to "choose between the machine that keeps you awake or the one that puts you in a coma." Alan, people are saying, *"chose the wrong machine."* I learn that Alan had lost not one but two kidneys as his chronic disease advanced. I vividly recall crossing paths with him at a supermarket in Alice Springs several months earlier. It had been years since I had seen him, and we were both delighted by the chance encounter. But the look in his eyes revealed a man consumed by the bodily turmoil and pain caused by the disease. A couple of days later, Nungarrayi and I were with one of Alan's brothers, talking over old times while sharing lunch in a quiet stretch of the sandy Todd riverbed. As we headed back toward our rental car, we saw Alan's silver Hilux whizz by, his figure hunched over the steering wheel, eyes fixed straight ahead. "Off to dialysis," his brother said.

The so-called diabetes epidemic in Aboriginal communities has been the target of several public health campaigns. People who are diagnosed are well-versed on the causes of the disease and will describe its prevalence in relation to postcolonial conditions—the consumption of too much sugar, fatty foods, and so on. Yet specific, individual instances of chronic illness and related death are always the subject of sorcery accusations.[18] Here I am struck by the resonance with Lisa Stevenson's observations in the Canadian Arctic, where Indigenous people frequently fail to cooperate with what she terms "the regime of life" and its register of abstraction.[19] Biomedical models of care only register so far in Warlpiri ways of going about life. People "know" what kinds of behavior lead to a healthy life, and they regularly attend the health clinic and seek medical intervention for all manner of bodily ailments.[20] But they are not sufficiently successfully hailed by the forms of biopolitical health care that would lead them to live life according to its precepts. Again, Stevenson provides a compelling sense of the ontologically different forms of interpellation at play here: a violent, abstract form that calls Warlpiri (like other Indigenous people) to adopt a fixed subject position and statistically stable identity versus another, more intimate form, albeit one with its own potential associated violence, a call that is made and felt directly and turns upon a reciprocally engaged mode of keeping company among kin.[21] Anonymous care versus life that requires and turns upon the care of known others to register one's actual presence in life and in death.

Life in the city brings people into dense encounters with forms of anonymous care and relatedly with the glittering commodity market and its promised liberations, but it provides few openings for their substantial participation. Sorcery narratives, in contrast, act as a glue that compels persons dispersed across space to a shared outlook and orientation. If there is a process by which a scattered desert community is gathered together, it is through collective assent to the powers of *marlpa* (company/kin) and *walaldja* (countrymen and countrywomen). In the present this relationality is supercharged by persistent sorcery fear. Here we might usefully draw upon Peter Geschiere's observation that sorcery "dynamizes kinship" through personalizing "shocking inequalities" and "creates a space, imaginary or not, that is beyond the state's authority."[22] Relatedly, he argues, sorcery gives "a central place to human actors while, at the same [time], hiding them from view."[23] In the vigorous debriefing that follows Alan's death, I am struck by the vast social distance between the cool bureaucratic practices of biomedical administration and the intense gathering of Warlpiri attention to navigate the circumstances surrounding death and its aftermath.

Nathan came home in the middle of the night and knocked on the window of the bedroom where I was sleeping, whispering to me to let him in. He immediately ran to the backyard; he sensed the presence of, then saw, two brothers standing out there. They are angry about losing their uncle. He proceeded to wake Nungarrayi, asking for smokes, asking her to cook for him, and then spent hours restlessly shuffling between watching television and listening to music until he finally settled down to sleep just before sunrise.

In the morning I log onto Facebook and learn the shocking news that a close colleague's sister, a renowned Pacific studies scholar, has died, just a few short weeks after receiving a terminal cancer diagnosis. Also strewn through my Facebook feed are reports of the evidence being brought before the Royal Commission into the Protection and Detention of Children in the Northern Territory, which is currently sitting in Darwin. A guard is questioned over an incident in which he had reportedly forced a child to eat feces, filmed the episode, and then posted the footage to social media channels. Another guard is questioned over reports that he asked a child for oral sex; the guard confirms he spoke those words but insists they were meant "as a joke." The piling up of reported brutalities in these commission hearings and the nonchalant attitude of guards under questioning breathe chilling new life into Hannah Arendt's observations of the banality of evil.[24] The commission will, in coming weeks, hear evidence of systematic use of force by guards, including regular use of tear gas, restraint chairs, shackles, and hoods, as well as punching, choking, smashing heads into walls, stripping children naked and locking them up without blankets, removing their clothes with a knife, and death threats. It will also hear of pervasive use of techniques of humiliation, including watching children shower and use the toilet. Racist taunts by guards are also common; inmates were called "stupid black cunts," "camp dogs," "oxygen thieves," "waste[s] of space," "little black poofters," and "fucking sluts."[25] The Royal Commission hearings provide a chilling glimpse of the workings of an institution that appears to operate as a factory for the production of less-than-human subjects.[26] Every Warlpiri family has been saddened, distressed, and angered by the revelations of systematic child brutality at the Don Dale detention center. Everyone is related to someone who has spent time as a child in detention.

Paperless Laws

Child detention is but one set of practices in an expanding law-and-order regime that has been rolled out in the Northern Territory over the past two decades.[27] A year before my first visit to Adelaide, on May 21, 2015, fifty-nine-year-old Mr. P Langdon, an extended brother of Nungarrayi, was arrested by police in Darwin, the Northern Territory capital, under the so-called paperless laws introduced by the Northern Territory government in December 2014. Under this legislation, police with "reasonable grounds" for assessing a person as having committed, or as about to commit, an "infringement notice offense" can arrest and detain that person for four hours or, if intoxicated, "for as long as they are judged to no longer be intoxicated." Infringement notices are conventionally issued for petty and relatively obscure offenses, including failing to keep a front yard clean, singing an obscene song, abandoning a refrigerator or ice chest, playing a musical instrument to annoy, or leaving dead animals in a public place.[28] The offenses under this category of infringement that receive most attention from Northern Territory police, however, are consumption of liquor in public and possession of small amounts of cannabis. Infringement notices commonly attract a small fine, not imprisonment. In the first seven months after the paperless laws were passed, police took 1,295 people into custody for some period of time. Close to 80 percent of them were Aboriginal.

Mr. Langdon had traveled to Darwin for medical treatment. He was enjoying the company of kin in a "long-grass" drinking circle when police arrested him and transported him to the Darwin lockup.[29] Three hours later he was found dead in his cell. The coroner's report into this death found that Mr. Langdon "was not causing any disruption before or during his arrest and at all times he was polite and courteous."[30] The maximum penalty for the offense of drinking alcohol in a designated area is a fine of seventy-four dollars. In Mr. Langdon's case he was issued with the fine and then handcuffed and placed in the iron cage at the back of the police van. The inquest found that a nurse overseeing his admission and using a cut-and-paste template falsely entered on his admission sheet that he had "denied health problems," despite reports that Mr. Langdon had requested a doctor and despite the nurse having access to medical records that would have alerted her to his multiple chronic health conditions. He suffered from cardiomyopathy, diabetes, and pulmonary edema and just months earlier had been diagnosed with an enlarged heart and congestive cardiac failure, most likely attributed to heavy alcohol consumption. He was placed in a cell, where he lay down to sleep. Two hours later, during a scheduled cell check, Mr. Langdon was found dead. Coroner Greg Cavanagh ruled that "Kumanjayi Langdon, a sick middle-aged Aboriginal man, was treated like a criminal and incarcerated like a criminal. He died in his sleep with strangers in this cold and concrete cell. He died of natural causes and was always likely to die suddenly due to chronic and serious heart disease, but he was entitled to die in peace, in the comfort of family and friends. In my view, he was entitled to die as a free man."[31] The coroner went on to criticize the paperless arrest laws as "retrogressive" and to recommend they be repealed. He observed that "a civilised society does not subject its citizens to [the] mortification [of arrest] unless there are no other reasonable options open."[32] Cavanagh's criticisms of the law are unusually strong for a coroner's report, yet his critique falls short of recognizing the larger systemic context in which these laws operate. First, Mr. Langdon did not die of "natural causes." He died of the bodily ruination precipitated by chronic alcoholism. The coroner may well have asked why chronic alcoholism is so widespread among dispossessed and disempowered Aboriginal people. Second, the new laws are not simply retrogressive; they dissolve the line between the work of policing and the court's adjudication of justice. As solicitor Jonathon Hunyor observes, the "paperless" laws are not an aberration but rather sit "comfortably with the prevailing culture of mass incarceration in the Northern Territory and reflect an increasing trend of laws designed to exert more coercive power by executive government."[33]

The Northern Territory attorney general John Elferink, who was also minister for justice and for health, was unmoved by the coroner's findings. He defended preventative detention and said people needed to "stop making excuses" for those people who "engage in self-destructive behaviour year in and year out." Elferink described Langdon as having gone on a "taxpayer-funded binge" after being sent to Darwin for medical care. "Why is that necessarily the police's or anybody's else's fault other than Mr Langdon's?" he asked. Both the minister and the police commissioner denied that Indigenous people are specifically targeted by the laws. Defending the new laws, the attorney general described paperless arrests as "catch and release"—a term commonly associated with fishing, the Northern Territory's most popular recreational activity and tourist attraction. Introducing the bill into the Northern Territory Parliament, the minister lauded the lack of paperwork that would be required by police enforcing the new law, which would allow them to "get on with their job."[34] Yet the paperwork required by police administering the "paperless" laws would turn out to be more complex than suggested. Significantly, decisions taken to release a person without charge or release with an on-the-spot fine would require more paperwork than taking a person into custody.[35]

The Don Dale revelations and the Northern Territory's paperless arrest laws are just two examples of Australia's vigorous embrace of what Didier Fassin variously describes as the "repressive turn," "a punitive moment," and "the carceral condition."[36] In the recent transformation of liberal democratic governance into new securitized forms, as the social state recedes, imprisonment expands. Ultimately, what is at stake in the expansion of incarceration, Fassin argues, is the management of inequality. So long as governments keep the attention of citizens firmly fixed on insecurity rather than inequality, they successfully efface the workings of power.[37] But there is something more than inequality being managed here that the massively disproportionate rates of Indigenous incarceration point to: a loathing of Aboriginal difference seemingly so pervasive in Australia that the presumption of Aboriginal people's lesser humanity and their need for harder governance is naturalized. Lurking more deeply still behind such presumptions is a form of settler innocence that assumes a self-righteous moral course in enforcing such a punitive regime. Ann Laura Stoler helps us see the connection between Aboriginal incarceration and chronic illness when she writes of the "after-shocks of imperial assault" that block livelihoods and health and entrench distressed sensibilities.[38] Ruination, she writes, is "an *act* perpetuated, a *condition* to which one is subject, and a *cause* of loss." It is also "a *political project* that lays waste to certain people, relations, and things that accumulate in specific places."[39]

I reflect upon these matters while observing a swirl of tension and distress growing in the wake of Alan's death. Some feel that the turning off of his life support occurred with unreasonable haste. Nungarrayi thinks he should have been left to let his own body take its course for a few more days. He needed more time to recover. Yesterday in the park we observed the separateness of seated groups of kin. Their unhappiness over this final decision was marked by social distance. The question of responsibility roams around. I am haunted by Nungarrayi's pressing claim: *he chose the wrong machine.* Sorcery pervades everything like a thick soup. Nungarrayi instructs Nathan to ensure "the brothers" keep a close eye on the body, to make sure there is no interference with it. There is also concern about anticipated fallout back in the Big Town, the expectation that further fighting and black magic might follow. Phone calls are made to caution relatives back home who expect to receive financial payments at a scheduled mining royalties distribution meeting in coming days. They are urged: "Do not let anyone buy cars on your behalf." Every fate, every illness, every accident befalling this community is interpreted through the lens of the ferocious magical power that fuels the disputes at the heart of The Troubles.

For Nungarrayi, there are periods in which the intensity of these forces recedes to a low simmer. In these quieter times she feels lonely and agitated. But the space of solitude is also the space that opens up other life possibilities and stimulates her to actively respond to the more mundane but nevertheless pressing calls of wider society. In this bifurcated reality the reason Nungarrayi regularly runs afoul of Centrelink and its mutual obligation "job search" requirements becomes clear. The force of The Troubles and concerns of kin are profoundly more compelling and urgent than the call of Centrelink and the circus of "job search" that consistently fails to deliver on its promises of transformed fortunes. There are no jobs. So long as she stays in Adelaide, there seems to be no escape from the drudgery of welfare dependency. Meeting Centrelink's requirements is inextricably tied up with the most basic need to acquire money to feed herself, as well as with her ambition to acquire unstigmatized Housing Trust rental accommodations.

FIGURE 4.1 Job Active in
Adelaide (photo by author)

Nungarrayi is caught in a pincer. The demands of welfare citizenship and responsibilities of kinship often appear as mutually exclusive, contesting social orders. On the face of it, the governmental imaginary for Aboriginal people from the desert anticipates a profound transformation in socioeconomic subjectivity, from kin-based welfare dependency to individualized wage earner.[40] But the reality is something quite different. The toughest challenge for those trying their luck in the city is the entrenchment of their marginalization. In the first two years of Nungarrayi's time in Adelaide, she was determined to push through her unemployed status. As a woman who had been proudly employed for most of her adult life, finding a job was a vital part of the process of establishing herself in the city and reanchoring her self-worth on the other side of so much trauma and destabilization. A work-for-the-dole opportunity opened up at a local church, where she was told she would be drawn into helping deliver programs providing assistance to local residents in need of support. She was upbeat in the lead-up to this placement. On the surface it seemed to promise work that would resonate with a position she had once held as a financial caseworker. While it would not add anything to her meager fortnightly welfare payments, it would get her out of the house and purposefully engaged among people. Disappointment hit hard when Nungarrayi presented herself for work only to find herself sitting at a table in an empty hall for hours on end with nothing to do. The woman responsible for overseeing her placement was disengaged and firmly rebuffed Nungarrayi's identification of various tasks she could complete. Nungarrayi called me several times during the week and a half she lasted in this placement, shooting time as she sat around, bored, bewildered, and irritated. Finally, she couldn't stand it any longer. She had an argument with her supervisor and refused to return. She complained to her job search provider and announced that she was changing companies.

This "work experience" adventure was continuous with a regime that required Nungarrayi to apply for twenty jobs a month to keep her fortnightly welfare payments coming in. The range of jobs she could apply for was limited by the contracts held by the job search provider. Nungarrayi's considerable and specific experience as a translator and community mediator in the Northern Territory counted for nothing in South Australia. When she relocated across state borders, her capabilities were assessed as equating to the terms of unskilled worker. Her caseworker had no interest and no capacity to go looking for a job placement for Nungarrayi that might actually make use of her expertise. As a consequence, she would apply randomly for positions as a poultry worker, kitchen hand, diesel mechanic, bakery worker, personal shopper, pizza maker, and pastry cook. Her applications for these "bullshit jobs" were never going to amount to anything aside from her own growing frustration with the system. The complete disconnect between Nungarrayi's particular working history and the abstract system that "manages" her entrenchment could be described as an instance of strategic neglect or systematic abandonment.[41] Yet she is no passive victim and continues to energetically and confidently hunt for resources that will help transform her circumstances. Somewhat remarkably, when she took action and "sacked" her job search provider, what followed was a productive collapsing of the distance between the practices of punitive governance and the call of kinship. Nungarrayi happened upon a company that employed a case manager she knew—who had recently relocated to Adelaide from a placement in the Big Town. Time in the desert had exposed this woman to the dynamics of Warlpiri extended family responsibilities, the frequency of deaths, and the nature of funerary obligations and related hypermobility. Nungarrayi would find navigating the punitive responses to her haphazard engagement significantly smoother, for a few months at least, via the intervention of this sympathetic agent adept at working the cracks in the bureaucratic field.[42]

We spend an entire day trying to locate Nungarrayi's sister Serena, whom we had failed to find on my previous visit. There is no sign of her in the parklands. One of the drinkers tells us she was sighted earlier in the day down the road, next to the detox center. We walk the two kilometers (one mile) to the other side of town, but no luck. We head back into the city center and cross paths with Magda and family, who have assembled at the bus interchange three hours early to say farewell to Alan's grieving family, who were booked to return to Alice Springs on the 6:00 p.m. bus. We do not linger there but keep moving and, after some vacillation over which bus to take, board one in the direction of the suburb where Serena has rental accommodations. The area into which we are heading is relatively unfamiliar territory for Nungarrayi. Communication with a friendly passenger leads us to get off the bus before it forks off in the wrong direction. We take a meandering two-kilometer (one-mile) walk to our final destination, checking Google Maps as we go. At my suggestion as we pass a market, we opportunistically shop for dinner ingredients. Finally, we reach the house. The door is opened by a smiling African man who greets Nungarrayi. Inside we are met not by Serena but by this man's wife, another of Nungarrayi's extended sisters, who tells me she has lived in Adelaide for thirty years. The couple had moved into the house just one day earlier to "keep Serena company." Serena, she tells us, is back in town, drinking in the parklands. It has been a long day. I call a taxi to take us home. As he arrives, the driver anxiously casts an eye over the unkempt state of the front yard and asks us up front how we will pay for our journey. I pass him my university corporate credit card.

In the city, temporality takes on its own distinctive distortions. "See how we roll" conjures the unpredictable spin of the day, as entire days, days rolling into weeks, are given over to the pursuit of resources, people, entertainment, and distraction. Conventional temporal structures of working hours, the particular rhythms of the working week and associated rituals of school attendance, weekends, regular meals, sleeping, and waking have no place in this social universe. I find myself marveling at how calm and orderly life in the desert seems by comparison to Nungarrayi's new situation. All of the same elements are in the mix, but a steadier rhythm of the day is established by a more or less collective assent to the patterns of community life. Unemployment, mobility, and stress may be pervasive in the desert, but the relatively contained setting of place, the rhythms of service delivery, more or less steady hours of operation for community organizations, stores, medical center, the regularity of afternoon football matches, the loud siren that declares school is in or out of session all contribute to a structured dynamic of the day and something that loosely approaches what might be described as integration of the social body.

Fragile Futures

Yet routine and steadiness can just as easily give rise to boredom.[43] Boredom breeds restlessness and a deep urge to travel in search of something more. Travel exponentially increases vulnerability. One premature death that hit me hard in recent years was that of Napurrurla, a thirty-four-year-old cousin of Nungarrayi who died suddenly of a heart attack following a drinking session in an Alice Springs town camp, one afternoon in February 2017. At the time, Napurrurla's death struck me as both utterly unbelievable and sickeningly inevitable. Within the Warlpiri realm she embodied the glittering, larger-than-life qualities of a rock star. In coming to terms with her death, I found it difficult to resist the clichéd question of how one who radiated such incandescent, pulsing life could simply stop living. On hearing the news of Napurrurla's death, I also had a stomach-churning sense of déjà vu. I was transported back ten years earlier to the news of the death of another radiant young woman, Napurrurla's close extended sister, the daughter of another friend. That sudden death was also heart related. That young woman's husband had died in a car accident a year or so prior to her death. They left behind a young teenage son and the woman's grief-stricken mother, whose life would now be utterly reordered as she acquired responsibilities as primary carer for this child and three other grandchildren who subsequently came into her care.

In the mid-1990s, these young women were part of a cohort who were an impressive force unto themselves. Aged then in their late teens and early twenties, a number of whom were mothers with very young babies, this group came together in a senior girls class in the school in a pilot education program that used a video conferencing network operating across five desert communities to deliver secondary-level curriculum from the correspondence school in Darwin. On leaving school these women had both skills and confidence that put them in high demand for the small number of paid jobs available around town. The place where they shone most brightly was at the community media center. They took to radio broadcasting, DJing with great enthusiasm. They were inspired to move into this work space by their biological and extended mother, who had been the first female radio worker, a matriarch of community broadcasting. They made that radio room their own and, in the process, pushed back against a prevailing order of aged and gendered authority in the Warlpiri public domain.[44]

The media center was a magnet for creatively driven people. Alan had also worked there as a translator, video maker, and editor until his failing health forced him to move to Alice Springs. Nungarrayi's ex-husband, Daniel, and her son, David, worked there in varying capacities. Napurrurla was the leading light among her peers and also the one who stayed. She worked for the media center for almost twenty years, right up to the time of her death. Tensions often erupted between Napurrurla and management over work schedules and remuneration. She regularly threatened to resign. But she always came back. Media work was too much a part of who she was. When the mobile phone network was rolled into the town, Napurrurla took to social media with zeal. She was the most avid and energetic Facebook poster I have known. She produced and uploaded hundreds of selfies, perfecting her preferred pose—pursed lips, large sparkling eyes, sassy fashion, and wicked ironic humor turning up one corner of her mouth. She posted her breakfast, her swinging moods, her love of family, her fierce independence, her on-again, off-again relationships, her critique of colonialism and police brutality, her proud Aboriginality. She posted that she was bored. She posted that she was drunk. She posted that she would fight anyone who offended her integrity. She posted that she was stuck in town and missed home and her family.

At the time of her death, Napurrurla had been traveling. She loved the anticipation of travel, but predictably she often got stuck somewhere for a period of days, high and dry, hungry, without money or transport, before making it home again. The hiatus of getting stuck, in limbo between places, signals the tipping point between the unpredictability and excitement of travel and the routine and deep grounding offered by home. As a charismatic and energetic person, Napurrurla lurched between these dispositions with great gusto. Arriving home after a period of being away was an occasion for passionate public celebration, for declarations of love of home and family. But the lure of the new, of elsewhere, was always present, always agitating, lodged at the core of her creative drive.

One afternoon in early 2013, Napurrurla spontaneously joined a drawing workshop associated with a research project I was conducting in the Big Town. She did so out of happenstance; she had come looking for her mother, who was working closely with me. In the course of a twenty-minute, humor-filled visit to one of the tables at which we were working, Napurrurla produced the drawing that I would select as the final image with which to conclude the book I was working on. This picture, which she made quickly and confidently, in several ways stood strikingly apart from those being made by the older women participating in the project. Her drawing was dominated by a large setting sun, a sparse desert landscape, and a road drawn in pinpoint perspective. She set a sole black figure striding purposefully along the road, flanked on either side by trees that looked as though they were dancing. I wrote that the maker of this drawing

> eschews classical iconography and gives us point perspective, the horizon, the lone figure—herself—walking along the road into the setting sun. The picture calls to mind the idea of Warlpiri women being "boss for themselves" explored by Diane Bell in her classic ethnography of women's ritual life. But [Napurrurla's] drawing also suggests a break in Warlpiri subjectivity, a break in the primary references through which a person sees their relationship to others and their place in the world. "Look at me as a creative independent individual," this picture seems to demand; "do not presume to characterise me through the prism of

kinship and Dreamings; do not look backwards in time in order to understand who I am; I am focused on the future."[45]

I went on:

> While [Napurrurla']s picture jolts the expectations of the viewer, it must be noted that the direction in which her figure walks is not towards Alice Springs, but rather westward, into the desert. In this sense, if this picture looks to the future it is a future that is less than clear. [Her] description of the drawing refuses to admit finality; she is walking and thinking, not leaving.[46]

I suggested that this drawing shared a sensibility with another striking drawing made six decades earlier by this woman's adoptive maternal grandfather, Jungarrayi, who was Nungarrayi's father's father. In 1953, Jungarrayi had created a beguiling drawing of light radiating through the fly screen that encased the window of the settlement superintendent's newly erected house. He had made the drawing for anthropologist Mervyn Meggitt, who was surprised to receive it. Meggitt's research was most closely shaped by discussions with senior men about country, mythology, and ceremonial themes. Jungarrayi's picture, I suggested, and Napurrurla's too, intervened in the history of Warlpiri people's engagements with anthropologists. Both pictures seemed to offer a glimpse, by no means a clear view, of large-scale forces that each drawing maker was grappling with, six decades apart. Both, I wrote, "seem to distil uncertain, future-focused, hope."

I wrote these words tentatively, at the end of a period Warlpiri friends observed had been especially dark. I was aware of the thinly stretched optimism I was loading onto Napurrurla and her drawing. She was luminous at the exhibition launch at the National Museum of Australia where we put the Warlpiri drawings on display in a yearlong exhibition in 2014–15. She enthusiastically participated in photo shoots and an interview in the Australian Broadcasting Corporation (ABC) radio studios in Canberra with her mother and me. She was excited as we drove in a convoy, three cars of her countrymen and countrywomen, from Canberra on her first-ever visit to the show. She posted memories of those events on Facebook a year later. She was fiercely intelligent and astonishingly quick-witted. She was a dazzling figure in the eyes of Warlpiri children.

Grief is often compounded by the worry and stress of trying to meet astronomical costs of transporting deceased bodies across the desert and at times across state borders. There are also considerations regarding where a body will be buried; where "sorry business" will take place; how money will be generated to purchase the blankets and other supplies that must be gifted to certain close relatives in the rituals associated with "finishing up." But beyond these concerns lie others that are much more basic: Who will care for those young children who have been left motherless? How will a family cope without the income from a senior relative's successful art-making career? Is it possible to host an initiation ceremony once those senior women with the authority to lead—women who held the dances and songs—have passed on? And, at a time when pervasive threats of sorcery collide and congeal with the practices of surveillance governance, are there *any* places to which people can retreat and feel unambiguously safe?

THE NIGHT BEFORE MY departure, Nungarrayi and I are sitting at the kitchen table when Nathan and his young wife walk through the door, along with the mother of Nungarrayi's youngest grandchild, Tyson. It was this young mother and child we had tried unsuccessfully to locate during our visit to Alice Springs five months earlier. All three adults are drunk. The purpose of the visit is announced: they have come to hand over Tyson into Nungarrayi's care. The mother looks uncertain, emotionally wrought. There is obvious tension between her and Nungarrayi. While Nungarrayi gets on with cooking a meal for everyone, I go and sit on the couch next to the young mother. She tells me she is twenty-two and has three children under the age of seven. She tells me she has been "growled by family" all over the place, telling her to give the boy to Nungarrayi. She is frightened that if she does not do this, "something might happen." But she is worried. She asks me quietly if Nungarrayi and Ram are trustworthy. The other young couple in the house have had their infant daughter removed from their care by South Australian Children's Services. Earlier in the day, while waiting for a bus in the city, Nungarrayi and I crossed paths with a father and son who were visiting Adelaide from the Big Town. I guessed the small child's age as five or six, but Nungarrayi told me he was nine. He had been caught multiple times breaking into the community store and was on the verge of being put into detention at Don Dale. In the absence of the child's mother or other relatives who could help take care of him, the father had brought the boy to Adelaide, hoping to keep him out of reach of Northern Territory police and the Department of Families and Community Services.

Once Nungarrayi has finished cooking and everyone settles down to eat, the house assumes a happy calm. They will all spend the night here, dissolving the mother's anxiety around imminent separation from her child. But I have a sleepless night, woken often by a dark mood I cannot throw off, as well as by the child's intermittent crying. With the break of day my anxieties settle somewhat. I can now see the situation differently. The mother is not coping with the care of three young children and makes that clear herself. Nungarrayi's determined action will keep this child out of state care and is having a galvanizing effect on her demeanor and sense of purpose. Ram too is genuinely delighted at the prospect of little Tyson living with them. After breakfast the visitors all leave the house, promising to return later in the day with the child and his belongings. As I pack my bag and prepare to fly back to Melbourne, Nungarrayi comes in and sits on my bed. As we talk over the events of the past five days, she points to my new Nike running shoes, which she has been eyeing since I arrived. "You've got to give those ones to me," she says. In the instant it takes me to flash a vision of my abundant wardrobe as well as my ability to replace these particular shoes if I so desire, I hand them over. Two hours later we meet up again in the city. I have left the house with Nathan's ID and bank cards in my wallet; I had forgotten that he had given them to me for safekeeping a couple of days earlier. The two are happy to have an excuse to come into town. As they approach the spot near the bus stop where I am sitting waiting for them, Nungarrayi cheekily smiles and points to her feet. She is wearing my shoes.

On the phone several weeks later, I tell Nungarrayi I have not been able to get the song "Don't Say Goodbye" out of my head. This time she presents the song that I had heard as a more or less literal refrain for Alan as a melancholy ode to her hometown. "I left my hometown. I don't want to say goodbye. In my memory I'm still there."

5

Forces of
Containment

Back to the Ground

We are close to the end of our four-and-a-half-hour drive. As the infrastructure of the Tiny Town comes into view, Nungarrayi noticeably relaxes. The
tension that spiked between us a hundred kilometers (sixty miles) back along
the road—my plea to break our journey, her retort that we couldn't stop—has
dissolved. Nungarrayi supposes out loud that she has not visited this place in
ten years. She is highly animated at the prospect of seeing her extended sisters
and other family we have come to visit. As I park our rental car in front of a
house that she directs me to on the western edge of town, two women come
out to see who is calling on them. We have given them no forewarning of our

visit. Once they recognize who we are, they break into wide grins and yell out excitedly to others in the camp.

We have come to see Nungarrayi's brother Justin, in the hope of traveling with him on to their paternal estate. He lives here in a house with his wife, several grown children, and grandchildren. Residing in the recently refurbished house next door is Justin's wife's brother and his family: his wife, who is another of Nungarrayi's close extended sisters, and several children in their care. The two sisters-in-law immediately set about raking the yard around us. This energetic cleanup is without doubt triggered by my presence, and discussions quickly ensue about sleeping arrangements. I reassure the women that we have brought our own swags. As the sun sets, we cook a barbeque with meat we purchased in Alice Springs and sit around the fire. It is an idyllic scene—lots of laughing, catching up on family news, stories of the movements of geographically dispersed kin, funny stories about drunken people, accounts of recent road accidents, people in the hospital. Nungarrayi is in her element, holding court. I get drawn into a conversation with two sisters. It's a mutual delight for us to see each other for the first time in several years. They show me elaborately decorated pictures they have made and stored on their phones, assemblies of children, grandchildren, deceased parents and grandparents. I had known one of these women as a gifted radio broadcaster in the late 1990s. She tells me she doesn't like going to the Big Town anymore. There is too much fighting. She tells me she has lived in the Tiny Town with her husband for five years.

It is a glorious late spring evening. There is no mobile phone coverage, and the tempo of the place is noticeably calmer and quieter than at the Big Town 150 kilometers (less than 100 miles) down the road. Our hosts have made sleeping arrangements for eight of us; bed frames, mattresses, and swags are set on freshly raked ground, lined up side by side along the fence, heads oriented eastward as is customary Warlpiri practice. I once assumed this easterly sleeping orientation to be influenced by cosmological order but came to understand through experience that it reflects basic environmental sense—to sleep with one's head pointing in the direction of the rising sun means one won't be woken by rays of light hitting one's eyes. Great care is always taken with the positioning of individual sleepers in any sleeping arrangements, responding to interpersonal politics of the day, and ensuring the safety of vulnerable people from the ever-present threat of nocturnal malevolent spirits.[1] On this occasion Nungarrayi will form one end of the line of sleepers, offering protection to me, as I lie to her right. Her brother's wife will occupy the other end of the line. As Nungarrayi continues to regale our hosts with all manner of gossip carried from Adelaide and Alice Springs, I retreat to my swag, feeling soothed and sleepy in the easy, jovial company of the camp. I am woken several times through the night by noisy, scrappy camp dogs, but each time I realize that I am snug and fall back to sleep. We wake to a clear desert day with a light breeze. As I look left from my bed, I see the dramatic red mountain range bathed in sun. Signs of people emerging into the day are indicated by music streaming quietly from a stereo over the back fence. The first song I register is Rod Stewart's "I'll Be Staying."

Finding Place

What is home? What is country? How does one respond to places and people who have been formative in one's life after periods of being away? Michael Jackson wrote directly on this question in *At Home in the World*, a book that explores his experience living in the northern Warlpiri town and working with senior men on sacred site surveys across the Tanami desert over several months in the late 1980s and early 1990s. Jackson interprets Warlpiri orientation to the desert through the prism of cosmology and complex kin-based politics, inflected by a Heideggerian privileging of experience and "being." Jackson's exploration confronts settler colonial displacement and its politically fraught aftermath, but his quest to come to terms with ideas of home ultimately levels attention on the teachings of Jukurrpa, Warlpiri Law, and the stories through which Warlpiri know their places, which invariably deploy a temporal order W. E. H. Stanner famously described as "everywhen."[2] The force of this narrative body of law is to be found in the social order that collectively enacts it but also, significantly, in what Warlpiri insist is its unchanging nature. When I turn to scholarship that takes this paradigmatic approach to place, looking for guidance and inspiration, I find myself increasingly frustrated by an apparent disconnect. Narratives of unchanging law only have so much interpretive power in circumstances where place-based attachments are so profoundly under pressure.

In vigorously pursued debates among anthropologists over the interpretation of Aboriginal ways of reckoning place, the concept of practice has been pitted against phenomenological experience. For Fred Myers, questions of Aboriginal placemaking must be approached through social mediation, most particularly the practices through which persons are taught and disciplined to relate to places in specific ways. Places come to be objectified in shared social practice. Places are ritually activated through the painting of objects and bodies, as well as in song and dance, and in the politics of negotiation that frame those activities. Myers rejects the implied passivism and ahistoricism of the Heideggerian concept of "dwelling" promoted by Tim Ingold, Jackson, and others, but he narrows the space between himself and these phenomenologically inspired writers when he observes, "It is through dwelling in a landscape, through the incorporation of its features into a pattern of everyday activities, that it becomes home to hunter gatherers."[3]

Places acquire or gather meaning in lived experience. The experience of dwelling in a place is primary in the establishment of one's sense of oneself. As Nungarrayi's life and indeed Warlpiri history indicate, experience of place enfolds layers of disruption, fragmentation, and trauma. Experience can cut across—just as it can affirm—the coherent order of nurturing relationships of care and, through them, Warlpiri Law. A person's associations with places unfold dynamically through time, and this is where the course of life and politics transcends the analytic efficacy of phenomenology. The storying of place simultaneously involves *making* place.[4] Through their shared orientation to places, people recognize each other as people of *that* place, people who have inherited certain ancestral potencies, attributes, physical features, and personality traits that are enfolded in the storying of a place. Storying is inextricably entwined with and interpreted through experience. In this way, place and persons are mutually, simultaneously produced, just as they may be cleaved apart.

The Tiny Town we are visiting has its own history of being made through the determined actions of a group of traditional owners who wished to leave behind the complex tensions that permeated life in the Big Town and to establish for themselves and their families a renewed desert-focused life. The town has its origins as the first Warlpiri outstation. People have lived here in small numbers since 1975. They campaigned hard for government support for this move and secured committed community advisers and others to deliver essential resources.[5] Yet Warlpiri narrate the origins of this place somewhat differently. As I am reminded one afternoon by Nungarrayi's extended sister Giselle, the widow of a recently deceased Pentecostal minister, this "community" was made not by government but by God. One night long ago, when people were living at the site of the old outstation, a large cross appeared before them in the sky. That is when they knew this place was the promised land. Over time the outstation grew into a town with a population of approximately 250, a number that has swelled in the aftermath of The Troubles.

This thinly sketched history indicates that if *practice* in the Bourdieusian sense is to be a compelling concept through which to glimpse the processes at work in the contemporary constitution of place or "country," it is not only ritualized practices that must be accounted for. What "structuring structures" shape placemaking practice in the volatile, hypermobile times of the present? Writing a decade ago of the Pintupi, whose lands lie to the west, Myers argued that despite displacement and the loss of site-specific knowledge that settlement gave rise to, underlying "formative forces" of place are still at play.[6] Crucial to Myers's analysis is people's continued physical orientation to their ancestral estates. Ute Eickelkamp, writing more recently of Anangu shifting relations to the desert, observes a stronger situation of rupture. Pointedly, Eickelkamp argues that as a consequence of the undermining of their "sovereign position as knowing subjects," people have *"ceased to be the makers of their own world."*[7] However, to observe ontological transformation is not to suggest that places have ceased to be ontologically significant. As proximity, visitation, and interaction with desert places recede as organizing principles for life, she writes, "the significance of *envisaging the self into place* cannot be overstated; it potentially transcends the importance of being there in the flesh."[8]

While the force of physical places may recede, the force of kinship constitutes its own generative process through which persons orient toward, and envisage themselves into, place. It is in this sense that the emotional associations of home or country rest not necessarily in localities but with *particular assemblies of people associated with those localities*. It is clear from my time spent with Nungarrayi in Adelaide that place is involved, affirmed, and reordered in more spatially distanced constellations of kin. Under such circumstances, placemaking practice is by no means restricted to ceremonial gatherings and the making of paintings. It is also vested in the fraught politics over landownership, native title, and mining royalties; in public exhortations to authority over community affairs; and in the production and exchange of music, videos, and family portraits. There are many things at stake in these practices, but ultimately, appeals to place-based identification are appeals to an anchored and specifically related self. People related through place share what George Herbert Mead describes as "significant symbols" through which they communicate and confirm order and value, and thus place operates as vital ground from which to make sense of the larger order of things.[9] Kinship carries associations of place, but what those associations amount to and how they travel with a mobile person across an expanding social field are less assured.

If places in the present are entities that continue in some way to "hold" persons, they can do so only through a person's active attending to place. When a person moves, by choice or circumstance, places become disembedded, internalized in the form of memories, nostalgic longing, recalled associations. Importantly, such disembedding does not originate with forced displacement. As Barbara Glowczewski observes, the melancholy sadness associated with leaving places behind is part and parcel of the affective dynamic of mobile Warlpiri hunter-gatherer life.[10] Warlpiri songs "teem with feelings of grief when one has to turn one's back on a place."[11] Nungarrayi's experience shows that such long-ing deepens when one is forced to leave, and especially when one leaves as a person fractured from the polity. A person dealing with traumatic rupture and the related weight of loss and longing must inevitably confront the entangled identification of person and place from which she is now separated.[12] Nungar-rayi's emotional investment in place as anchor of herself enacts such a redemp-tive, creative response.[13] She cycles back to the same sequence of memory, one from her childhood in which she camped for an extended period at her father's outstation in his nurturing care and that of her grandparents. This is an exis-tentially crucial envisaging of herself into place. She undertakes this work on her own, during private moments of distress, in my company, and, where the stakes are highest, in interactions with kin who will recognize and confirm the authority and significance of her claim.

The Work of Relatedness

While Nungarrayi dwells vividly in her mind in certain places, in her home-town, on her ancestral estate, the places she longs for as constellations of a particular social world are no longer reachable. The arrangements she mourns belong to another time, another generational setting of authority and care, an-other governmental imaginary. At times she refutes what she detects as my nos-talgic longing and place-based sentimentality. "You can't live your whole life in one place," she tells me, dismissing my concern for the existential cost of her dis-placement to Adelaide. "I want to be here," she insists. Her attitude in moments such as these is not unlike the attitudes of her sisters who currently live in the Tiny Town. They are pragmatic as they rationalize their own relocation. There's too much fighting at the place they once called home; that's why they are here. But there are signs that the apparent tranquility of this little community is also fragile. For this too is a place that exists only in relation to other places and the persons who reside there and pass through—a place linked to other places through practice and especially in the present to frenetic, volatile mobility.

Nowhere is the sense of destabilized calm more apparent than in the small cemetery perched on the edge of the Tiny Town. Here are the graves of local legends, the men and women who led the movement to establish the outsta-tion in the late 1970s. Most of these people lived well into old age, through multiple world-changing transformations. We have come here to visit the new-est graves, those of a man and a woman in their early thirties who were killed in a car accident in Alice Springs several months ago. Nungarrayi and I had danced together in 1996 at the ceremony where this man, whom she called

FIGURE 5.1 Tiny Town cemetery (photo by author)

son, was initiated alongside her son, David. I had known him as the son of an aging ceremonial leader, a hot-tempered child whose demeanor underwent a striking transformation after he emerged from the bush camp as a newly disciplined, quietly proud, initiated young man. These graves and several others are piled high with plastic flowers. Riotous, joyous color obfuscates the terrible circumstances of these premature deaths. As we head back toward the gate, I spot the earth mound of another recent grave. I am pulled up short when I realize whose grave this is and confront its white wooden cross snapped in half, with the pieces strewn on the ground nearby. The cross bears the name of the man to whom I dedicated a previous book. I imagine it being pulled from the heaped earth and snapped in half in a fit of alcohol-fueled rage. How to make sense of this reckless, sacrilegious act? The man in question was an exceptionally philosophical, calm person. I had heard whispers of conflict over his estate.

Nungarrayi is wound up as she moves around the camp and streets of this place. She asserts herself forcefully among her extended network of sisters and related kin. I listen on as she holds court on all manner of issues as we sit around the yard on plastic chairs. She instructs her relatives to think about ways of developing their Tiny Town—they should campaign for mining royalties to be spent on tractors, and they should establish paid work for cleanup teams to be employed. She is keenly projecting herself as a leader. The rhythms of camp life turn upon the comings and goings of people. None of our hosts have jobs to go to. There is plenty of time for talk. The mood of the camp cycles through hazy bouts of reverie, excited and hilarious gossip, speculation about when the shop will open, discussion of travel plans to attend a funeral that will be held tomorrow at the Big Town. Among our camp is the younger brother of Mr. Langdon, whose death in custody and related inquest were explored earlier. He is a shy, good-looking man with a lovely open smile. I learn that he served a lengthy prison sentence in Adelaide, from 2007 until sometime in 2015, suggesting a conviction involving a death. He tells me he first went to jail when he was fifteen and is due to face court again this coming week for outstanding warrants on charges of drunken disorderly behavior in Alice Springs. He tells me that he got pulled up for these outstanding warrants when he tried to purchase grog for relatives who had no identification. Following his release from jail about eight months ago, he traveled home to the Big Town but soon relocated to this quieter place to keep out of trouble and find work. He makes it clear to me that he is especially keen not to go back to jail.

Our visit coincides with school holidays. Kids roam around. On the second morning of our visit I watch on with discomfort as a small boy slowly kills a native pigeon, blow by blow. He lands his first blow with a stone and slingshot, rendering the bird unable to fly. Then he stalks after it with a deflated plastic football, taking aim, again and again, as the poor bird hobbles around the yard trying in vain to seek shelter beneath a car body, cowering next to the inner wall of a tire. But there is no escape. I console myself that this is a young hunter in the making as I watch the boy saunter back and forth. When he finally presents his catch to his grandparents, offering for their approval a large cooking pot in which the still alive but badly injured bird flaps around, he is criticized for being cruel. His grandfather tells him they might call the rangers.

Late in the afternoon, five of us, all women, drive out to a large floodplain that is currently covered in water, seeking relief from the unseasonably warm weather. We are heading for an emu dreaming place owned by the deceased husband of one of Nungarrayi's sisters. On Nungarrayi's request, I have purchased two frozen kangaroo tails from the store, and when we arrive at our destination she sets about energetically cutting wood, lighting a fire, and cooking the tails while the other women watch on. I wander around exploring the surrounding landscape. It is a beautiful spot—a long sand dune flanks a claypan edged by silver-barked eucalyptus. As I watch Nungarrayi wield the ax, I marvel at her unabating energy. For most of the day she has been in full-flight "talking story."

FIGURE 5.2 Kangaroo tail picnic (photo by author)

All of her stories are laden with moral weight: they are about people who are not caring properly for children, not sharing, not looking after old people, not having a "proper" basis for claiming ownership of country. She is stirred up and restless, a force of energy and talk. As she leads the direction of certain discussions, the talk is all about shoring up her version of reality, her way of reading situations and by extension, I surmise, securing an image of herself as a morally attuned person, in sync with her family, despite her prolonged physical absence. I am reminded of Basil Sansom's and Myers's writings on the hard, public work that Aboriginal people conduct in order to reproduce their relatedness.[14] But this work is also gendered. A Warlpiri woman makes moral claims on others as part of the process of active care. A woman oriented to others through an ethics of caring is motivated to sustain an ecology of rich interaction with others, as well as her own personal development.[15] Kin relations are not given; they are not simply born into and carried through life, but require constant attention and shoring up. Relationships are fragile, contingent. At times people make impossible demands of each other, sometimes with dramatic, devastating consequences.[16]

Distress and rage at having one's demands—and thus one's relatedness—rejected and, conversely, the driving impulse to stand alongside kinsmen and kinswomen in situations where honor is at stake indicate the stakes of kin recognition. Similar emotional intensity is at play when women like Nungarrayi, as well as several of her sisters and their biological mother before them, decide to leave their close kin and country. Amanda was driven to leave the Big Town as she struggled with the overwhelming grief associated with losing her son. Such depth of feeling is further fueled when grog and fast cars are in the mix. The primary ingredient is passion for family, an ontological grounding of self which decrees that there is no life worth living outside the inextricable webs of kinship, regardless of the volatility and trauma they might enfold. Lisa Stevenson seems to have this same force of emotion in mind when she writes of the constant yet elusive presence of suicide in the Indigenous communities of the Arctic as inextricably caught up with a form of life "that refuses to be constrained by the hegemony or abstraction of life."[17] The attenuation of kinship, when the bonds of family are stressed and stretched by the experience of displacement, introduces new fragility into the reciprocal order of family care. As she prepares to join a traveling party departing Adelaide for Central Australia, Nungarrayi calls to ask if I can help her out with money so she can purchase food for the road trip. "Can't family help this time?" I ask, invoking the extended relations with whom she is catching a ride. "I don't like to ask family," she tells me. When the ground on which life is lived is so unstable, there is too much at stake to risk the possibility of rejection.

Axel Honneth takes the setting of the family as the primal space where authentic recognition—openness to the other and by extension to the world—is cultivated, takes root, and can be most clearly identified. If a subject's own autonomy turns upon intersubjective dependency, it follows that systematic experiences of *mis*recognition in any sphere of life will feed back into the primary and most intimate settings of subject formation. Honneth shows that individuals engage in struggles over recognition because "they want to recover basic social conditions that are essential to them as human beings."[18] When he writes of *all claims* for recognition involving struggle, Honneth appears to be most closely focused on public and political claims. He writes with attunement to and concern for contexts of oppression, implying that the achievement of recognition inevitably involves some violence being done. The violence he has in mind is utopian, a targeted violence that would break apart the representational orders that entrench disrespect and inequality.[19] The violence that currently pervades the Warlpiri universe is more complexly dispersed. Nungarrayi struggles against misrecognition on two fronts: that which circulates at the level of the national picture, and that which threatens to be unleashed in the ricochet effects of attenuating kinship.

Nungarrayi reminds me that the attack by her ex-husband left her with a serious head injury and she now has a plate implanted in her skull. She continues to see a psychologist about her head injury. I wonder about that blow to the head as I contemplate the intensified, sped-up version of herself I'm becoming accustomed to. Late at night as we settle down for sleep, a boy in an agitated state is brought to Nungarrayi to heal. His mother tells Nungarrayi he played computer games all through the previous night and for much of the day and has consequently made himself ill. Nungarrayi massages the boy's head as she performs a mixture of *ngankari* healing procedures and prayer. She makes invocations to Wapirra, to God, to make the boy well.

Just before sunrise on the second morning of our visit Nungarrayi wakes me and tells me she's been thinking all night about a close sister who resides in the Big Town who is grieving the recent death of a brother. We had been hoping that Nungarrayi's absent brother Justin would arrive back from Alice Springs and travel with us on to their patrilineal estate, but in recent days he has been spotted driving around Alice in a new car—the bounty of a recent mining royalty payments distribution. It will likely be some time before he returns to the Tiny Town. This morning she has a new idea. We should go and visit her country today, without her brother, "have a quick look around," and then drive on to the Big Town to camp with her sister for the weekend. I'm surprised because this suggestion to visit the place of her banishment comes out of left field. But I'm also enthusiastic, especially at the prospect of a weekend visiting old friends in the Big Town. Nungarrayi sets about making damper for the camp in advance of our departure.

Places beyond Reach

Nungarrayi and I had talked many times about wanting to visit her country in the course of this research. She cannot recall when she last visited. My own last visit was more recent than hers, in 2013 and in the company of two of her aunties and three of their daughters. On that occasion we had camped overnight at the outstation. The focus of our group's attention was a sequence of drawings made in the early 1950s by one of Nungarrayi's paternal grandfathers. Our visit had a clear purpose, namely, to stimulate the sharing of memories of the period when the extended family spent considerable time residing in the area, and to share whatever memories remained of the remarkable but elusive man who made the drawings. On that trip it was apparent that there had been no visitors to the place for some time. The bush track into the outstation was barely visible, overgrown in chest-high grasses and tough sprouting shrubs.

The expansive spinifex plain at the foot of the mountain range had not been clear-burned for some years, making it impossible to cross by car. We reluctantly abandoned the idea of visiting a series of sacred sites. I wrote afterward of the melancholy mood that I found difficult to shake during that visit—a sadness on being confronted by what I took to be the distance of my traveling companions from their places and my own dawning realization that physical proximity to a place in and of itself does not deliver or release anything. The places we had come to visit and honor remained tantalizingly close yet out of reach. Memories that may have broached such distance were overshadowed by more pressing issues of the day. All travelers on that expedition were heavily preoccupied with the fighting that was simmering at home. As we lay in our swags around the fire at night, it was the power of God as invoked through biblical readings that held sway over the group, not the power of Jukurrpa and storied country.[20] I found these to be disarming mediations of place, at least for that constellation of visitors at that time.

Today, as Nungarrayi and I drive onto her country, we head directly to the manager's quarters to make our presence known. This land has for the past decade been under the stewardship of the Nature Conservancy. Nungarrayi has not met the manager before. I know of this man by reputation; he has many years of experience working with Aboriginal communities and is highly regarded. Nungarrayi introduces herself as a "traditional owner" and without pausing for breath asks him straight up, "Where's the rent?" The two spend some time establishing each other's bona fides. He responds to her questions in a calm, direct, measured tone, explaining that something like rent was never negotiated in the native title legal process that was completed several years ago. "We spend lots of money but never make any," he says, as he explains the work of the wildlife sanctuary. I surmise that this is not the first time he has been grilled in such a way. The manager tells us that he is awaiting the arrival of a road train delivery of building materials and a large concrete pour later today. He is consumed by logistics surrounding construction of a new dwelling that will house the many scientists who come through to conduct research on the endangered species being protected on this reserve.

As we take our leave, the manager describes the layout of a network of new roads that has recently been graded to cater to the work of the conservancy. The station has attracted international media attention for its construction of two meter-high, forty-four-kilometer (twenty-five-mile) long, feral predator-proof fence and will soon declare the fenced area "feral free."[21] Nungarrayi is confident that she knows her way to the places she wishes to visit, but as I drive she quickly gets disoriented and as a consequence we miss visiting a number

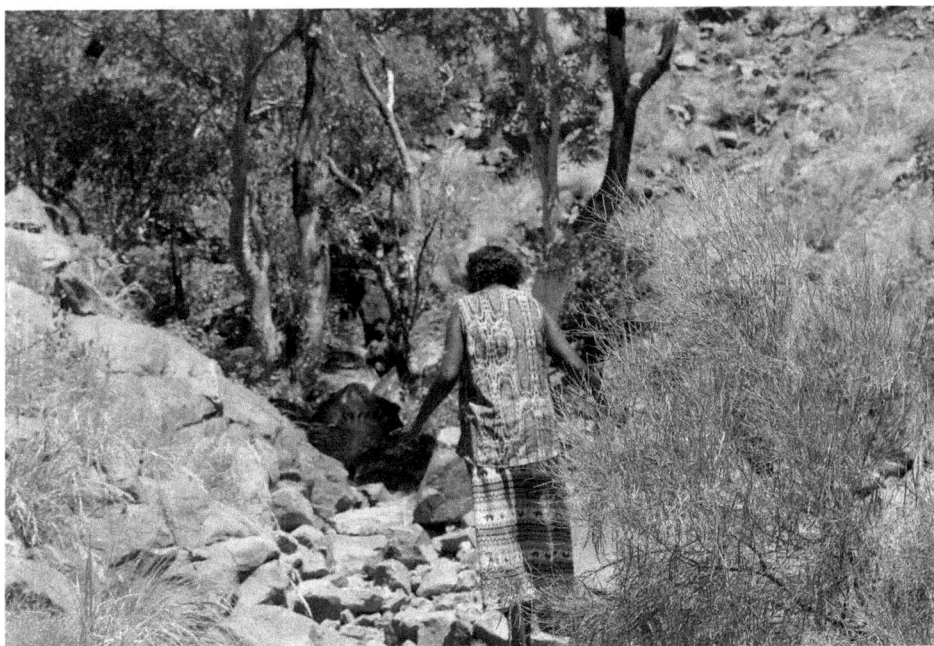

FIGURE 5.3. Back to country (photo by author)

of important places, including her grandfather's grave. As we skirt the perimeter of the mountain in our air-conditioned four-wheel-drive vehicle, I have a powerful sense of déjà vu. As with my previous visit in the company of her aunties, the oft-mentioned camping places, water holes, and places of ancestral activity are all gestured toward through the car window, but the places themselves remain beyond reach. The awe-inspiring presence of the mighty mountain range and its multiply storied places do not trigger fresh memories, but rather the retelling of stories I have heard before. Nungarrayi recalls a camping trip from her childhood during which she, her father, and other kin posed at various places for the camera of a Central Australian historian who took their photographs. We agree that we should try and track down those photographs. As we drive, I'm struck by the layered imaginaries and practices through which this land has been repurposed across the period of living memory: once a cattle station run by a pastoralist the Warlpiri knew as a kind and generous man; then, following recognition of Warlpiri land rights, an ancestral estate with two outstations and a series of interconnected sacred sites; more recently, following the death of the pastoralist and his donation of the land to the Nature Conservancy, a wildlife sanctuary encased in a security fence that cuts a vast swath through the spinifex plain and a new cartography geared to the interests of bird-watching scientists.

During our visit, the country does, however, throw up a surprise gift, a *jitti* stone of love magic. Jitti is mined at a woman's place nestled in the mountain. The stone lies directly in Nungarrayi's path as we finally get out of the car and climb the gentle incline to a sacred water hole. Leaving the vehicle's air-conditioned interior for the dry heat of the spinifex plain delivers a jolt to the senses. My vision goes hazy in the dazzling sunlight. I trail behind Nungarrayi, taking photographs. She calls out to her ancestors, announcing her presence: a woman from this place, accompanied by me, her *kardiya* (whitefella) friend. The air vibrates with the shrill hum of grasshoppers, and the occasional clear whistle of a bird Nungarrayi identifies as *mirlalypa* (guardian spirits) responding to her call, affirming her rightful presence. Spotting the stone on the ground ahead of her, she stops dead in her tracks and gasps. Overcome with emotion, she bursts into tears and calls out to me. Yet again, I'm taken aback by the fragility of her disposition. On visits to country over the years, I've observed offerings such as this being treated as nothing out of the ordinary; indeed, gifts of country are expected in the spiritually infused reciprocal engagement of people with their places. But in the upheaval of the present, such a tangible conferral of Nungarrayi's authority and her related capacity to call forth and engage ancestral power carries considerable weight. Our encounter with this stone and the country that offers it up will be a defining moment of the two weeks we spend in Central Australia, rupturing the rapid-paced trajectory that has thus far swept us along. The encounter with the stone seems to power-fully instantiate the conjuncture of separation, longing, and recognition that Nungarrayi's exile has made manifest.[22] What seems to be revealed in this en-counter is something very basic to what is at stake in distinctive Warlpiri-place relationships and the forms of recognition they bestow. In the days that follow, Nungarrayi will tell everyone we cross paths with about the stone. Finally, one day in an Alice Springs car park, she will relinquish the stone into the hands of her daughter. It will, her daughter tells us, bring her luck at cards.

Near the top of the incline we sit quietly by two rock holes that are slowly filled by a trickling spring. This is where Nungarrayi and her family collected water in the time before a bore was sunk and a water tank and windmill in-stalled near the outstation's tin houses. She bathes while I take in the breath-taking vista that rolls out below us. The country is spectacular, vivid green set against red rock. Wildflowers are in abundance. We track across to the ocher-colored cliff face, and Nungarrayi guides my eyes to see fading, delicate black line drawings made by her grandfathers. We make our way back down the hill

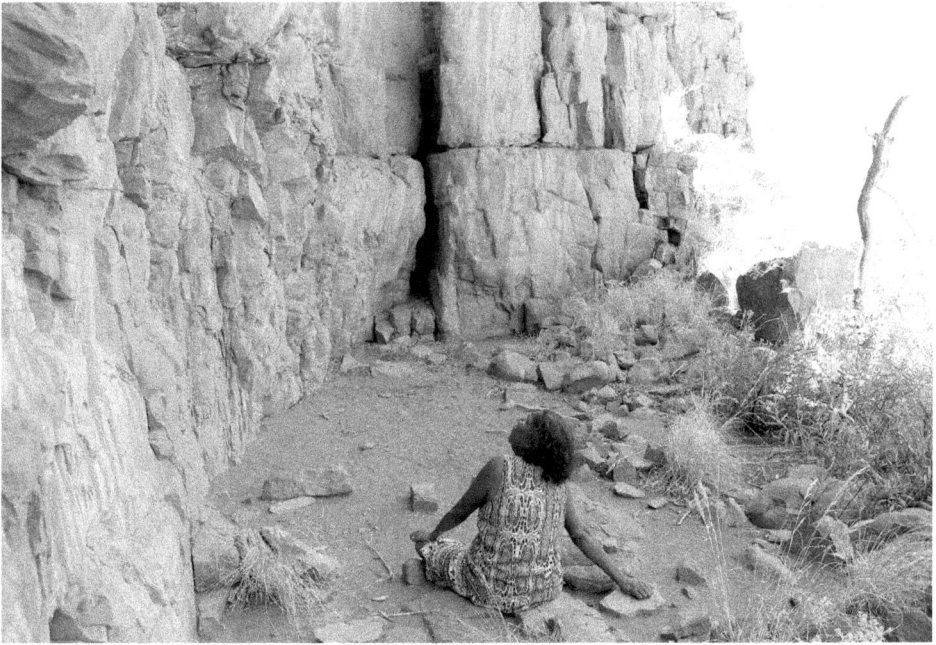

FIGURE 5.4 Grandfathers' place (photo by author)

and decide to drive across to the second outstation on the other side of the mountain range. By now I am getting bleary-eyed, and we settle into a quiet reverie, she dozing, me navigating the narrow bush road. We hit upon a change in geology, and the gentle red sand gives way to a rocky, bone-jarring track that is heavily impinged upon by large acacia shrubs whose branches rhythmically whack the windscreen and the panels of both sides of the car. After half an hour of this, we emerge suddenly from the bush into an opening, and there stand the long abandoned near-pristine houses. Nungarrayi makes clear she has no interest in getting out of the car. Was this detour a simple going through the motions for my benefit? Feeling tired and flat, I cannot help but wonder how different our visit might have been in the company of her brother.

"Time to go," she tells me, as I turn our car toward the road that leads to the Big Town. The languid afternoon drifts as I drive. But as we near her hometown, I sense Nungarrayi stiffen and become increasingly agitated. As we approach the house of close kin on the eastern edge of town, she has what seems to be a panic attack. "No room! No room!" she screams as she doubles over in her seat. A young woman appears and escorts us across the road to Nungarrayi's sister's house. Nungarrayi instructs me to park the car behind the house while the two of them go inside. To my astonishment, within thirty minutes of driving into town we are back on the road and heading toward Alice Springs. I am surprised to realize that I am also relieved to put the town behind us. Nungarrayi's anxiety is infectious. An hour down the road we stop at the roadhouse to eat burgers. Then, as night closes in, I drive the remaining two hours to Alice Springs. It has been a long day. By the time we turn onto the Stuart highway, twenty kilometers (twelve miles) out of the regional center, I am exhausted and on the verge of hallucinating. Our unplanned arrival coincides with the eve of the World Masters Games, and Alice Springs is abuzz with aging sports tourists. Hotels are fully booked. I discover that this is the most expensive and difficult week of the year to find accommodations. I secure the last available room in a hotel at twice the usual nightly rate. As I settle down to sleep, Nungarrayi heads out, restless, looking for action. I'm woken by her knocking on the hotel window at sunrise, with stories of a strange Nakamarra woman, an extended daughter, who followed her around all night.

Our encounter with the jitti stone stays with me as the flip side of Nungarrayi's panic attack and our flight from her hometown. Taking stock of this long, remarkable day, I wonder what has become unhinged. Being in the presence of place is an experience that can be disorienting, overwhelming, just as under other circumstances it can be comforting and reassuring. Places not only draw people close but also push people away, making them feel estranged. Places are pervaded by forces that are powerful, volatile, and unpredictable. There is something other than ancestral energy at work here. Fear, fragility, and instability have become entwined in the social mediations of place. They grind and clash against memories that conjure security and certainty. Yet, destabilizations of the present are also pushed back upon by countervailing *stabilizing* forces—the recognition calls of bird-spirit ancestors, the activating and authorizing appearance of jitti stones, houses and infrastructure that hold comforting memories but of themselves offer no comfort in the present.

In a thoughtful incursion into anthropology's spatial turn, Nancy Munn argues back against the abstract deployment of the concepts of place and space, offering an alternate reading that focuses on "the centering subject," the "spatially and temporally situated actor—through whom and in whose experience the integrity of space and time emerge."[23] She explores a series of case studies that show how ancestral power, understood as fixed in country, can be transposed into a moving space, such as "a Law [initiation] truck" and its travelers. But crucially, all of Munn's mobile examples presume more or less bounded fields of action and socially certain subjects. Her analysis is applied to situations that appear remarkably stable when set against the fragmentation, hypermobility, and dangerous magical power with which Nungarrayi must contend. If place signals "at homeness," an affiliation consonant with stable identity, in the present Nungarrayi's claim to place asserts itself as a call against destabilization, an anxious refrain in her seemingly inexhaustible, determined presentation of self.[24]

Place Uncontained

Searching for a clear-eyed perspective from within the vortex of my journeying with Nungarrayi sometimes feels like wading through spiderwebs. Ethnographic experience is compelling: it lands me in the thick of the whirl, it seductively lures me along, but it provides no distance, no interpretive anchor points. Compounded intergenerational trauma is increasingly being brought to my attention in the storying that animates our travel, and with it the need for a longer temporal view than ethnography allows. Instances of child separation, departures and premature deaths of parents, and incidents of incarceration pile up. Critical criminologists argue that in order to comprehend these practices in the present and recent past, it is necessary to look back across the history of settler colonial governance. Russell Hogg describes the exceptional application to Aboriginal people of a series of intersecting welfare-penal institutions throughout the twentieth century. Aboriginal family and community were regarded as institutions that threatened social order and civilized values, the principal means by which Aboriginality and culture were reproduced and, thus, "something that had to be eliminated rather than cultivated and supported."[25] These creative acts of settler destruction return us to Honneth's observation that recognition struggles always involve violence. Here it is worth highlighting the reciprocity of negative recognitive practices—violence is done to Aboriginal people and their practices *because* they fail or refuse to recognize and respond to the authority of European law.

The starkest, most literal case of an "elimination" attitude being applied by settlers to Warlpiri came with the Coniston Massacres of 1928, when mounted and armed police and settlers led a terror-fueled rampage across the southern Tanami Desert, shooting and killing upwards of a hundred men, women, and children in retribution for the murder of dingo trapper Fred Brookes.[26] The Coniston killings were not simply a catastrophic event; they marked the beginning of the end of hunter-gatherer occupation of the desert. Through policy regimes of "protection" and "assimilation" that were implemented over the following four decades, the social institutions that supported life in the desert were intensively targeted for transformation. The government settlement would be the site of a constellation of practices geared toward remaking Aboriginal subjectivity.[27] The forms of containment and policing of movement practiced on settlements through the mid-twentieth century also insulated desert people to some extent against criminalization and penal incarceration.

If the policy eras of protection and assimilation were geared toward both containing and fragmenting Aboriginal social order, from the early 1970s a new approach emerged. The belated constitutional inclusion of Aboriginal people and the legal recognition of land rights in the Northern Territory were followed by government support for an "outstations movement," enabling those whose rights in land had been granted to return to live on their ancestral lands in residential groupings of their own making.[28] On Warlpiri country, aside from a few exceptions, the outstation movement was relatively short-lived. Part of the perceived failure across many desert estates had to do with a mismatch between government and Aboriginal expectations, at times with devastating consequences.[29] The new policy had been born of government acknowledgment of the failure of large settlements of the previous era to put in place safe and fulfilling social arrangements. At the same historical moment that the Australian Commonwealth recognized Aboriginal land rights, it also passed legislation that would actively foster those same people's participation in new kinds of placemaking activity. The superintendents of the previous generation departed, and settlements were newly named Aboriginal "communities." Aboriginal people would be legislatively required to be involved in the creation and governance of their new social entities.[30] A proliferation of committees, boards, and councils sprung up, drawing upon the authority of senior people to participate in the governance of myriad community activities. The structural flow of government resourcing in support of "communities" and "outstations" rested upon a further misrecognition. It required people to commit to their outstations located near ancestral places as if they were permanent residents; it asked that they identify as *either* outstations or community people. Warlpiri, like other Aboriginal people of the region, had never been fully sedentary in any particular place and had no intention of being so now. People wished to live dynamically, to move between different places as social demands and interests drew them thus.

While the amount of time spent in and around outstations waxed and waned, for many Warlpiri the lure of travel to places farther afield also beckoned strongly. Such travel was in part fueled by a resurgent national and international interest in Aboriginal cultural production, especially desert painting.[31] As senior men and women enthusiastically embarked on their first long-haul flights to attend exhibitions displaying their art, they absorbed the strikingly different circumstances in which people lived and the brutal effects of inequality in large cities. These experiences shaped their own distinctive comparative vantage. During my early interactions with senior women, I was left in no doubt that Warlpiri women viewed themselves as well-traveled chroniclers of life in an expanding social field. The first "story" shared with me by the widely recognized leader of women's ceremonial activity was an account of her visit to New York, her sadness at observing the lot of homeless people in that city, and a declaration that Warlpiri were lucky because they had "everything."

Through much of the 1980s and 1990s, community leaders actively worked to cultivate an arena of activity that was governed by what they described as "two-way law." A women's night patrol was established by a formidable group of senior women who wished to assert their own authority in relation to the control of wayward children, drunken men, and instances of domestic violence, and to generally keep peace and mediate between their community and police.[32] An outstation-based program to tackle youth petrol sniffing and other substance misuse became a regional model and ultimately achieved wide acclaim.[33] Attempts at pragmatically conjoining elements of Warlpiri and European authority gave people some cause for optimism. For a while it seemed possible to shape local organizations and institutions with the principles and practices of place- and kin-based orientations and priorities.

The progressive opening up of place, through increased Warlpiri mobility but also through transforming government imaginaries, has had multiple, contradictory ramifications. Paradoxically, with the end of assimilation, the governance of Aboriginal people has increasingly been dealt with through criminal justice, delivering growing numbers of people into prison.[34] The dehumanizing traumas systematically established in the earlier period through displacement, disempowerment, and child removal have carried deep consequences into the present. Many crimes committed by Aboriginal offenders can be interpreted as responses to the experience of being treated as lesser humans. In Hogg's words, they are "overwhelmingly crimes of poverty, despair and defiance."[35]

References to "two-way law" not only carry an appeal for a different attitude to legality but also invoke the possibility of social containment—the idea that as Warlpiri navigate the complex terms of an expanding world, they can continue to apply their coherent, place-based body of customary authority to it. The challenges and creative possibilities of such a vision have animated many intercultural projects. Alice Springs–based psychotherapist Craig San Roque, for example, worked closely with Nungarrayi's now-deceased extended father, and through years of dialogue the two men came to mutually articulate the distinct and related elements of a complex that anchored individuals psychologically and organized a Warlpiri worldview. Japaljarri initially presented this complex to San Roque in the visual language of a painting comprising five elements: country/*ngurra*; family/kinship/*waladja*; cultural stories/story system/*jukurrpa*; individual vitality/spirit/psyche/soul who inhabits this matrix; and law/the entity that binds the entire complex together.[36]

In their interactions, which were especially focused on the challenge of responding to trauma, the two men homed in on the fifth element of the schema, the essential, binding function of Warlpiri Law. Japaljarri was frank in acknowledging that the binding power of Jukurrpa was disintegrating or, more tangibly, that it was being *displaced* by the Supreme Court, which grants no authority to customary law and its fundamental role in the psychological disposition of persons individually and collectively. San Roque writes of the symbiotic relationship between a collectively held attitude he describes as the "carrying of care" and the well-being of an individual. These two men were engrossed in an intercultural exploration of the accommodations that might realistically be achieved between these two legal systems. San Rocque writes of the intercultural "recognition zone" as a malleable, vital space that needs to be critically fostered, and of the blindness that characteristically pertains to recognition across cultural difference. "What will bind us together into the future?" he asks.

Kinship's New Containments

Here in Alice Springs, Nungarrayi frequently returns our conversation to the topic of her ex-husband, and one day she suggests I go and visit him in jail. I'm surprised. It is my loyalty to her that has kept me from doing so thus far. She makes it clear she is curious to know how he is faring. Visiting jail is a strangely banal affair, notwithstanding the security complex to be negotiated. On the day of my visit the front office is attended by a muscular uniformed officer with a German accent and a blond buzz cut who processes my admittance, and Les, the Aboriginal liaison officer who took my call when I phoned earlier that morning and who facilitated my request for a "special" visit. The mood of the office is cheerful, tempered by the muted authoritarian aura that pervades the space, and the uniformed officer's expressionless gaze when he tells me I will take nothing with me and bring nothing out. Les smiles as he tells me he was amazed I managed to get approval for a visit in just a few short hours. I had been careful to include my university professorial signature in the request I emailed to the prison warden that morning. After placing my bag into a locker, I am buzzed through a series of extremely heavy iron doors, pass through a metal detector, and then follow a painted line that leads across a wide concrete courtyard to the doors of the visitor center. An officer opens and closes the door for me, and as I enter the room, I come face-to-face with Daniel, who sits on a bench in prison-issue dark blue track pants and orange jumper. He looks fresh, with a recent cut to what I register with surprise is now a head of entirely silver-gray hair.

Daniel tells me he had no idea who was coming to see him and greets me with a slightly quizzical, muted smile. He volunteers that he isn't worried about the court case for which he has now spent two and a half months waiting on remand. "This woman," his most recent partner, had "lied." He had been "somewhere else on the night in question." He is yet to see the charge sheet or be visited by a lawyer. He is scheduled to attend court in three weeks. We are the only people in the visitor's room, and we are cursorily watched over and listened to by an officer stationed at a desk a couple of meters away. Daniel and I have not been face-to-face for seven years. This is the first time I've seen him since he nearly killed Nungarrayi. For a long time, I had told myself I couldn't see him again, at least not without giving him a piece of my mind. But recent days spent in Central Australia, as well as Nungarrayi's own urgings, have softened my attitude.

The visitor's room is furnished with four metal tables and bench seats that are bolted to the floor. Signs on the wall advise visitors they are permitted to embrace and kiss prisoners on arrival and that it is then permissible to hold hands across the table for the duration of the visit. A coin machine issues cans of drinks and packets of chips. Daniel has always been a quiet man. We spend lengthy periods of the hour-long visit sitting together in silence. I ask him about the conditions in the jail. He tells me he shares a cell with ten men, all on remand. Being on remand means being in lockdown, except for an hour or two of exercise each day. The only stimulation in the cell is a television with faulty transmission. I ask if he watched the recent Australian Football League grand final. "Sort of," he says. The poor transmission signal made it difficult to watch because the picture kept going out of sync. As we talk on, the out-of-sync television stays with me as a compelling metaphoric image for the experience of incarceration and its severance from participation in the outside world. Daniel tells me with a pained expression that he tries to keep his mind off everything to do with life outside.

I ask Daniel if he will talk to me about what went wrong between him and Nungarrayi. He pauses and then tells me she got sick of him and wanted to go with another man. He underscores this by telling me she told him as much. When I ask after his brothers, he tells me they are all sick with kidney problems and from too much drinking. When I ask who he is close to in his life now, he says only his two daughters. But he is currently without phone numbers for either of them. He thinks they do not know he is in jail. He doesn't want them to know why he is here. I tell him I will ring those phone numbers through to him. I ask him how he passed time during his earlier four-year sentence. He tells me about the landscaping "work gang" he joined that maintains the gardens at Desert Park. But he transferred to Darwin prison on request when he "got sick of being in Alice" and was advised he would have a better chance of finding work in Darwin after his release.

I tell him about the book I am writing and ask him to think about whether he would talk to me about how he sees the changes in his life, how he got from where he was when I knew him in the mid-1990s to now. He indicates little enthusiasm for this proposition, and his responses to my prompts show little sign of the reflective philosopher I once enjoyed ruminating with on all kinds of subjects. In response to my carefully phrased but nevertheless searching questions, he vaguely casts around, deflecting, "lots of reasons . . ." As we sit and talk, a group of prisoners are ushered through the room. These men all faced court yesterday and are now being transferred from remand to incarceration proper. Among them are two men I know from the Big Town. They are demure and keep their eyes focused firmly ahead. Daniel tells me with a smile that another close relative was brought in last night. Incarceration is such a normal part of life for Warlpiri men it makes sense to identify prison as a significant site of identity formation. The incidence of incarceration also means that newly processed inmates are commonly imprisoned in the company of kin. It is not unusual to hear men describe a short prison sentence as allowing them "a rest" from the stresses of home. In prison they have the novelty of eating and sleeping in a structured routine that is strikingly different from the tempo of life on the outside. There are opportunities to play music, make art, read books, and tend gardens.

But being on remand, as Daniel has been for the last two months, is a grueling kind of limbo. Remand lasts as long as it lasts, often a period of several months. It is only after one has been convicted and sentenced that one can participate in programs and activities that give structure to and help pass the time of confinement. For now, Daniel has nothing to do but lie on his bed in the cell and try not to stew over how he got here. Having told me earlier that he doesn't have access to the library, toward the end of my visit Daniel volunteers that he has been reading a book about the Iraq War. Did I know it was all about oil, not terrorism? We joke a bit about Donald Trump and the bewildering circus of the recent US presidential election. The prison guard advises us that our time is up. I promise to return again, if I can, before I leave Central Australia.

In the days that follow, Nungarrayi returns our discussion to Daniel quite often. She has told me several times that she would have stayed with him "forever" if he hadn't "fucked everything up." She says even his kids are sick of him now. His daughters tried to get him to come and live with them, but he wouldn't do it. She tells me that prior to this current stint in jail, there were sightings of Daniel sleeping "anywhere" across town. On the ground outside the Caltex petrol station. Anywhere. The implication is one of *shame*—or, more precisely, that he has *got no shame*, that he has lost his way, that he is no longer being held in the world by the love and support of family and the self-esteem such support sustains. *Wiyarrpa*, poor thing, dear one—this is the most common Warlpiri refrain of empathy, emotional attunement, and longing, which gets applied to people and country alike. I find listening to these stories deeply upsetting. They have accrued additional weight since Nungarrayi shared with me some of the detail of the trauma Daniel was exposed to as a child, that he exhibited throughout their marriage and refused to speak about with her.

SHAME, *KUNTA*. IN WARLPIRI and broader desert reckoning, this term conjures an emotional state as well as a social disposition. To be ashamed is to be embarrassed, but also to act with proper reticence, even courtesy in respect of others. Kunta effectively holds a person in place, in a properly arranged assembly of others. In anthropologist Sarah Holcombe's words, kunta "discourages the individuation of authoritative behaviour."[37] But shame and its loss can also be at work in the way persons respond to their own disempowerment, as well as submit to their subjection by the carceral regime. Desert people grow up with a pervasive sense of the inevitability of imprisonment as a normalized experience and contained space of life. Brutality, indifference, and lack of empathy between prison guards and Aboriginal inmates are established and enforced in these practices. Writing of the encounter between Alice Springs police and Kwementyaye Briscoe, an Anmatyerre man who died in custody, Holcombe speculates on the cycle of brutality that the regime of policing self-perpetuates. "Is the failure of police to care for the drunk Aboriginal persons they take into custody," she asks, "partly a product of Aboriginal people's own failure to care?"[38] If Holcombe's question assumes its own affirmation, I cannot help but wonder, what brings about a failure of such profound depth and consequences? Surely there is something to explore here in the distancing between self and other that perpetuates its own entrenchment—a distancing that undercuts reciprocity *and* demands constant navigation.

6

See How
We Roll

Failure of Care

I am agitated as I prepare to fly to Adelaide in late February 2018. I had visited two months earlier, just a week after Nungarrayi had relocated to a new house. Finally, after years of determined lobbying across several bureaucratic agencies, she had secured a Housing Trust rental house allocated in her own name, a house to call her own. I had expected on that visit to find Nungarrayi elated, but instead she was exhausted and unwell, run ragged by sleep deprivation and the incessant demands of energetic two-year-old Tyson, and perhaps also by the effects of sustained drinking, although that side of things was not so clear. She had tried and failed recently to get her son, David, to take over the care of his son. The house was in a shambolic state. Shortly thereafter, she lost her latest mobile phone, so we had not had much communication. Recent posts to Facebook indicated that she had been fighting with some unidentified sisters. Against this backdrop I was bolstering myself for a fractious visit.

The taxi I hail from Adelaide airport is driven by a woman in her midfifties who introduces herself as Amanda. As she pulls the cab away from the curb, Amanda tells me she has been driving taxis for twenty years. The Adelaide Festival will commence in the coming days. It is peak tourist season for the city, and as she drives Amanda offers me tips on where to find cheap accommodations. We skirt the central business district and pass the newly opened, vast, and glittering Royal Adelaide Hospital, which has been subjected to a barrage of media criticism for cost blowouts and an astonishing litany of design, construction, and health delivery systems failures. Amanda reflects out loud on the dicey nature of present-day hospital care. She tells me of a friend, "a gentleman" who was, like her, as she put it, "low income and single." He died a year earlier at the age of fifty-eight, following many years of failing health associated with a chronic condition and a surgical procedure that left his colon strapped to a bag. A series of cascading illnesses had set in motion a cycle of admissions in and out of hospitals and aged care facilities. Amanda had been deeply saddened on visiting her friend in a nursing home and observing the cumulative effects of poor food and poor-quality care that made him sicker than he had been prior to admission. The larger intent of her story is clear, and she spells it out for me—her friend had struggled as a single person whose insecure employment left him perched just above the poverty line. He had no extended family to provide nurture and support, and he was not eligible for a tier of government-sponsored medical treatment, prescriptions, and additional support that might have actually made a difference to his well-being. Amanda is emotional as she describes the circumstances of her friend's institutionalization. In the end, she puts it to me, he died as a result of the failure of care.

A demonstrably thoughtful woman, as she drives, Amanda moves on to reflect more broadly on society's failure to deal with the unfolding challenges of an aging population. She suggests that "Asian families" seem to be so much better than "Anglo/Caucasian families" at looking after their aging relatives. For that matter, so are Africans, Greeks, and Ukrainians, she continues. "And Aboriginal people?" I interject, interested to see how she will respond. She pauses. "That's another thing I think about," she says. "I know it's controversial, but I think everyone should have to learn the Aboriginal dialect of the people of the area in which they live. It's the least we can do." She tells me about a recent female passenger, an Aboriginal woman from Central Australia who lives in Adelaide and "speaks twenty-three languages" and is constantly in demand for her translation skills.

"Don't get me wrong," says Amanda, "I don't like having them in my car. When I do it takes days to get the smell out." The city-based Aboriginal people she deals with are "very difficult." She has had people in her car who have gotten out of the cab at the end of a ride and refused to pay the fare. "That's for the lost generations, sister," they tell her as they flee. She tells me that her boss owns a company that transports Aboriginal patients from the airport to hospitals and medical centers. She says it's always such an ordeal to get them into the bus. "They get stuck in the airport toilets," marveling at the "water going 'round and 'round in the toilets and the hand basins." "They never seen running water before," she tells me earnestly. Those people coming in from the bush "only know thunder box and riverbed." And they don't speak English. They are still not learning English after so many generations. She explains, "The missions tried hard. They had the right ideas, but it just didn't work out. I don't know why." Amanda is a monologist, keen for an ear rather than interchange, so after a few failed attempts to engage I sit back and listen.

She recounts the time she picked up a "tribal elder" from the airport and drove him to the hospital where his wife was receiving treatment. She "just knew" he was a man of significant standing; he was "majestic" and "carried himself with great dignity." They drove past a scene of Aboriginal people drinking and fighting. "Driver," he addressed her respectfully, "I'm ashamed of my city brothers." "I'm over the lost generations," she says to me. "Don't get me wrong. It was a terrible thing we did, taking those piccaninnies away from their mothers. But you've got to find a way to move on." Why are things so bad? Is it a failure to understand on our part, or a refusal to budge on theirs? As we pull up in front of Nungarrayi's rental house, Amanda circles back. "I really think we should all have to learn local dialects. It's the least we can do. It will be hard. Who knows where that will lead . . . ?" As I get out of the car, I'm struck by the uncompromising interculturalism Amanda brings to the challenges of the present. Her delineation of ethnically marked attitudes toward care may well be tainted by Orientalist and nostalgic imaginaries, but her suggestion that white Australians must step up to the plate in order to transform the structured relationship of their belonging is unusual. She puts me in mind of George Herbert Mead's observations regarding the social formation of empathy and the idea that when a person learns a new language, she "gets a new soul."[1] The way Amanda holds together a genuine concern for the larger implications of unremedied settler colonial injustice along with empathetic insights into exacerbating failure of social care unsettles expectations of the cultured workings of neoliberalism. Loïc Wacquant, for example, draws attention to the new forms of "statecraft" that work to "re-engineer" and "redeploy" collective representations, social relations, and subjectivities in tandem with enforcing radical changes in economic and social policy.[2] He argues that the resurgence of inequality is met not only by new punitive techniques of governance but also, crucially, by particular forms of symbolic violence—communicative practices that encourage popular animus toward welfare recipients and symbolic contests between marginalized groups over worthiness of entitlement, thus reinforcing material and symbolic divisions across the community. Rather than reproducing such divisions, Amanda's reflections fuse a kind of hard-light-of-day realism with primitivist imaginaries and crosscutting empathetic challenge. She presents the idea that openness to difference in the face of historical injustice, gross inequalities, and failure of care might trigger something vital, something potentially transformative.

Punishing the Poor

As Nungarrayi and I embrace inside her front door and I drop my bag on the floor, I am delighted to find that Ram is here. However, it does not take long to get a sense of his emotional state. I detect slow-burning rage that has been building under the weight of his having been stuck in closely managed unemployment and training for many months of regulated visits to his job search provider, Job Futures. The cruel irony is an obvious one that he now fully grasps: there are no futures on Ram's employment horizon. He describes the tense scene in the office where "clients" like himself have to wait lengthy periods, sometimes as long as two hours, for their allocated meeting, only to then be ushered in and out of a perfunctory five-minute "checkup" with a case manager. If a "client" fails to turn up for such a scheduled meeting, they will be punished for "breach of contract," often resulting in cancellation of up to eight weeks of payments. Desperately keen to find work, Ram does not miss appointments. Yet, at his last scheduled meeting, with its predictable anticlimax, Ram had finally had enough and, in his words, he "flipped out." As I sit on the couch, he paces up and down, describing the situation to me:

> Job Futures, I go there. I have an appointment to go there, to see one guy, his name is like . . . Darryl, my case manager. He called my name to come through. I had to wait forty minutes. He tell me to come there, to sit down in the chair. He asked questions for me. "What you doing at

the moment?" I tell to him, what I'm doing. "You have that computer," [I say to him,] "to see my details." He know already. I tell him. But he know; "you go to school," [he says]. "How many days you go school?" I go like, four weeks, five days a week, I telling to him. "You have to keep going," [he says]. I tell him: "Why you guys force me to keep going there? I come here for you guys to help me to get a job. I keep doing that [training, English language courses]. What for? No income for that." Even sometime, I have to tell him: "I want a proper job." He says, "Which job you want to work?" I telling to him, "I'm really interesting for construction work." He tell me, "Do you have experience for that?" I say, "Yes, back in my home country I have experience. I was building a house." He says, "OK, Ram. We find for you works." I telling to him, "How long you guys keep telling me the same thing?" My mouth, my voice is gone.

I go there, [when I go there I am hopeful] my feelings is a little bit happy. [But] I go there and it's the same shit. This bloke tells me the same thing, no job. I come here, you guys speak "I give you job," but nothing. Same shit. "I don't want to listen to your story like that. Put me in a true job. I want to speak to your boss. I have to speak to them. I'm not going to keep coming like this." Nothing, five minutes interview. Sitting waiting for two hours. Then go home. I'm not doing that. If you only want to keep talking, "I give you job, I give you job," like that, find for yourself a job. "You guys give me headache." I was really arguing with that bloke. I said [to him], "Give me your place [seat in front of the computer] and I'll find job. If you were me, [how would you feel to have this experience?] You call me here, you make me angry. Don't say it like that: "I find you a job, I find you a job." I was telling him, I was talk, talk, talk, for him. He was just watching. He didn't talk. In the middle, he just shut up his mouth. He had nothing to say. I was feeling really, really angry.

Ram tells me that as a result of his outburst, all the Job Futures staff are now frightened of him. No one wants to talk to him. No one makes eye contact with him when he enters the building. No one cares about his situation. He has been in Adelaide five years, without any sense of his situation budging. Two weeks after Ram unloads his frustrations on Job Futures staff, a mobile phone video recording of an incident involving a distressed man erupting at staff and clients at the Centrelink office in the neighboring suburb of Salisbury goes viral on digital news outlets and social media. The chief executive officer of the South Australian Council of Social Service responds, declaring that "current circumstances" are a "perfect recipe for deep frustration," and that "punishment" has become integral to the political practice of managing the unemployed.[3] This is punishment of people who are already stigmatized, that works by containing a person, restricting their social mobility and simultaneously undermining their sense that a different life might be possible. In Wacquant's observation, governance of this kind reproduces "the very social disorders, material insecurity, and symbolic stigma" it is ostensibly "supposed to alleviate."[4]

I ask Ram if he knows anyone who ever got a job from a job search provider. He doesn't. I ask if he talks with his family about his frustrations. He makes clear that there is considerable shame associated with his situation, as the only son in a family with nine older sisters. He also conjures up the alienation associated with his experience:

> We coming from another country. I don't know the history or all about this country. Maybe I feel lost, or what. I'm thinking, I'm sorry, God is with me, but no people are with me. I'm Christian man. No people love me in the heart. I want to do good things in the world. I want to do things better. Not hard drinking, fighting. I want to make it. I forget. I have to sleep. I cannot forget. My brain give me a headache. My brain is fucking give me a headache. Five years . . . I come here. It's been like long time. I like to stay in the jungle. No one there. It makes you feel happy. No headaches.

The depth of Ram's distress is palpable. He conveys the despair generated by governmental techniques that are experienced as if they have been consciously designed to hold people in limbo, endlessly deferring their futures. For a man like Ram, so determinedly focused on establishing a productive and honorable life for himself, the scenario is torturous, both physically and mentally. The systematic failure of case managers to respond to Ram *as a person*, with his own singular life trajectory and aspirations, is what ultimately triggers his distress. In a similar way that the life of taxi driver Amanda's friend was minimally sustained but ultimately taken away by the institutional forms of "care" he received, Ram's acceptance by the Australian government as a resettled migrant in need of prolonged training is delivered as a form of slow violence that entrenches his exclusion.[5] Ram is fully cognizant of the implications of his status. "Maybe I feel lost . . . no people are with me. . . . No people love me in the heart."

Fault Lines to Belonging

It has been several months since Nungarrayi's son, David, was released from prison. In the lead-up to his release, she waited in anticipation, certain that he would travel to Adelaide to visit her at the earliest opportunity. But weeks and months passed, and David never arrived. In the meantime, Nungarrayi assumed responsibility for the infant son David has not yet met. In a happy coincidence, David and his new wife, Monica, are due to fly into Adelaide from Alice Springs just hours after my arrival. Ram leaves us to go visit friends, and Nungarrayi and I catch a bus into town to meet the couple from the airport. It is close to ten years since I have seen David, and he has since grown into a large man. His wife is nineteen years old and hails from a small desert town. She is pregnant, and all are excited at the prospect of a new addition to the family.

In a remarkable logistical feat, we also collect David's son, Tyson, as we travel home from the city by bus. Nungarrayi has been working her phone, communicating with the child's mother, who appears on the platform as our bus stops briefly at an interchange, and hands him and his stroller swiftly through the double folding doors into Nungarrayi's arms. Tyson had spent the previous week in his mother's care while she was visiting Adelaide. She is "still an alcoholic," Nungarrayi tells me. It is clear that the little boy is delighted to be back in Nungarrayi's company. I marvel at how much he has developed in two months. He has acquired a lot of language, predominantly Warlpiri, and a confident ability to move himself around. He is physically affectionate, especially with Nungarrayi but also with me, whom he seems to remember. He is feisty and fearless, and as they snuggle together his grandmother coaxes him into the dispositions of a little Warlpiri warrior. As we ride the bus, he stands, hands pressed firmly to the large window, sharply observant of the environment whizzing by. I'm transfixed by this little force of energy, but also taken aback as the social cartography of his language acquisition begins to unfold. He points out BWS (BeerWineSpirits) liquor stores along the highway and excitedly exclaims "pama!" (grog). He notes passing police cars and trucks, and occasionally even proffers a provocative "puck you!" in the direction of seemingly random vehicles. He is curious about his "papa," who sits in the seat in front of him but is also shy and reserved.

My anxious anticipation that I would find Nungarrayi in bad form was misplaced. She is in the best shape I have seen her since I started visiting Adelaide three years ago. Perhaps as a result of her week of respite from the vigorous Tyson, she looks radiant and well-rested. But, more important, she seems relaxed, settled into herself. Is this what the transcendence of exile looks like, I wonder? If so, it has occurred through particular means—the substantial reassertion of kinship as the source of purpose, honor, self-worth, and anchorage in the world. Caring for this little person is utterly exhausting, but also injects indisputable drive and meaning into the grind of daily life. In the meantime, other possible lives beckon—with Ram, who has recently come back on the scene and who still fantasizes about the two of them heading out of Adelaide to explore the wider world; but also, now with another "new friend," an Anglo drinker called Jason, with whom Nungarrayi spent the previous day at the beach, a new favored picnic and drinking spot.

I sleep badly that night: restless and wired, notwithstanding that it is probably the quietest night in a Warlpiri household I've ever enjoyed. In the morning, we have a slow start to the day, waiting for David and Monica to wake and emerge from their bedroom. I spend an hour in the backyard with Tyson, observing the little boy rummage around energetically, selecting things to play with from the detritus of the heavily rubbish-strewn backyard. I watch as he takes to a clear patch of lawn and becomes deeply absorbed with a half-filled bucket of water and an empty laundry detergent container and lid, carefully scooping water from the bucket into the lid and then pouring it with great care and concentration into the container. He is more or less oblivious to my presence.

I am disturbed by the state of the backyard. Plastic bags of garbage are piled high not far from the porch. The weather is warm, and the rubbish stinks. Today is rubbish collection day, but the household's overfilled bins remain parked next to the house and have missed being emptied. I reluctantly decide to intervene and make a phone call, ordering a large skip-bin to be delivered the following week. I tell Nungarrayi what I have done, and she responds with talk of what she will do once she has that skip, and once she gets her "friend" to come and mow the lawn. The previous night, as I was preparing to cook a meal, I had made a cursory move to clean the kitchen. Nungarrayi finally has the house she has longed for, but the transformative possibilities she once invoked around the idea of her "own" house appear to have dissolved. Yet, I remind myself, it is *my* mind that fixes upon and fills the details of these transformative imaginaries. My affective presence may have even called out the expression of such fantasies in the first place. It is my judgmental attitude that places household cleanliness and order at the center of a picture of a positively transformed life (although I recall that Ram has also been bewildered by Nungarrayi's inability to keep her house clean). As I reflect upon Nungarrayi's relocation from the desert to the city, I cannot help but read the state of the house as a failure to cope with the most basic ordering principles of daily life. But the more significant outcome surely is that, in the face of what I read as her failing cosmopolitan transformation, Nungarrayi has assumed responsibility for Tyson. For the foreseeable future she is reveling in this role and in the related affirmation she receives as matriarch and host to her visiting son, David; his new, pregnant wife; and her extended son Nathan. Care of kin has been firmly recentered as *the* force of her life.

In the city parklands that afternoon we happen upon an especially upbeat scene. Patrick is holding court in the seated circle of drinkers. He declares his country and Jukurrpa to all who will listen, narrating in shorthand the dramatic story of two sons who killed "the little favorite pet" kangaroo of their father. This killing unleashed their father's grief and vengeance, which he wielded with great fury in the form of fire set upon his sons, resulting in them being burned to death. I am familiar with this epic Warlpiri tragedy and also with the pair of striking ghost gum eucalyptus trees that stand in the desert where the sons are immortalized. As I sit beside him, Patrick, buzzing on booze, presents the story in short form to me and to the assembled group, over and over again. He gestures around the circle, identifying the dreaming of each of his countrymen and countrywomen by turn, pointing them out one by one. "That's my dreaming, fire. That one, wallaby. That one blue-tongued lizard. That one butterfly. Solid man, that one . . ." Some countrymen ignore him; others proudly accept these public bestowals. It is a common practice of this congregation of drinking kin to invoke their displaced traditional ownership of distant countries. Dignity is found in such shared declarations of emplacement. Public testimonies gather together those who are assembled in mutual affirmation: this is where we come from, this is what it means. On any particular day the sociality of the drinking circle might waver between such scenes of warm collective proclamation, tight-knit celebrations of care and closely related identity, and countersituations of unraveling chaos. I have become at least partially attuned to reading the small signs, the trigger points that might quickly turn a genial gathering into its antithesis with argument and fighting, poised on the edge of disaster.

There are a couple of terribly disfigured bodies among the group, bodies scourged by grog and its inevitable imbrication with physical violence. One man has a grossly distorted bottom lip, swelled by cancer and the surgery that removed it. His torn shirt reveals a back that is deeply scarred as a result of some separate battle or accident. The skin of his face glows with a recognizable greasy, grog-soaked sheen. Alongside him sits a radiant, beautiful, open-faced woman. The scene reminds me of Basil Sansom's observation of the "stylish ease" of the lives of Aboriginal fringe dwellers living "longa grog" in Darwin's fringe camps in the late 1970s. "Ease," in Sansom's description, "stands for life lived out on the basis of common Aboriginal understandings that are uncompromised."[6] By this, he seems to gesture toward grog's anesthetic affects: the way in which a company of drinkers come together in collective retreat from the stresses of their lives to immerse themselves in the immediacy of convivial social space. The discursive production of relatedness, the public proclamations, the storying that carries it along are all constant work enacted as a counterforce against the inevitable fission of any assembly. There is much at stake in this work of making and remaking of relationships—at base, a community of acknowledgment and care and a person's very existence as a person.[7]

Jukurrpa-proclaiming Patrick addresses me, drawing my attention back to him: "Nangala, I'll show you all those Jukurrpa. I can put them in a painting. Butterfly, two butterfly, twins. Others talk about money, about buying flash cars, kangaroo tails, grog. I got a lot of butterfly Jukurrpa. My Jukurrpa caterpillar. Longer than the pyramid, Egyptian pyramid. We got sacred ground there. Older than pyramid." Michael Taussig follows Walter Benjamin in observing that storytelling is an outgrowth of place. Relatedly, he suggests that in the turbulent circumstances of the present, as displaced persons and illegal immigrants assume the role of storytellers, "place assumes the status of phantom limb."[8] The congenial celebrations in the parklands appear to rebuff such a chilling vision of absence, but having read these words, I find it hard to shrug them off. A related disquiet and sense of disjuncture unfolds as I reread Sansom's culturally relativist, socially bounded account of Aboriginal drinking camps nearly four decades after its publication. Sansom's vivid descriptions of the distinctive language and physical means by which campers negotiate the moral terms of daily life among themselves jar with more recent writing on violence that insists on a wider vantage.

There is another crosscutting element to this scene that I have been observing build over recent months—the steady drift of African drinkers into the same area of the parklands, and the tentative but largely good-humored interactions evolving between the two groups. The two groups establish the centers of their respective gatherings at a respectful distance, while keeping company, sharing exchanges, and moving around freely. Among the Africans today is a strikingly tall young woman wearing a skin-tight white dress embellished with golden studs. The vibe between the two parties of drinkers is friendly, with people exchanging cheerios, until the woman in the white dress ventures across the delicate invisible demarcation that separates the groups and hits up a Warlpiri man for a cigarette. His wife swiftly intervenes and makes clear to the African woman that she has overstepped a line. "I'm not after your man, I've got my own man, I just want a cigarette," says the African woman. "You walk that way. You go that way for a cigarette, don't come after my husband," responds the wife. After some period of banter between the two women, the tension finally dissolves and the situation ends with the Warlpiri woman asking her husband for a cigarette on behalf of the African woman, thus demonstrating to her the correct, gendered etiquette for any future requests. The woman in the white dress is accompanied by more demurely dressed Amy from Tanzania, who quietly tells me she is twenty years old and has been in Australia

FIGURE 6.1 "Can I have a smoke, please?" (photo by author)

since 2012. She came to the parklands today with other resettled migrants she has only recently met. She says forlornly that she wants to go to the university and get a job, but it's too hard. So now she just drinks instead.

I have been sitting with Edna, a woman in her seventies and an extended mother of Nungarrayi, who tells me she was born in the northern Warlpiri settlement. She married a Pitjantjatjara man and lived with him until he died. She then married a Warlpiri man whom she eventually left. I'm astounded to learn from her that after a period of living in the Big Town she ran away to Darwin in the company of Nungarrayi's biological mother. Nungarrayi sits beside me, unmoved as she listens in. Edna stayed in Darwin for twenty-seven years and finally left the Northern Territory with a white partner. She lived with him in Sydney for four years before coming to Adelaide, where he left her. She is waiting for a house but might go back to Darwin. As we talk, I watch another party of desert people bearing boxes of beer being helped out of an expensive European car by a well-dressed white woman. Two uniformed police officers come by. They know a lot of those assembled by name. One of the officers wants to know who I am and is quick to tell me that "this group by and large doesn't give trouble." The police have come down to assist several people with Centrelink and travel-related queries. Their interactions are all very jovial. Meanwhile, more people are congregating nearby. Among them are two African men. One lies down on the grass to sleep; the other sits watching the police with a brooding look on his face.

Comfort in Exile

Early in the evening we catch a free ride home in the bus operated by the Aboriginal Sobriety Group. According to its website, this service aims to "reduce harm arising from the use of alcohol and other substances" and "maximize the wellbeing of individuals affected by drugs and alcohol by taking them to places of safety."[9] As we settle into the back seats of the minivan, our happily drunk crew play music very loudly through a wireless speaker and talk even more loudly over the music, while continuing to drink bourbon and Coke from plastic water bottles—in direct transgression of the bus's prohibition, which is emblazoned across the passenger door. The driver and his coworker cheerfully mind their own business. Everyone in the back is highly animated. Nungarrayi is very pleased to finally have her son come to visit, David's young wife, Monica, is clearly chuffed by her new situation as a pregnant married woman on holiday, and Nathan is happy to be reensconced in the family unit after several weeks roaming with others.

Monica is looking through her phone's social media feed. Prompted by the appearance of an image, she turns our conversation to a recent rape case involving a two-year-old girl that has been all over mainstream media in recent weeks.[10] She tells me the baby girl was her cousin. Nungarrayi has not yet heard of this incident. Both she and Monica burst into tears as Monica describes the bare outline of the case. Nungarrayi turns to me with a look of incredulity. "How can people do these things to little kids?" I shake my head, speechless. I tell her that new grog laws are being introduced in response to this case. "That's good," she says. I ask, "Is this really about grog? What about all that mob drinking every day in the parklands?" "They right," she responds firmly, "they look after each other. Those ones who rape kids are sick people."

The outspoken relative of my companions has been all over the media following revelations of this incident. In an opinion piece in the *Australian* she rails against the widespread refusal of political leaders to place the blame for child abuse on families and communities. Blame, she argues, is "seemingly placed everywhere but the shoulders of the perpetrators or the families whose responsibility it is to provide love, care and stability for their children. . . . There has been a culture of silence for too long."[11] The newspaper's editorial takes up and promotes this argument, lecturing its readers that "the colonisation grievance should not be used to silence the cries of children." This incident, coming more than ten years after the federal government's Northern Territory Emergency Response promised to take radical action to protect suffering children, was met with a very public prime ministerial visit to the regional center where the incident allegedly occurred, more claims by politicians of a "tsunami" of child sexual abuse, and a stream of related online commentary that endorsed the picture of dysfunction and attributed blame to remote communities and Aboriginal culture.[12] The vigorous hypermediated public response was followed, just as quickly, by silence.

As we approach her suburb, Nungarrayi asks the driver to drop us off in the car park that flanks Salisbury Park, directly opposite a hotel and bottle shop. David and Nathan head across the road to purchase more grog while the rest of us wander into the park. The men soon return, David carrying a large cardboard box containing a four-liter cask of wine, a large bottle of Jack Daniels whiskey, and a large bottle of Coca-Cola. When I see him weighed down with this bounty, I register that he is actually looking unwell. As if to confirm my unspoken assessment, he tells me, "I think I might give up drinking, Nangala." "Right," I say. We saunter home, slowly and with much pleasure, through this fabulous park. David continues to splash grog into each drinker's plastic bottle as we walk along. I am genuinely taken aback by this landscape. It is expansive, with a creek running through it and edged by rich red cliff faces with protruding palms, as well as a grove of thickly planted strappy gums. Scattered across the green-grassed fields are a number of majestic river red gum trees with vast girths. We are just two blocks from Nungarrayi's house. She has brought me here by design, knowing I will be moved by this beautiful place in close proximity to where she lives.

We amble along, posing for photographs I shoot on my mobile phone and exchanging greetings with the dog-walking couples with whom we cross paths. As we leave the park and walk through a small copse of trees that separates the park from the neighboring suburban street, young Tyson calls out to Nathan. Nungarrayi tells me quietly that the word he speaks is exchanged between these two when they see spirit figures. It confirms their special shared ability to see. Nungarrayi climbs through the front window to unlock and open the door. I turn around to see Monica vomiting on the footpath. It is nearly 8:00 p.m. by the time we arrive home. Nungarrayi retrieves pork chops and a bag of vegetables from the freezer and makes a delicious fragrant stew. The evening passes with David and Nathan dancing in the small lounge room to music

David sends from his phone to Nungarrayi's speaker. I recognize it as the same speaker through which she played music for me on my very first visit. But gone is the dome that once transformed a room into a disco with tiny multicolored, rolling lights.

The next morning, as my taxi pulls away from the curb and I give Nungarrayi my final wave, the driver asks me, "Is she your friend?" I tell him a little about our friendship and the book I am writing. "About her life?" he asks. "Now that's a book I would like to read. I've picked her up a few times," he tells me. "She tells me she comes from the desert and that it is really different there." The driver falls silent for a while. "Can you tell me why they live so unhygienically?" I offer what sounds to my own ear like a thin and unconvincing account of the relatively short time frame of Warlpiri adaptation to life in the city. Taxi driver Amanda's fantastic stories of the innocence of "tribal people" rush back to me, as does W. E. H. Stanner's famous provocation to Australians in the midst of the assimilation policy era: What if Aboriginal people did not know how to "un-be" themselves? I tell the driver, "Sometimes I think people just don't see the rubbish. They see other things. Life is pressured and they are very caught up in looking after family."

But such ways of looking after, transposed to the city with drinking as a central preoccupation, are weighing heavily on me at this stage. I feel tired and at a loss. Having arrived at the place where I had decided somewhat arbitrarily to bring this story to an end, I find we have come full circle. Nungarrayi has transcended her exile by supplanting kinship firmly at the center of her life. This is no heroic ending, but rather one in which exile seems to be generalized and entrenched rather than superseded. I am amazed to learn that the idyllic and close-knit camp we enjoyed during our short stay at the Tiny Town in October 2016 has since been transposed to the city; Nungarrayi's extended sister and brother-in-law who hosted our visit have been staying with Magda for nearly a year. As a result of some alcohol-fueled altercation several months ago, Nungarrayi is not speaking to either of them. Her relationship with Magda, once so pivotal to her endurance of life in Adelaide, has suffered directly as a result. I also learn that Nungarrayi's lovely teenage niece, her brother's daughter, with whom we camped and whose image is captured in several of our photos, was killed—strangled in a fight, just months after our visit. I also learn that Aunt Audrey's husband, the warm and quiet Arrernte man who presided over the Alice Springs town camp with such gentle authority, died after being hit over the head by a young, drunk kinsman.

Nungarrayi, meanwhile, has slowed down. She has also put on weight, something she had told me enthusiastically on my arrival. Something in her has settled; the fast-paced anxiety that set the dynamic for so much of our time together over these past three years has gone. But I have an agitated sense that the household is just a hair's breadth away from a situation that could trigger a new crisis. I am sickened to have my hunch confirmed weeks later. One night after a big day of drinking, Nungarrayi provokes an argument with David. By her own telling, she needles him and needles him and needles him until finally he explodes and beats her, breaking her arm and leaving her with a serious head injury. She is hospitalized, and he is remanded in prison for two months, on charges laid by police that she will later drop.

FOLLOWING A DAY OF meetings disconnected from my research with Nungarrayi, I go out in search of a badly needed laugh at Adelaide's Fringe Comedy Festival. The so-called World Comedy I happen upon in a nearly empty room in a city bar is delivered by two overweight and disappointed-looking Englishmen. One of them opens the show by declaring that this is his first visit to Adelaide. "I'm staying at Salisbury North," he says. "Why?" yells someone from the audience in disbelief. "Every day I leave the train station and I know I've arrived home when I get to 'shit fuck cunt.'" He pulls out his mobile phone and shows the audience a photo of these words spray-painted in blue on the wall of a Salisbury shop. The small audience, all but me, laughs in bitter recognition and sympathy. "Yes, but" I want to ask, my mind still full of the sense of space and light and beauty of that landscape, "have you been to Salisbury Park?"

In retrospectively tracing the arc of Nungarrayi's displacement across the period of my visits, I identify what appears to be a crucial juncture. It is the point at which her frustration at failing to cut through—failing to secure paid work, failing to acquire the diverse forms of capital with which to be recognized as a participating citizen—reached its climax. Six months after the public altercation with the disapproving Indian woman, when Nungarrayi appealed directly to the woman to recognize her as a woman from this place, "the oldest living culture," and her subsequent arrest for drunken disorderly behavior, she was confronted with the primary needs of kinship. In taking on the role of primary carer of Tyson, Nungarrayi was presented with an honorable cause and legitimate reason to retreat from the more challenging project of cosmopolitan self-alteration. In so doing, she shifted her own status from morally stigmatized and unemployed to guardian of a child in need, and knowingly intervened in the space between her family's fragile future and the coercive workings of government. There is a kind of double movement here. Nungarrayi's taking on of Tyson could be read as a response to what Mead might describe as the recurring negative expression of the conversation of gestures. "The question of whether we belong to a larger community," Mead argues, "is answered in terms of whether our own action calls out a response in this wider community, and whether its response is reflected back into our own conduct."[13] Rejection and exclusion are profound experiences to process at the level of the self, especially for one attempting to establish a new and expanding ecology of relationships. Nungarrayi has responded to these rebuffs by retreating to the familiar social world of family. In this setting there are few constraints on her capacity to live a strenuous and active life of caregiving—the foundations of a moral, satisfying life. Her new identity still requires her to navigate the terms of the city as a precariously placed Warlpiri woman, but from an ethical disposition that now enfolds deeply held purpose, confidence, and pride. The lines of belonging have once again been redrawn.

7

Free to
the World

No Place like Home

On Saturday, November 9, 2019, news broke on national media that a nineteen-year-old Warlpiri man Kumanjayi Walker had been fatally shot in his family home. Over the following days, the larger story emerged. Alice Springs police had pursued the man and attempted to arrest him for breach of parole; it was said that he removed his electronic tracking device and fled the facility where he was detained on a community control order. At the time of the shooting, many of his family were returning from the town's cemetery following a funeral for a senior relative. Kumanjayi Walker had returned home to attend this funeral. When police forced their way into the house, relatives say, he was lying on a bed looking at family photographs. The precise details of what occurred next are sub judice in a forthcoming murder trial. Immediately following the shooting, police bundled Kumanjayi Walker's fatally wounded body into the back of a police van and hurriedly retreated to the local police station where they locked themselves inside and refused to interact with his family or community leaders. Just hours earlier, the Northern Territory health department had closed the health clinic and evacuated all medical staff following a series of reported threats to staff safety. There were no medical staff in the town to attend to the man's injuries. The Royal Flying Doctors Service refused to send a plane until police could assure the safety of staff attending. Hours later, an ambulance finally arrived by road. Meanwhile, dozens of anxious relatives kept vigil outside the police station through the night. The following morning, police confirmed that Mr. Walker had died.

News of the shooting death was met with a national outcry. The Northern Territory acting assistant police commissioner traveled to the town to address a meeting of hundreds of angry and distressed relatives and residents. He told the crowd that he was "very sad." He said the police were wearing body cameras and "everything was recorded." "A full investigation will reveal the truth. We want to help the community find the truth." He went on, "There have been concerns about having police in the community. The police are here to help, protect, to work with you. . . . I know you are angry and sad and upset. . . . But I ask that you don't try and hurt the police."[1] Warlpiri residents who assembled for this meeting anticipated high-level media attention. They had unfurled banners declaring "Black lives matter," "Stop police brutality," "We stand with Walker," and "Always was always will be Aboriginal land" as backdrops to the space from which police addressed the crowd, so as to be captured by cameras. Multiple video recordings of the meeting were streamed live. Photographs were carefully staged and posted online, with pleas to friends to "share widely." Community leaders addressed the police, angry at the disrespect they had been shown and the lack of communication, distressed that Kumanjayi Walker's body had been removed from the town without allowing relatives to attend to it and undertake vital mortuary procedures, and alarmed at the expanded presence of police. The following day, the Northern Territory chief minister flew to the town and promised that "consequences would flow." A day later the twenty-eight-year-old constable who allegedly shot Walker three times was charged with murder. There was initial rejoicing over this charge until it was revealed that the officer had been released on bail, spirited out of the Northern Territory to his family home in Canberra, where he remained, suspended from duty on full pay.

The police response to Kumanjayi Walker's killing consolidated alarm and fear and confirmed this shooting as the progression of an ever-intensifying policing regime. Forty members of the Territory Response Group, a heavily armed, military camouflage–wearing special forces unit linked to the Commonwealth's antiterrorism tactical response complex, were immediately dispatched to the town. Over the days and weeks that followed the shooting, there were many reports of police harassment and intimidation. Roadblocks were established on the Tanami Highway to monitor the movement of people in and out of the desert. Aboriginal drivers were interrogated over their residence and mobility. Vehicles were searched and some were certified as unroadworthy on dubious grounds. A family with small children had their vehicle stopped and were ordered not to drive their car or risk being arrested. They were left to wait by the side of the highway for another ride, in searing heat without a supply of drinking water. In the town itself there were reports of police intimidation of community leaders. Small children were threatened. Posts to Facebook declared people felt unsafe and that "this place no longer feels like home." A young Warlpiri man had been shot and killed, and the officer who discharged the firearm had been charged with murder, but the intensified police response suggested Warlpiri themselves presented the danger.

This situation mirrored a trajectory observed by critical anthropologists and criminologists who identify policing and carceral regimes not as "technical appendages for fighting crime" but rather as "core political capacities through which the Leviathan governs political space, cuts up social space, dramatizes symbolic divisions and stages sovereignty."[2] Earlier sections of this book have explored the expansion of the carceral regime in the Northern Territory as a core dimension of shape-shifting settler colonial relations over the past century. The neoliberal intensification of policing in the Northern Territory dates from 1997, when mandatory sentencing provisions were legislated. Dubbed the "three strikes" laws, mandatory sentencing was instrumental in systematically delivering Aboriginal youth and adults into detention for petty crimes against property. Virtually all young people detained under these laws are Aboriginal.[3] But, as we have seen, it was not just Aboriginal *bodies* being stalked by these governmental/policing techniques. Federal legislation introduced a decade later associated with the Northern Territory Emergency Response radically reordered at two levels the governance of Aboriginal *places*. First, this legislation removed the permit system that had been established under the Aboriginal Land Rights Act (Northern Territory) of 1976 that vested authority in traditional owners over the movement of visitors across Aboriginal land. Second, new laws dissolved distinctions between public and private space, allowing police to enter Aboriginal houses without a warrant and apprehend persons. The rolling out of this regime and its intrusion into intimate spaces of people's lives enact the "endless horizon" of security practice of which Joseph Masco writes.[4]

Kumanjayi Walker's shooting and its aftermath deepened an affective sensibility that had been released by the declaration of the 2007 Northern Territory Emergency Response, when fear pervaded the desert that the government was coming, once again, to take children away. Recent incursions have unraveled the certainties of place—contingent and short-lived though they were—that were established during the self-determination era. Government and police now work in tandem to proliferate dispersed social insecurity. As the social supports associated with "self-determination" and "community" have progressively been withdrawn from desert towns, they have been replaced by new mechanisms that ensure governed subjects are constantly on guard, alert, and anxious.[5] Might the neoliberal reordering of Aboriginal policy constitute a version of the "revanchism" that Wacquant writes of, a political manifestation of the will to reverse territorial losses incurred by the nation-state, following a war or social movement?[6] The reversal of the moral sentiment of land rights and self-determination sees the Australian state acting literally to *take back* control of Aboriginal space and bodies through the withdrawal of delegated authority and the fracturing of the idea of inalienable Aboriginal landownership.

Simmering in the background of the dramatic scenes surrounding Kumanjayi Walker's death were slow leaching pressures of another kind. The Big Town was running out of water. For more than a year and a half, the water supply has been showing increased salinity levels; it is unpleasant to drink and is listed by the power and water utility as at "severe risk." On the back of this "water crisis," a Northern Territory governmental decree has halted all development with population implications. A planning application to build new housing for staff of the town's renowned youth program was rejected; the government's rationale cited "pressure on the dwindling potable water supply."[7] Lack of rainfall and overextraction associated with large-scale gold mining in the Tanami Desert are identified as the causes. Meanwhile, a separate investigation has revealed elevated uranium levels in the water supply of a nearby Warlpiri town.[8]

These circumstances echo the situation that precipitated the forced relocation in the early 1950s of more than a hundred Warlpiri. Overcrowding and incidents of "tribal fighting" had resulted in several deaths. Surveys had declared there to be insufficient water supply to support a growing population. The Commonwealth government pragmatically resumed a lapsed pastoral lease and transferred a quarter of the population to that site. But seven decades on, there are no new frontiers, no lapsed pastoral leases, no potential new places to which a sizable community could be relocated. Even if such places could be identified, attitudes—governmental and Warlpiri—have changed. The desert is no longer a place to which people retreat. It contains precious sacred places, but it no longer provides sanctuary. Any future relocations are likely to be out of the desert, into regional and metropolitan Australia. In this Warlpiri are not alone. The dilemma of their place in Australia now joins up with the larger unfolding calamity of climate change. Temperature rises are making large swaths of inland and northern Australia uninhabitable. The water shortage is a crisis unfolding across the country. A series of small residential areas and regional towns started to run dry in late November 2019. Governments are blindsided by these challenges and deflect the idea that they can intervene in matters they variously attribute to short-term weather fluctuations, natural disaster, or market mechanisms.

Recognition's Distancing Effects

If intensifying security regimes and climate change present the most tangible threats to small Aboriginal towns and their ways of life, transformations in the scope of national politics present another. In the decade since the federal government's "national emergency" successfully supplanted a new imaginary of dysfunction for desert towns and their residents, the relatively abstract campaign for constitutional recognition of Australia's Indigenous people has displaced the more tangible politics of the land rights era. As national attention to remote life through flash point media exposés around violence and child abuse waxes and wanes, concern for life in the bush, and more specifically for the idea that territories of Aboriginal ownership and occupation are places worthy of reverence and respect—places where life is differently organized—has also receded. In marked contrast to the preceding era, in which the interior and north of the country and the forms of cultural production they sustained were primary reference points for Indigenous political activism, the post-Intervention period has seen a shift in focus to city-based cosmopolitan agendas. Recognition of "first peoples" in the Australian constitution has become the main game in Aboriginal politics.

Meanwhile, life in the city for Nungarrayi has involved escalating criminalization. After seven months of caring for her infant grandson, she released the toddler into the care of her stepdaughter. Consequently, Nungarrayi has reassumed the status of unemployed "job-seeking" client. "Visiting family" has taken on a new intensity, a more or less daily ritual of traveling to the city parklands to keep company and drink with her relatives. One day in February 2019, as we walk through her local shopping center, we cross paths with an aging, slightly disheveled lawyer who greets Nungarrayi with a smile and the question, "You keeping out of trouble?" I learn of a pending court case involving her new boyfriend, who had an altercation with a bus driver that resulted in a smashed windshield and a minor road accident. The argument was triggered by a transaction between Nungarrayi and the bus driver over the purchase price of a ticket. I learn of her boyfriend's precarious couch-surfing homelessness, the death of his mother to cancer several years ago, as well as the negativity, aggression, and unhappiness that pervade his relationship with Nungarrayi. I learn of a warrant in Nungarrayi's name for an assault charge laid against her by one of her close sisters several years ago, a warrant that could be acted upon and result in her arrest as soon as she sets foot in the Big Town. I learn of the social hierarchies recognized by precariously placed people—Nungarrayi tells me that having rental accommodations issued in one's name, as she does, enables one to be placed on "Home D" (home detention) following a conviction, whereas homeless people will always be sent to jail. The talk around Home D is new; it has a flicker of reckless bravado about it and has come into her life with her new boyfriend.

Unemployment, homelessness, creeping criminalization: Nungarrayi's world increasingly opens out onto terrain Wacquant analyzes in terms of the "double regulation" of poverty via the intertwined state practices of punitive welfare and hyperpolicing/incarceration.[9] The situation for desert people, whether they stay proximate to their own territories or move farther afield, shadows the triple selectivity of the US carceral system, where, Wacquant observes, policing occurs first by class, second by race, and third by place.[10] Bodily injury and physical violence are also in the mix. In France, Didier Fassin asks, why do police punish as they do, in excess of what the law allows? He continues:

Why would officers purposely put handcuffs incorrectly on to suspects they have arrested so as to painfully twist their arms and make fun of their complaint while taking them into the precinct for questioning, sometimes causing nerve compression that can be irreversible? Why would they take them into custody in filthy and cold rooms without letting them go to the toilets, have something to eat, or even sometimes take their medicine? Why would they intentionally drive their vehicle in a rough way when they extradite prisoners to a faraway jurisdiction so as to have them bang around or get car sick? Why would they debase them with offensive remarks and threaten them with dismaying prospects?[11]

Fassin identifies the elements of these practices that escape rational analysis and tap a dimension of emotional experience Nietzsche describes in terms of "voluptuous pleasure": "To punish is to produce a gratuitous suffering, which adds to the retribution, for the mere satisfaction of knowing that the culprit—or the one presumed such—suffers. In the assimilation of punishment with pain and, even more, in the unnecessary torment that is added to it, one cannot not recognize the expression of cruelty." Fassin's provocations regarding policing's excess could just as well be posed to the practices of child detention and Aboriginal deaths in custody in Australia as to the French carceral system. But it is not only police who punish. Such brutalities are internalized by the criminalized subjects of those practices who, triggered by stress, wield their aggression against their own.

Stretching Thin

Across the time of this research, Nungarrayi has made several attempts to visit her hometown, the country that "pushes her back." She has journeyed interstate in the company of kin with the intention of attending family funerals and mining royalty meetings and to visit her daughter and grandchildren. Three trips were aborted midway. Halfway between Adelaide and Alice Springs, en route to a funeral in the Big Town, she got into an argument with the husband and wife in whose car she was traveling. When they stopped for fuel at an outback roadhouse, she stormed off in a moment of rage, and the car moved on without her. She was rescued by her daughter and son-in-law, who had to make a ten-hour round trip to collect her. On a second journey to attend a family funeral, she made it as far as Alice Springs, but no farther. On a third trip she made it "home" and spent two days in the town but became seriously unwell. On her arrival back in Alice Springs, she was briefly hospitalized with breathing difficulties and a chest infection. She called me, run-down, agitated, and emotional. I responded to her call for help by purchasing an air ticket for her to fly back to Adelaide. She missed the plane and called me from the airport, deeply distressed, pleading with me to buy another ticket so she could take the next flight. I told her I was not able to help. Weeks of frosty silence followed.

In late 2017, I was in north Australia at a conference and twice failed to answer or return her calls. She left a message on my phone one evening, telling me she never wanted to talk to me again, telling me she wanted to speak to my boss, and threatening to withdraw from our research project. I called her the next day, braced for a full-scale argument. But she made light of the message she had left on my phone. She had been drinking, she explained, just mucking around. But she wants money. Something has shifted. I feel we have hit the thinnest possible end of "friendship," and I have no idea how to turn this situation around.

Encountering Recognition

In July 2019, the two of us travel to Australia's national capital, Canberra, to visit a major repository of Indigenous archives whose holdings include several significant collections of photographs associated with her family. Nungarrayi makes the trip from a tiny town in the Western Australian desert where she has spent the past two weeks visiting one of her close sisters. I spot her in the airport arrivals lobby as I descend the escalator; she is engrossed in animated discussion with the person whose dyed-pink hair and rainbow onesie suit strikingly set them apart from the long line of dull gray-suited travelers on my flight to the capital. Nungarrayi is relaxed and effusive as she embraces me. She introduces me to the onesie wearer, whom she knows from their work in youth suicide prevention programs in Central Australia.

We are staying in a two-bedroom apartment at the University House on the Australian National University campus. The apartment is extraordinarily spacious, larger than Nungarrayi's house. Its construction dates to the immediate postwar period when the university was opened. The foundations of the parliamentary capital city had been constructed only two decades earlier, and a lack of available housing caused the university to build residential accommodations for its foundation staff. We have to carry our luggage up two flights of stairs to reach our rooms, and Nungarrayi flips out as we finally reach the door, reminding me that she is asthmatic and can't handle the load. As she moodily takes to the couch in the large lounge room and rips off the top of a takeaway container of Chinese food we purchased en route from the airport, I trudge off to see if there is a possibility of us moving to a ground-level room. On my return she says it's all OK. She surmises that we should drag the mattresses from the bedrooms out to the lounge room and sleep side by side, under the ceiling heater. I don't respond, knowing how much physical effort would be required to relocate heavy mattresses and also the consternation a Warlpiri-style camp would cause housekeeping and hotel management.

We have come here to look at two collections of photographs, one created by an Anglo-Australian man who had married into Nungarrayi's extended family in the 1970s. The other collection was produced by a renowned amateur historian who traveled extensively through Central Australia in the same period. Nungarrayi remembers a particular camping trip on which this man accompanied her father, grandfather, and herself and photographed them at a series of sacred sites. I am hopeful of what we might uncover and what discussions between us these photographs might stimulate.

The institute that holds these collections has undergone its own transformation over several decades. It was established in the early 1960s by the Australian government as a statutory organization that would fund and direct "salvage" research across Australian Indigenous communities. Over time, management of the substantial and voluminous photographic, film, sound recordings, paper, and manuscript collections deposited into the institute's care has become the main order of business. This shift in operations has been accompanied by a major transformation in staffing. Gone are the ambitious research programs and research funding allocations, and relatedly the research fellowships for predominantly white anthropologists, archaeologists, historians, and linguists. The institute has been rapidly indigenizing its staff, who oversee researchers' requests to access collections, community and family history projects, and library and archival services.

I have a long association with the institute as grant recipient, onetime employee, researcher of its collections, published author with its press, curator of an exhibition utilizing its collection, and editorial board member of its flagship journal. This history of association gives me a privileged conduit to a small number of long-standing staff who respond to my requests outside of the usual bureaucratic avenues that have wait times of many months. But on this trip, it is also clear that Indigenization has hit a tipping point and research per se has been displaced by the redemptive practice of community outreach. The cultural shift I detect connects up with a wider disenchantment that I, along with other anthropologist-friends of my vintage, have been struggling with in recent years, as we have confronted the displacement of anthropology by Indigenous standpoint. In a complex of paradigm shifts that are messily entangled with the forces traced by this book, discipline-based expertise is being increasingly marginalized and deemed irrelevant. Attitudes on the ground in Aboriginal communities, in the public domain, as well as those that govern the allocation of national research funds and approval of institutional ethics protocols have all been shifting accordingly.

On our first morning, as Nungarrayi and I sit together in a small, windowless office in front of a computer monitor, clicking slowly through twelve hundred digitized photographs, an Indigenous woman with long gray hair comes in and effusively greets Nungarrayi. She introduces herself as "mob from Queensland." She speaks excitedly about a painting from Nungarrayi's community that she wishes to include in an exhibition she is curating. She would like to talk to

Nungarrayi about this, to "make sure all the community are happy." By coincidence, one of the makers of the painting is Nungarrayi's grandfather. She responds with enthusiasm and is clearly pleased to be approached thus, as a woman of authority. Nungarrayi, aware that the woman has completely ignored me, introduces me and our project to her. Nungarrayi suggests to the woman that the two of them can meet tomorrow morning, after she has finished her "own family work here."

Here, at the Indigenous Institute in the national capital, as a woman recognizably from the desert, Nungarrayi encounters respect of a particular kind from enthusiastic Indigenous project officers. She initially basks in the reverent attention but soon tires of the intensity of these interactions. The planned meeting with the Indigenous curator does not eventuate. "I've got a headache," she whispers in my ear toward the end of an hour-long presentation we have been urged to attend one lunchtime, a report on a staff community consultation field visit to outback Queensland. As we congratulate the staff on their work and leave the room, she begs me to take her off to a club in the city where she can play poker machines for a couple of hours on her own and "have a rest." I sneak off to enjoy my own time out, shopping at a favorite boutique.

Nungarrayi is often on her mobile phone to relatives during our time in Canberra. She is edgy, and her fragile dislocation is easily activated. There is a momentary flash point when she detects negative recognition in an exchange with an Asian woman working a counter in the Canberra Centre food court. When the woman plates Nungarrayi's food and fails to hand her cutlery, Nungarrayi turns to me, distressed, and says, "Nangala, she's only doing this because I'm . . ." Her voice trails off as I point to the cutlery supplies and condiments sitting on the counter. We are both very tired. The weather is unseasonably cold. We sit quietly at a table. I drink hot tea and eat sweet biscuits while she eats curry and rice. But there are social high points on this trip as well, including dinners with old friends, three other anthropologists and a long-standing community adviser we both know well, and an intimate dinner when the two of us eat an Indian feast at an otherwise empty large restaurant.

Our visit to the archives, however, is ultimately unremarkable. There are no new discoveries. No epiphanies. No eureka moments. There are plenty of digitized photographs, but none of them are new to Nungarrayi. Nor do our interactions with these photos bring about a shift in mood. If anything, the experience of whizzing through the digital files, flicking through scenes of life from decades earlier, in the Big Town and the desert, pictures of deceased loved ones, pictures of her younger self, entrenches a quiet melancholy. We fail to locate a set of pictures Nungarrayi often recalls as she describes a particular country visit and related sequence of childhood memory. We apply ourselves to the work of documenting as many of the photographs as we can so that named persons are logged in the archive for anyone who might access these collections in the future. But at a certain point this no longer feels like work in the service of our own project.

A Broadening Horizon for The Troubles

Back in Adelaide, six months later, Nungarrayi is convinced that the fighting that triggered her departure from the Big Town is now over. She thinks I have been unnecessarily fixated on The Troubles and encourages me to think about the fighting differently. We are sitting on a bench in Salisbury Park on a cool, windy day as she puts it to me in these terms:

> When there's a family-to-family fight, it's just reality, you know, it's in the Bible. It says it in the Bible: two brothers, one's a loving brother, one's not loved. Isaac chose his own son, and other son, offerings. . . . One gives an offering to God, other one doesn't. One young brother has faith in God, that's why his father loved him so much to work with him and look after flocks. They fight among each other.
>
> We always say, it's like it says in the Bible: because you won't tell the truth when you kill your own brother . . . Wapirra [God] punish that son. He says go away, not to return to this land. Go and make your family . . . because he done a bad thing for his young brother, and never told his father. . . . And even for Joseph. Twelve sons in the family. He was the loving baby child out of the family. Well, "Coat of Many Colors," Dolly Parton's song, Joseph, he was really loved by his father. A lot of those brothers they didn't like him, they traded him to Caesar. Father always cried, wondering where he is. One day it was all drought in Egypt, they had to travel far distances for the . . . they had to trade that young fella. He became trade in Caesar's family. And, every once a month when they ran out of food, they would come with all the camels. You mob came to get food, he made them look silly. He made them suffer. They went back, no, we didn't get anything. Joseph . . . he had to come out in the open. Father said, you answered my prayers.

My more or less agnostic upbringing and lack of musical theater education leave me not fully grasping the comparison Nungarrayi makes, although I'm very much taken by her move to de-exceptionalize The Troubles. The bare outline of Joseph's story strongly evokes Nungarrayi's situation. More precisely, it

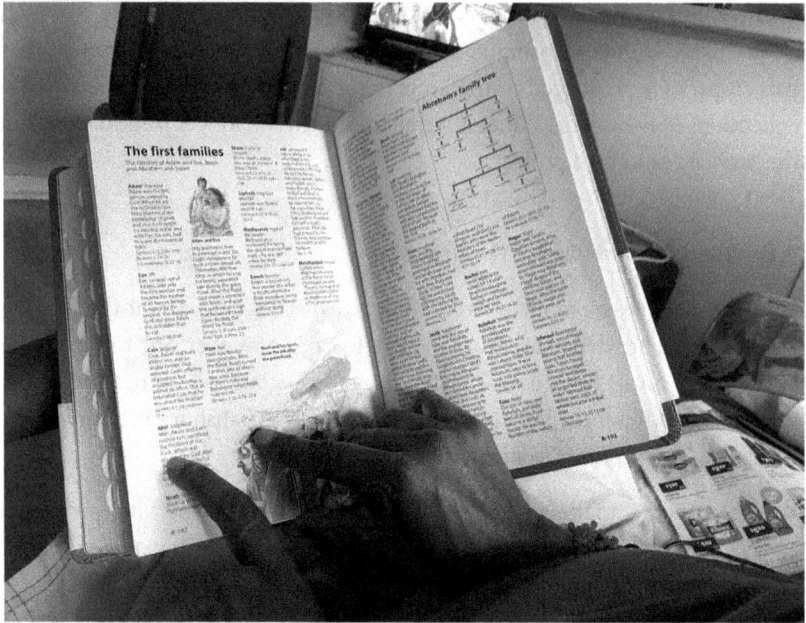

FIGURE 7.1 The first families (photo by author)

is redolent of the transformative fantasy of exile she presented to me when we first came together in Adelaide: a favored child is bestowed with unique powers by his father, triggering jealousy among his immediate kin. The anointed one is forced into exile and unjustly imprisoned. He overcomes his plight by deploying his special powers to interpret the dreams of those in authority, and finally achieves great power in a society in which he is a foreigner.

In reaching for a comparative frame, I find myself drawn in a different direction, not across cultures and religious traditions but to the great annals of Warlpiri mythology, where instances of treachery, betrayal, high passion, and violent warfare are integral to the making of the world, such as in this recounting of a great battle by one of its senior female custodians:

> In anger they killed each other [two brothers]. Then they made peace with each other. . . . Furiously they came close from there, from [W——]. Where that place is, there they fought and killed each other, killed each other. We are the right people for here. He came up from the west, he came to revenge his older brother, the younger brother came up from the south, and then from the west, from the place in the west, from [N——]. It is still marked by the tree that is always eaten. They used to

be people. This is where they used to kill. Here the people belonging to [Y——] killed them. Consequently, the ones from over there came for vengeance. Two groups of people set out to perform the revenge, our . . . relatives from [K——], and the people from [W——], both peoples came here for revenge. Here, there, where that tree stands all eaten, the tree all of whose leaves the people eat. Two armies set out for revenge. Here they killed each other all together, the [N——] people, at [Y——] they killed each other, the yam people and the water people. At this place they fought out the vengeance. They killed each other, they killed each other, they killed each other, they killed each other, they killed each other.

Then the two men made peace.

And now they stand at that place, the two trees. At the end they made peace. After they had struck each other with deep and open wounds, thus they spoke to each other.

"This is enough of killing each other, brother."

"Brother, enough of these big wounds. You see me standing here with all the dead. Let it stop."

"Here let us make peace with each other, the two important ones, the two elders. We two, let us make peace."

"Enough brother?"

"They have all died. I am going back to [W——]."

"Yes. I will stay here at [Y——]."

"Yes."

They went. They went south, they went south, they went south. They went back. That one went along singing, that one we know to be there from the place belonging to the song who sang himself back to the south. He went back singing. Thus, he went along, singing himself back.

There, the two foremost men bade each other farewell. There one of them sang himself. The bone of his leg had pierced the flesh. He got the *nyirawu* vine. With it he healed himself. He bound up his leg, he joined the muscle again, he reunited the bones, he joined the muscle again, he joined the muscle again, the tendon he joined together.

Then singing he went along. He did not die, because he had joined the muscle, because he had reunited it, because he had sung himself.

The two of them went into their homes. The two of them went into their homes, into there.[12]

The Troubles reverberate with the drama, poesis, violence, and ultimately the hopeful redemption of this world-making story. But notwithstanding the vital role of repetition in Warlpiri aesthetics, and insistence on the unchanging nature of Jukurrpa, the time of The Troubles is the time of a new kind of placemaking. The processes and practices continue to unfold in ways that are difficult to get hold of, even as I write. Nungarrayi continues as we sit side by side on the picnic bench, "I just want to see changes at my home community, be a big family like we used to be. Loving each other, not fighting." She insists that everything was OK in the 1980s. The Intervention changed everything. "Can't even go on the road to sleep over," she says. "Can't go hunting no more. Always scary [in the town and the desert]." She insists, however, that the intractable feud entangled with the recent fear of the bush has now been resolved. Relations between those who had been deemed enemies are now friendly, respectful.

Kin relations are vital to life in the city, but they are ordered differently. The intense flow of interaction that establishes the structure, sensibility, and priorities of life in the desert can no longer be taken as given. In the city, it falls to Nungarrayi herself to seek out her relations and the affirmation they offer. The city offers up other instances of recognition and solidarity, other kinds of company. One day as Nungarrayi rode the bus into town, she took a seat near two Nepali girls. The girls' brothers-in-law were sitting at the front of the bus while she and the girls sat in the back. An African man had moved to sit with the girls. He was making a move on them. Sensing their discomfort, Nungarrayi intervened. The African man was not impressed, and he poured a drink over her head. The Nepali men leapt from their seats at the front of the bus and came to her defense. Nungarrayi smiles as she recalls this encounter. She was pleased with this scene of solidarity.

In the two weeks prior to our visit to Canberra, Nungarrayi had been visiting a close sister who lives in a tiny town deep in the Western Australian desert. I spoke with both of them by phone several times, and it was clear that the visit was deeply rejuvenating for Nungarrayi. When she left Adelaide on that trip, she walked away from the stress of her new relationship as well as a constellation of governmental requirements and responsibilities. Hosted by her sister, she was able to get by without welfare income for some time. As we drive around Canberra the morning of our departure, Nungarrayi tells me that she has been "breached" again for missing a scheduled appointment during her time away, and as a result the electricity to her house has been disconnected. After three phone conversations she convinces her job search case manager to reactivate her payments and trigger the power being reconnected. On a cold winter night as she prepares to board her flight from Canberra back to Adelaide, Nungarrayi phones Ram and asks him to go around to her house and turn on the power so that she will have hot water when she arrives home.

New Stakes of Placemaking

I have completed the final section of this book at a time when the stakes around security, mobility, and containment have been dramatically heightened. The time of the COVID-19 pandemic presents especially dire conditions for displaced people for whom the possibility of keeping moving offers the only hope of survival. Global mobility is a primary vehicle for the highly contagious virus, and curtailment of movement is now subject to unprecedented government intervention and policing, globally. In Australia, Aboriginal people are singled out as having heightened vulnerability; the prevalence of preexisting chronic illness across desert communities indicates the arrival of COVID-19 will have devastating consequences. The Northern Territory has imposed bans on "nonessential" travelers crossing the border. Small Aboriginal towns are subject to further protection orders and require those who are authorized to enter to first self-quarantine in a designated "excluded area" for fourteen days. In the time of pandemic, hotels emptied of tourists as well as offshore detention centers are repurposed as quarantine stations. Police enforce new government directives associated with mobility and new requirements for "social distancing."

Yet for some Aboriginal subjects of the COVID-19 security regime, the initial enforcement of these orders is experienced as an intensification of the "hard" policing to which they have become accustomed. Fear of the invisible virus, stoked by the constancy of dramatic social media updates and alarming mathematical projections, further entrenches perceptions that there are now *no* safe places to retreat to. The containment orders of COVID-19 from one perspective echo the policing of Aboriginal people's movement across the desert during the earlier twentieth-century "protection era." As government authorities and missionaries moved to establish settlements, they were also concerned to contain the spread of disease—disease that had been contracted and spread through interactions with settlers and prospectors, but attributed by some commentators to Aboriginal people themselves.[13] However, as 2020 unfolded, the response to the pandemic delivered a remarkable statistical exception: not a single Aboriginal infection or death in remote Australia was attributed to COVID-19. For the period of lockdown, small towns were reported to be quiet and calm, with residents thriving on improved diets as a result of the federal government's enhanced pandemic welfare payments. Between May and September, individuals received biweekly payments not only at double the normal rate but also with all of the punitive mutual obligation requirements suspended. For this brief, surreal period, from the vantage of these places, it was as if the government had stepped in to compensate for the failure of capitalism.

Two important places for Nungarrayi, the Big Town and northwest Adelaide, were both made in the service of twentieth-century extractive capitalism. The government settlements that were subsequently transformed into Aboriginal towns effectively opened the desert to gold mining and pastoralism by removing the people and their mobile ways of life that stood in the way of development. The postwar satellite town that was promoted to its prospective new residents and industrial labor force as "the city of tomorrow" was by the 1970s "a city with a disabling past."[14] The government policies and manufacturing practices that launched northwest Adelaide were abandoned just a decade later. Its newly established industries and workforce were sacrificed to globalization and technological transformation, although it would be another three grueling decades of slowdown before the iconic Holden car factory finally closed.[15] The abandonment of Aboriginal towns came later but might be interpreted through the progression of related processes.[16] After the two-decade window of support for small, decentralized residential areas began to close in the mid-1990s, there followed cases of essential services and related support being withdrawn from outstations, with catastrophic consequences for their residents.[17] Systematic dismantling seemed assured in the March 2020 announcement by the Western Australian government that it would disconnect basic utilities in twenty-five small Aboriginal towns that were no longer considered financially viable or safe for their residents.[18]

Once those who have lived differently are "liberated" into the community of abstract citizenship, what kind of agency can they claim?[19] Responding to such a question requires tackling an influential analysis that sees substantive cultural difference as inextricably tied to the colonial production of indigeneity.[20] Against the repressive weight of recognition regimes, as well as more recent identity politics stoked by precarity and existential insecurity, identity is promoted as an immanent and improvisational project. The immanent turn in critical scholarship acquires galvanizing appeal at a time of resurgent xenophobia and the expansion of brutal transnational regimes of surveillance, incarceration, and exclusion. Implied in such projects is the idea of actively embracing the fractured conditions of one's existence and fashioning tactics for endurance drawn from whatever is to hand. This book has tracked Warlpiri life in the shadows of legal recognition, and it might appear to share much ground with these projects. However, it is also clear that to focus only on that which is immanent is to overlook the recursive moves that people make under conditions of duress as they tap vital repositories of tradition, practice, sentiment, and ways of seeing.

Nungarrayi's endurance of exile involves intensely felt and intuitive returns to the terms of her desert subjectivity and related intergenerational inheritances, even as she insists that she embraces a new life on her own independent terms. In thinking about her circumstances, and relatedly about my fixation on the optimistic possibilities of exilic transformation, I am haunted by a series of exchanges I had several years ago with an especially astute man. Japangardi was a retired schoolteacher, football coach, ceremonial leader, and artist. It was Japangardi's grave that I was taken aback to find desecrated on our visit to the Tiny Town. He was a close and incisive observer of interactions between Warlpiri and non-Aboriginal people. During the mid-1990s he spoke with me at length about the experiences of his forebears who had been driven from their hunting grounds and into brutal subjugation by settlers and prospectors in the 1920s. His grandmother had as a young girl survived the horror of watching her father shot dead in the punitive raids led by mounted police and pastoralists that would come to be known as the Coniston Massacres. Japangardi also shared his observations of his people's intergenerational adaptation to the evolving terms of life on government settlements, the places that would later become "communities." At the heart of Japangardi's attention to the past was a relentless desire to come to terms with ongoing legacies of settler colonial domination and, in more concrete terms, how it was that Europeans consistently claimed an upper hand in their dealings with Warlpiri. Yet, as in so many similar contexts, and as the Palestinian poet Mahmoud Darwish reminds us, Japangardi encountered *kardiya*, whitefellas, not as an undifferentiated Enemy, an abstract Other, but as human beings met in their specificity under conditions of cohabitation.[21] Japangardi was optimistic, future-focused. He remained open to the possibilities of forming relationships of trust, transformative relationships with kardiya. He was especially influenced by a close friendship he enjoyed with an art teacher when he was a young man. In his words, the new ways of picturing, of seeing the world, that he learned through the exchanges with this man played a vital role in his acquisition of the ability to be "free to the world."

Japangardi's creative drive consistently pushed the bounds of acceptable practice, cutting across conservative Warlpiri social conventions. Like several renowned Indigenous critics of colonial and settler colonial dispossession, Japangardi regarded the acquisition of close knowledge of white people's ways as a vital strategy if Warlpiri were to reclaim some semblance of power over their own lives.[22] In applying his focus to contemporary dilemmas, Japangardi was moved to look to what he regarded as core Warlpiri principles and tenets learned on the ceremonial ground, to marshal these to new purposes. He spoke to me about his endeavor to come to terms with the "hidden agendas" of white people's ways, telling me of the epiphany he had while at Teacher's College while watching the Warner Brothers film *The NeverEnding Story*: "I could see, you know, I was looking for this notion of a hidden agenda. [I was thinking,] What are these people doing to make this work? I remember [the teachers] taught us how to get this idea of a hidden agenda. We were watching *The NeverEnding Story*. . . . Every time you watch a movie, we're thinking [what's happening] inside. You can see the picture, but inside, what's there? . . . Picture's all right, but what's really there? There gotta be two, maybe three answer to the plot." As he reflected on it further, the narrative of *The NeverEnding Story* struck Japangardi as an instance of *jaalparra*, a Warlpiri term that identifies a series of ways of referring to objects and persons that are indirect, distant, polite, and in some contexts secretive. Jaalparra is enacted in prohibitions around use of the names of recently deceased persons. It refers to other forms of indirect and parabolic speech that invoke an individual person through reference to their country, car, relatives, bodily dispositions, or clothing. Jaalparra ways of talking enact Warlpiri social etiquette. They also allow sensitive matters to be discussed such that some listeners will be kept from understanding their specificity. Jaalparra in this sense puts certain things out of sight, below the surface. It might be understood as a technique for the wielding and withholding of power.

Japangardi's analysis shares ground with Anishinaabe scholar Gerald Vizenor's notion of survivance as "a theory of irony."[23] It also resonates with the practice of cultural redevelopment that philosopher Jonathan Lear speculates on, in his exploration of the transcripts of Crow Chief Plenty Coups that were recorded in the wake of the Crow being violently dispossessed of their land and their capacity to organize their lives and their world.[24] Japangardi's creative work might also be read as "gestures of religious rebellion, born of defiance and despair," as Nicolas Rothwell writes of a larger-scale "fluid frontier episode" of cultural reorientation that gave rise to the Western Desert art movement.[25] During one of our interactions, Japangardi made a series of drawings that he insisted were appropriate for public display. Other senior men insisted otherwise. At stake in these politics is a weighing of the heavily freighted terms of secrecy and revelation, a testing or stirring of the powers of creation, in the ultimate hope that the force of these powers might be made apparent to and be properly acknowledged by the larger society. This fault line of conservatism versus its transcendence is not about the preservation or rejection of the past. Despair, as Rothwell indicates and as Darwish puts it most poignantly, has a distinctive creative strength: "Despair can begin creation anew because it is capable of finding the necessary splinters, those of the first things, of the first elements of creation. And this force, this impetuosity, reverses the roles [between victor and loser], and in the despairing, one finds himself again a position of strength."[26] Himself an exiled poet, this master craftsman, Japangardi, looked for the power that lurks beneath the surface of things—a way of seeing honed on the ceremonial ground *and* in the classroom—and applied that to the transforming world around him. He took up the Warlpiri concept of jaalparra and stretched it to apply to the new world of intercultural problems. In this creative redeployment of a concept drawn from a body of moral philosophy he would describe as "Warlpiri way," Japangardi attempted to guide his country-men toward a new field of intercultural coexistence. He found a way to reach deep into "culture's thick understanding," to stretch it thin and apply it in novel ways to novel challenges.[27]

Japangardi was concerned about a generalized loss of care among his coun-trymen for the quality of artworks they were producing. He told me he was critical of people bringing "rough work" into the art center—boomerangs and other wooden objects that were not finely worked, not properly planed or sanded, not made with the appropriate reverent attitude. He could tell, "just by looking at something," whether it had been made "just for money." The key marker of quality, he offered, was care—one could clearly see when a boomer-ang or a painting had been "truly cared for" by its maker. There is something here of what Michael Taussig describes as "yielding to the very life of the ob-ject," an achievement of a kind of attention that refuses the abstraction and fleeting nature of capital—things made to sell—and that rather insists on "the sensuous particular."[28] The ultimate significance of such an attitude, Japan-gardi suggested, was that it is only when one cares, when one really thinks about what one is doing and handles the craft of making with sustained at-tention, that one can feel good about oneself. This idea of pride in one's work, with its close symbiosis of socially constituted personhood and self-esteem, had been central to Nungarrayi's sense of herself.

Locating Resources for Remaking a World

Scholars of displacement and forced migration often identify nostalgia, diverse modes of looking back to times and places now out of reach, as central to exilic experience.[29] Yet Paul Carter alerts us to the possibility that what we gloss as nostalgia might actually involve a theory of integration.[30] In a different set-ting of racialized violence, Laurence Ralph invokes a similar process at work when he writes of the "qualia of pain," the qualitatively distinct experiences of embodied violence, pain, and police torture that black Chicagoans come to terms with as they produce communal narratives of injury and in so doing produce their social world.[31] Nungarrayi's and Japangardi's respective everyday and philosophical wrestlings with the terms of displacement are suggestive of a similar process at work. These grapplings with cultural inheritance operate in a different register to the reifications of culture we might gloss as strategic essentialism, or conversely repressive authenticity.[32] Displacement necessarily involves a newly distanced, reflexive relationship to erstwhile practices, ways of relating, and principles for life. Nungarrayi, in her postexilic situation, conjures the kin-based ground of her subjectivity, while Japangardi undertakes a sharply focused excavation and redeployment of Warlpiri principles of visuality. Each of them is hopefully engaged with an expanding field of social life while understanding that the possibility of being "free to the world," as Japangardi would describe it, turns upon a close and considered practice of "looking back."

For some scholars, the urgency of humanitarian crisis and of environmental calamity is carrying anthropological theory forward, imbuing it and the lives it engages with volatility and uncertainty, while deriding attention to the past as so much misguided distraction. What is less often recognized is that the supercharged temporality and associated future-focused directionality of becoming shares an uncanny resemblance with the cultural logic of techno-capitalism and its digitally networked means of operation.[33] To make mobility, "flight," and transparency (of lives) as the basis for a cross-cultural liberatory practice is to overlook that this form of mobility is associated with its own qualitatively distinct way of being human—one that turns upon the temporary contract, fluid subjectivity, and flexible relations to place. Modeled as liberation from entrapment, the "becoming" analytic paradoxically entrenches the sensibility of displacement rather than enabling a critical vantage upon it.

Transnational structures of brutal and systematic exclusion that prevent so many of the world's people from being able to pursue lives with dignity continue to draw their force from models of cultural difference. As anthropologists continue to track and expose the expanded workings of these repressive regimes, we face an additional challenge: how to adequately attend to the coexistence—including within individual persons—of differently constituted orientations and ways of relating, including embodiments of structural violence and domination. At stake are concerns that go to the heart of the anthropological project: What is it to be a person, a community, or human in the present? What makes a life livable? What are the terms by which a differently ordered world might be imagined and brought into existence?[34]

THROUGH THE COLLECTIVE TRAUMA and stress prompted by the police shooting of Kumanjayi Walker, Warlpiri leaders presided over their grieving and angry community with composed dignity. They worked tirelessly to maintain calm. They led a convoy of dozens of vehicles into Alice Springs and initiated the largest public demonstration residents of that town could recall. They interpreted the shooting as the logical outcome of their collective disempowerment and issued public statements pleading for respect for the sanctity of Warlpiri law and the reinstatement of their relative autonomy. They were awaiting a coronial inquest and court case associated with Kumanjayi Walker's death.

Then came COVID-19. Just four months after the killing of Kumanjayi Walker, checkpoints have again been set up on the Tanami Highway to surveil the movement of desert people. The small Aboriginal towns that were deemed "prescribed communities" under the Northern Territory Emergency Response legislation have now been declared "designated areas" under the Federal Biosecurity Act. They are effectively in lockdown. Any travelers, including Aboriginal residents of those areas who have made the return journey into Alice Springs, will be placed in quarantine for fourteen days. Under the conditions of this international "emergency," their situation is no longer exceptional. The biosecurity regime and the policing practices that enforce it have been deployed across Australia's major cities and in locally varied forms over large parts of the world. Global hypermobility has been brought to a dramatic halt. Yet history ensures that some Warlpiri and other Aboriginal people will experience the interventions geared toward protecting their vulnerability not as gestures of care, but as a threat, one that strikes at the heart of their lifeways.[35] "Social distancing" is not only a perverse prospect from a Warlpiri perspective; it is social death. In the time of biological life, in the enforcement of pandemic emergency provisions, public health has become yet the latest frontier of settler colonial containment. From another angle COVID-19 might be seen to comprise magical qualities attributed to The Troubles—but also the workings of state power—invisible, rapidly moving, proliferating, uncontainable, deadly, world-changing.

In the final weeks and months in which I have been completing this book, Nungarrayi and I have had only sporadic and relatively fleeting contact. The interstate border closures and citywide lockdowns imposed by state and federal governments have made in-person visits impossible. But our gradual moving apart began months before the pandemic arrived. When I try to put my finger on trigger points for the affective shift in our friendship, three incidents come to mind. The first was the extended drinking binge that reached its climax with her being severely beaten by her son, precipitating her hospitalization and his imprisonment. The second was Ram's displacement by Nungarrayi's new love interest. The third was a series of terse, alcohol-fueled altercations between the two of us over money. Each of these incidents reveals the stress and unrelenting pressures of life under conditions of displacement and entrenched socioeconomic impoverishment. Each also stakes a challenge with profound consequences for our friendship. Yet my attention to these incidents also reveals the moral weight *I* have attributed to them, the classed differences between us, and relatedly the fault lines of *my* desire. Here I confront the limits of empathy, the narrow cast and self-righteousness of my residual liberal sensibility—qualities and constraints that also cast a shadow over the history of anthropology. Ram's coming into Nungarrayi's life signaled to me a virtuous meeting of attractive abandoned subjects. Here was a story of our times, a story of shared injustice and love across cultures, a beautiful story worth telling. Her new relationship with an angry, alcoholic, Anglo-Australian man carried, in my mind, no such virtue.

There is no redemptive transformation to be celebrated here, no "settling" into a new life. Nungarrayi's entreaty to me to "see how we roll" is not simply a mischievous incitement to join her in open-ended adventure. It invokes an attitude toward life described by Michel de Certeau, whereby disempowered people have no choice but to dwell in the immediacy of their lives, and find cracks, social spaces in which to "slip and slide," resist authority, and seize back some semblance of control.[36] Ultimately our friendship—at least for now, for the time of this book—is more or less constrained by the uneven terms of this social landscape. Our friendship cannot but be a resource to hustle. But this will not be the end of it.

Afterword

MELBOURNE, AUGUST 2020, COVID-19 LOCKDOWN STAGE 4: Through the first half of August, Nungarrayi phones me several times. She calls one day to put me on the phone with her extended daughter Georgia, a woman in her early thirties whom I have known since she was a child and who has lived a highly mobile, drinking life for the past decade. Georgia has turned up in Adelaide, and today the two women are sitting on the riverbank in Salisbury Park, drinking happily and well-ensconced in sentimental mode. Nungarrayi puts her phone on speaker so that we can engage in a three-way conversation. She peppers me with a series of questions. Remember our trip out bush? What did we see? What happened to you in the night after we visited? She draws me out as I narrate for Georgia some of the key moments of that trip to her grandfather's country—Nungarrayi's call-and-response with *mirlalyipa* ancestral spirits on our arrival; the little bird that woke me in the night chirping outside the window of my Alice Springs hotel room; the *jitti* stone that appeared at Nungarrayi's feet as she approached the mountain. As I talk she confirms each of my recollections with small cries of pleasure and growing excitement.

The next day Nungarrayi texts me a stream of carefully assembled photographs: her smiling, deceased paternal grandparents; her son, David, paired with her ex-husband, Daniel; David and his dearly missed best friend/brother; herself with Tyson; and a selection of selfies. Later that day, when I call her back, she asks if I can print the photos for her in color, mount them on a board, and mail the ensemble back to her. I tell her this work will have to wait until after Melbourne's draconian stage 4 lockdown is lifted—all retail centers beyond those offering "essential services" are closed for the duration. I joke with her about the constraints of life in Melbourne under lockdown, with its 8:00 p.m. curfew, tight limits on lawful reasons for leaving home, five-kilometer restrictions on how far one can travel, police and army walking the streets, and exorbitant fines issued to those found breaking the rules. I also share with her my growing distress about the impact of the declared "state of disaster" and enforced isolation on people across the community. A hard border closure between the states of Victoria and South Australia has been in place for several months. It is unlikely the two of us will be able to see each other in person before year's end, at best.

The pandemic generates unexpected conjunctures between older experiences of displacement and the new experience of being stuck in place. As the freedom to move about at will and visit places of special association is withdrawn from the citizenry, circumstances would appear ripe for comparative empathetic reflection on the traumatic consequences of containment, as well as the significance of place per se to ontological security. Yet notwithstanding a proliferation in reports of diffuse forms of neighborliness, COVID-19 appears not to have activated empathy with significant transformative capacity. As we are all forced to retreat into shrunken and technomedia-intensified versions of our social worlds and deal with the associated existential, psychological, and economic fallout, there is a related tendency to focus on those elements of life that lie within one's immediate sphere of control.

Memory has assumed an expanded role in the time of "stay at home." George Herbert Mead reminds us that memory images are not simply produced by a person, but a person in relation to a particular environment as remembered. Accordingly, consciousness, he argues, is not simply a state of individual awareness, but the outcome of interactions between a person and her environment, "and cannot simply be located in either."[1] By environment, Mead invokes place as part of a larger social universe of interaction—the conversation of gestures through which selves internalize and respond to a community of others, and in so doing govern their own conduct. When Nungarrayi assures me that she is OK and that "country is all right," regardless of where she is, she seems to invoke something akin to this analysis. Country is always within her. It is held by her and her relatives; it is a vivid constellation of forces, foundational to her very being, that continues to shape the person she is, influencing her actions in myriad ways, not least her attention to the new country and people around her.

As I reflect out loud on the phone about how long it might be before we can next meet up, Nungarrayi bursts into tears. "Nangala, you should come here to me. You should bring Jungarrayi and Japaljarri [my partner and son] and we should all go and live out bush. We got all those houses. Plenty of room. Fresh air." We dialogue back and forth, building the picture of how we will subsist on bush foods and collect fresh water flowing from the perennial spring, and of the activities that will fill our days. It's a beautiful and very appealing image.

Notes

INTRODUCTION

1 Female names commence with *N*, male names with *J*, such that brother and sister are Nangala and Jangala, Nungarrayi and Jungarrayi, and so on.

2 A. Vanstone, "Beyond Conspicuous Compassion: Indigenous Australians Deserve More Than Good Intentions," in *A Passion for Policy: Essays on Public Sector Reform*, ed. J. Wanna (Canberra: ANU Press, 2005), 39–46; H. Hughes, *Lands of Shame: Aboriginal and Torres Strait Islander "Homelands" in Transition* (Sydney: Centre for Independent Studies, 2007).

3 Commonwealth of Australia, "Our North, Our Future: White Paper on Developing Northern Australia," Department of Industry, Innovation and Science, Canberra, 2015.

4 C. Wahlquist, "Fears Western Australia Will Close Remote Indigenous Communities by Stealth," *Guardian*, July 14, 2016, https://www.theguardian.com/australia-news/2016/jul/14/fears-western-australia-will-close-remote-indigenous-communities-by-stealth.

5 P. Taylor, "Remote Communities Making the Move to Town," *Australian*, July 16, 2019, https://www.theaustralian.com.au/nation/remote-communities-making-the-move-to-town/news-story/ac74fcdfab0c34968f02d2a9f1aeffic.

6 S. Standen and T. Joyner, "Squalid Homes Demolished, Residents Relocated from Aboriginal Reserves, in Shadow of Big-Money Mines," *ABC News*, July 13, 2019, https://www.abc.net.au/news/2019-07-13/squalid-indigenous-housing-in-shadow-of-big-money-mines/9940500.

7 L. Allam and N. Evershed, "Too Hot for Humans? First Nations People Fear Becoming Australia's First Climate Refugees," *Guardian*, December 18, 2019, https://www.theguardian.com/australia-news/2019/dec/18/too-hot-for-humans-first-nations-people-fear-becoming-australias-first-climate-refugees.

8 H. C. Coombs, "The Future of the Outstation Movement" (working paper, Centre for Resource and Environmental Studies, Australian National University, Canberra, 1979); C. A. Blanchard, *Return to Country: The Aboriginal Homelands Movement in Australia* (Canberra: Australian Government Publishing Service, 1987).

9   E. Povinelli, *Economies of Abandonment: Social Belonging and Endurance in Late Liberalism* (Durham, NC: Duke University Press, 2011).

10 On "orbiting," see N. Pearson, *Our Right to Take Responsibility* (Cairns: Noel Pearson and Associates, 2000).

11 Pearson, *Our Right to Take Responsibility*; S. Grant, *Australia Day* (Sydney: HarperCollins, 2016); M. Langton, "Trapped in the Aboriginal Reality TV Show," *Griffith Review* 19 (2008): 143–62.

12 P. Sutton, *The Politics of Suffering: Indigenous Australia and the End of the Liberal Consensus* (Melbourne: Melbourne University Press, 2009).

13 Observing the fallout from this process on the ground in Central and North Australia, I was moved, along with my partner, economic anthropologist Jon Altman, to design and coedit two volumes of essays engaging these fraught politics. The first book, *Coercive Reconciliation: Stabilise, Normalise, Exit Aboriginal Australia*, collected thirty responses by Indigenous and non-Indigenous activists, academics, and commentators, as a rapid response to the dramatic announcement of the Northern Territory Intervention. A second book, *Culture Crisis: Anthropology and Politics in Aboriginal Australia*, brought together anthropologists in vigorous debate over the interpretation of the circumstances of remote Aboriginal Australia and the legacy of anthropology's contributions to this policy domain.

14 M. Meggitt, *Desert People* (Sydney: Angus and Robertson, 1962); D. Bell, *Daughters of the Dreaming* (Sydney: Allen and Unwin, 1983); P. Vaarzon-Morel, ed., *Warlpiri karnta karnta-kurlangu yimi / Warlpiri Women's Voices: Our Lives, Our History* (Alice Springs: Institute of Aboriginal Development, 1995).

15 M. C. Hartwig, "The Coniston Killings" (honors thesis, University of Adelaide, 1960); T. Roberts, *Frontier Justice: A History of the Gulf Country to 1900* (Brisbane: University of Queensland Press, 2005); T. Bottoms, *Conspiracy of Silence: Queensland's Frontier Killing Times* (Sydney: Allen and Unwin, 2013).

16 J. Long, *The Go-Betweens: Patrol Officers in Aboriginal Affairs Administration in the Northern Territory 1936–74* (Darwin: North Australia Research Unit, Australian National University, 1992); T. Rowse, *White Flour, White Power: From Rations to Citizenship in Central Australia* (Melbourne: Cambridge University Press, 1998).

17 S. Wild, "Recreating the Jukurrpa: Adaptation and Innovation in Songs and Ceremonies in Warlpiri Society," in *Songs of Aboriginal Australia*, ed. M. Clunies Ross, T. Donaldson, and S. Wild (Sydney: University of Sydney, 1987), 97–120.

18 Rowse, *White Flour, White Power*; M. Hinkson, *Remembering the Future: Warlpiri Life through the Prism of Drawing* (Canberra: Aboriginal Studies Press, 2014), 78–80.

19 L. Campbell, *Darby: One Hundred Years of Life in a Changing Culture* (Sydney: Australian Broadcasting Commission Books, 2006); P. Burke, *An Australian Indigenous Diaspora: Warlpiri Matriarchs and the Refashioning of Tradition* (New York: Berghahn Books, 2018); M. Hinkson, "Beyond Assimilation and Refusal: A Warlpiri Perspective on the Politics of Recognition," *Postcolonial Studies* 20, no. 1 (2017): 86–100.

20 N. Munn, *Walbiri Iconography: Graphic Representation and Cultural Symbolism in a Central Australian Society* (Ithaca, NY: Cornell University Press, 1973); T. Swain, *A Place among Strangers: Towards a History of Australian Aboriginal Being* (Cambridge:

Cambridge University Press, 1993); M. Jackson, *At Home in the World* (Durham, NC: Duke University Press, 1995).

21 Munn, *Walbiri Iconography*, 214.

22 F. Myers, *Pintupi Country, Pintupi Self: Sentiment, Place and Politics among Western Desert Aborigines* (Berkeley: University of California Press, 1991); B. Glowczewski, *Desert Dreamers* (Minneapolis: University of Minnesota Press, 2000); F. Dussart, *The Politics of Ritual in an Aboriginal Settlement: Kinship, Gender, and the Currency of Knowledge* (Washington, DC: Smithsonian Institution Press, 2000); J. Biddle, *Breast, Bodies, Canvas: Central Desert Art as Experience* (Sydney: UNSW Press, 2007).

23 U. Eickelkamp, "Finding Spirit: Ontological Monism in an Australian Aboriginal Desert World Today," *Journal of Ethnographic Theory* 7, no. 1 (2017): 235–64; J. Biddle, *Remote Avant-Garde: Aboriginal Art under Occupation* (Durham, NC: Duke University Press, 2016); F. Myers, "Unsettled Business: Acrylic Painting, Tradition, and Indigenous Being," in *The Power of Knowledge, the Resonance of Tradition*, ed. L. Taylor et al. (Canberra: Aboriginal Studies Press, 2005), 3–33; Y. Musharbash, *Yuendumu Everyday: Contemporary Life in Remote Aboriginal Australia* (Canberra: Aboriginal Studies Press, 2008).

24 Elizabeth Ross and Jeannie Herbert, as interviewed in Hinkson, *Remembering the Future*, 88–91.

25 P. Willis, "Patrons and Riders: Conflicting Roles and Hidden Objectives in an Aboriginal Development Programme at Kununurra (WA)" (master's thesis, Australian National University, 1980); E. Michaels, *For a Cultural Future: Francis Jupurrurla Makes TV at Yuendumu* (Sydney: Artspace, 1987).

26 N. Peterson, "An Expanding Aboriginal Domain: Mobility and Initiation Journey," *Oceania* 70, no. 3 (2000): 205–18.

27 Burke, *An Australian Indigenous Diaspora*.

28 Musharbash, *Yuendumu Everyday*.

29 On Northern Ireland, see A. Feldman, *Formations of Violence: The Narrative of the Body and Political Terror in Northern Ireland* (Chicago: University of Chicago Press, 1991).

30 V. Das, *Life and Words: Violence and Descent into the Ordinary* (Berkeley: University of California Press, 2006); S. Caton, "Coetzee, Agamben, and the Passion of Abu Ghraib," *American Anthropologist* 108, no. 1 (2006): 114–23; A. Simpson, *Mohawk Interruptus: Political Life across the Borders of Settler States* (Durham, NC: Duke University Press, 2014).

31 J. Comaroff and J. Comaroff, "Millennial Capitalism: First Thoughts on a Second Coming," *Public Culture* 12, no. 2 (2000): 291–343; J. Comaroff and J. Comaroff, "Occult Economies and the Violence of Abstraction: Notes from the South African Postcolony," *American Ethnologist* 26, no. 2 (2003): 279–303; A. Kleinman, V. Das, and M. Lock, eds., *Social Suffering* (Berkeley: University of California Press, 1997).

32 Simpson, *Mohawk Interruptus*.

33 D. Goldstein, "Toward a Critical Anthropology of Security," *Current Anthropology* 51, no. 4 (2010): 487–517.

34 Goldstein, "Toward a Critical Anthropology of Security," 487.

35   T. Lea, "When Looking for Anarchy, Look to the State: Fantasies of Regulation in Forcing Disorder within the Australian Indigenous Estate," *Critique of Anthropology* 32, no. 2 (2012): 109–24; Povinelli, *Economies of Abandonment*.

36   M. Hinkson, "Media Images and the Politics of Hope," in *Culture Crisis: Anthropology and Politics in Aboriginal Australia*, ed. J. Altman, and M. Hinkson (Randwick: UNSW Press, 2010), 229–48.

37   L. Bessire, *Behold the Black Caiman: A Chronicle of Ayoreo Life* (Chicago: University of Chicago Press, 2014), 14.

38   M. Taussig, *The Corn Wolf* (Chicago: University of Chicago Press, 2015), 9.

39   J. Om, "Another Yuendumu Exodus to Adelaide," *ABC News*, February 12, 2011, https://www.abc.net.au/news/2011-02-15/another-yuendumu-exodus-to-adelaide /1943676; "Yuendumu Campers Pack Up and Go," *ABC News*, March 14, 2011, https://www.abc.net.au/news/2011-03-11/yuendumu-campers-pack-up-and-go /2661492?site=alicesprings.

40   L. Wacquant, "Crafting the Neoliberal State: Workfare, Prisonfare, and Social Insecurity," *Sociological Forum* 25, no. 2 (2010): 197–220.

41   Y. Musharbash, "Sorry Business Is Yapa Way: Warlpiri Mortuary Rituals as Embodied Practice," in *Mortality, Mourning and Mortuary Practices in Indigenous Australia*, ed. M. Tonkinson and V. Burbank (London: Routledge, 2017), 34–56.

42   A. Mbembe, *Necropolitics* (Durham, NC: Duke University Press, 2019), 29.

43   H.-G. Gadamer, "Friendship and Solidarity," *Research in Phenomenology* 39, no. 1 (1999): 7–8.

44   A. Honneth, "On the Destructive Power of the Third," *Philosophy and Social Criticism* 29, no. 1 (2003): 20.

45   A. Honneth, "Integrity and Disrespect: Principles of a Conception of Morality Based on the Theory of Recognition," *Political Theory* 20, no. 2 (1992): 189 (emphasis added).

46   H. Vigh, "Motion Squared: A Second Look at the Concept of Social Navigation," *Anthropological Theory* 9, no. 4 (2009): 421.

47   J. Biehl and P. Locke, "Introduction: Ethnographic Sensorium," in *Unfinished: The Anthropology of Becoming*, ed. J. Biehl and P. Locke (Durham, NC: Duke University Press, 2017), 8; J. Biehl and P. Locke, "Deleuze and the Anthropology of Becoming," *Current Anthropology* 51, no. 3 (2010): 317–51.

48   M. Agier, *Borderlands: Towards an Anthropology of the Cosmopolitan Condition* (Cambridge: Cambridge University Press, 2016); K. A. Appiah, *The Lies That Bind: Rethinking Identity* (London: Profile Books, 2018); S. Mehta, *This Land Is Our Land: An Immigrant's Manifesto* (New York: Farrar, Straus and Giroux, 2019).

49   M. Hinkson, "Locating a Zeitgeist: Displacement, Becoming and the End of Alterity," *Critique of Anthropology* 39, no. 3 (2019): 371–88.

50   E. Povinelli, *The Cunning of Recognition* (Durham, NC: Duke University Press, 2002).

51   G. H. Mead, *Mind, Self, Society: From the Standpoint of a Social Behaviorist*, ed. and with an introduction by C. W. Morris (Chicago: University of Chicago Press, 1934).

52   P. Virilio, *The Great Accelerator*, translated by Julie Rose (Cambridge: Polity, 2012); S. Khosravi, *Precarious Lives: Waiting and Hope in Iran* (Philadelphia: University of Pennsylvania Press, 2017); G. Ramsay, "Incommensurable Futures and Displaced Lives: Sovereignty as Control over Time," *Public Culture* 29, no. 3 (2017): 515–38.

53 P. Vaarzon-Morel, "Pointing the Phone: Transforming Technologies and Social Relations among Warlpiri," *Australian Journal of Anthropology* 25, no. 2 (2014): 239–55; M. Taussig, *The Nervous System* (New York: Routledge, 1992); M. Auge, *Non-places: An Introduction to Supermodernity* (New York: Verso, 1995); P. Virilio, *Speed and Politics*, translated by Mark Polizzotti (Los Angeles: Semiotext(e), 2006).

54 J. Latimore, "Steve Bunbadgee Hodder Watt: Jacinta Price under Fire from Aboriginal Women," *@indigenousX*, February 6, 2018, https://indigenousx.com.au/steve-bunbadgee-hodder-watt-jacinta-price-under-fire-from-aboriginal-women/; "Ten Things You Need to Know about Jacinta Price," *Welcome to Country*, February 9, 2019, https://www.welcometocountry.org/things-need-to-know-jacinta-price/.

55 A. Wright, *Tracker* (Sydney: Giramondo, 2017).

56 A. Wright, "What Happens When You Tell Someone Else's Story?," *Meanjin*, Summer 2016, https://meanjin.com.au/essays/what-happens-when-you-tell-somebody-elses-story/.

57 V. Crapanzano, "Review: Life-Histories," *American Anthropologist* 86, no. 4 (1984): 953–60; K. Dwyer, *Moroccan Dialogues: Anthropology in Question* (Baltimore: Johns Hopkins University Press, 1982); S. A. Tyler, "Post-modern Ethnography: From Document of the Occult to Occult Document," in *Writing Culture: The Poetics and Politics of Ethnography*, ed. J. Clifford and G. Marcus (Berkeley: University of California Press, 1986), 122–40.

58 Miyarrka Media, *Phone and Spear: A Yuta Anthropology* (London: Goldsmiths University Press, 2019).

59 E. Tuck and K. W. Yang, "Decolonization Is Not a Metaphor," *Decolonization: Indigeneity, Education and Society* 1, no. 1 (2012): 1–40.

1. JOURNEYING WITH

This chapter is a revised and expanded version of "In and Out of Place: Ethnography as 'Journeying With' between Central and South Australia," *Oceania* 88, no. 3 (2018).

1 M. Hinkson, "In the Name of the Child," in *Coercive Reconciliation: Stabilise, Normalise, Exit Aboriginal Australia*, ed. J. Altman and M. Hinkson (Carlton: Arena, 2007), 1–13.

2 L. Abu-Lughod, "Writing against Culture," in *Recapturing Anthropology: Working in the Present*, ed. R. Fox (Santa Fe, NM: School of American Research, 1991), 147.

3 Abu-Lughod, "Writing against Culture."

4 L. Berlant, *Cruel Optimism* (Durham, NC: Duke University Press, 2011) (for "dissolving assurances"); M. Jackson, *Critique of Identity Thinking* (New York: Berghahn Books, 2019).

5 P. Sutton, *The Politics of Suffering: Indigenous Australia and the End of the Liberal Consensus* (Melbourne: Melbourne University Press, 2009); J. Altman and M. Hinkson, eds., *Culture Crisis: Anthropology and Politics in Aboriginal Australia* (Randwick: UNSW Press, 2010).

6 J. Beckett, "Frontier Encounter: Stanner's Durmugam," in *An Appreciation of Difference: WEH Stanner and Aboriginal Australia*, ed. M. Hinkson and J. Beckett (Canberra: Aboriginal Studies Press, 2008), 89–101; I. Clendinnen, "The Power to Frustrate

Good Intentions: or, The Revenge of the Aborigines," *Common Knowledge* 11, no. 3 (2005): 410–31; R. Manne, "W. E. H. Stanner: The Anthropologist as Humanist," in W. E. H. Stanner, *The Dreaming and Other Essays* (Melbourne: Black Inc., 2010), 1–18.

7 J. Casagrande, ed., *In the Company of Man: Twenty Portraits by Anthropologists* (New York: Harper and Brothers, 1960).

8 Beckett, "Frontier Encounter," 98.

9 Beckett, "Frontier Encounter," 98.

10 D. Bates, *The Passing of the Aborigines: A Lifetime Spent among the Natives of Australia* (London: John Murray, 1938).

11 B. Hill, *Broken Song: T. G. H. Strehlow and Aboriginal Possession* (Sydney: Vintage, 2002).

12 R. M. Berndt, "Areas of Research in Aboriginal Australia Which Demand Urgent Attention," *Bulletin of the International Committee on Urgent Anthropological and Ethnological Research* 2 (1959): 63–69.

13 Sutton, *The Politics of Suffering*.

14 Abu-Lughod, "Writing against Culture."

15 U. Eickelkamp, in discussion with the author, July 2017; U. Eickelkamp, "Finding Spirit: Ontological Monism in an Australian Aboriginal Desert World Today," *Journal of Ethnographic Theory* 7, no. 1 (2017): 235–64; J. Biddle, *Remote Avant-Garde: Aboriginal Art under Occupation* (Durham, NC: Duke University Press, 2016); S. E. Holcombe, *Remote Freedoms: Politics, Personhood and Human Rights in Aboriginal Central Australia* (Stanford, CA: Stanford University Press, 2018).

16 H. Powdermaker, *Stranger and Friend: The Way of an Anthropologist* (New York: W. W. Norton, 1966); D. Mayberry-Lewis, *The Savage and the Innocent* (Boston: Beacon, 1968); H. Buechler and J. Buechler, *Carmen: The Autobiography of a Spanish Woman* (Cambridge, MA: Schenkman, 1981); J. Sexton, *Son of Tecún Umún: A Maya Indian Tells His Life Story* (Tucson: University of Arizona Press, 1981); M. Shostak, *Nisa: The Life and Words of a !Kung Woman* (Cambridge, MA: Harvard University Press, 1981); P. Rabinow, *Reflections on Fieldwork in Morocco* (Berkeley: University of California Press, 1977).

17 V. Crapanzano, "Review: Life-Histories," *American Anthropologist* 86, no. 4 (1984): 956.

18 On the 1980s "crisis of representation" and the new interpretivist attention to writing, see J. Clifford and G. Marcus, eds., *Writing Culture: The Poetics and Politics of Ethnography* (Berkeley: University of California Press, 1986); C. Geertz, *Works and Lives: The Anthropologist as Author* (Cambridge: Polity, 1988). On experiments with modeling dialogical engagement, see V. Crapanzano, *Tuhami: Portrait of a Moroccan* (Chicago: University of Chicago Press, 1980); V. Crapanzano, "Hermes' Dilemma: The Masking of Subversion in Ethnographic Description," in *Writing Culture: The Poetics and Politics of Ethnography*, ed. J. Clifford and G. Marcus (Berkeley: University of California Press, 1986), 51–76; K. Dwyer, *Moroccan Dialogues: Anthropology in Question* (Baltimore: Johns Hopkins University Press, 1982); S. A. Tyler, "Postmodern Ethnography: From Document of the Occult to Occult Document," in *Writing Culture: The Poetics and Politics of Ethnography*, ed. J. Clifford and G. Marcus (Berkeley: University of California Press, 1986), 122–40. On individual creativity, see R. Rosaldo, S. Lavie, and K. Narayan, "Introduction: Creativity in Anthropology," in *Creativity/Anthropology*, ed. R. Rosaldo, S. Lavie, and K. Narayan (Ithaca, NY:

Cornell University Press, 1993), 1–8; N. Rapport, *Transcendent Individual: Towards a Literary and Liberal Anthropology* (London: Routledge, 1997). On autobiography, see J. Okely and H. Callaway, eds., *Anthropology and Autobiography* (London: Routledge, 1992). On life writing as social history, see J. Beckett, "George Dutton's Country: Portrait of an Aboriginal Drover," *Aboriginal History* 2, no. 1 (1978): 28; J. Beckett, "Walter Newton's History of the World—or Australia," *American Ethnologist* 20, no. 4 (1993): 675–95; B. Myerhoff, *Number Our Days* (New York: Simon and Schuster, 1978); G. Cowlishaw, ed., *Love against the Law: The Autobiographies of Tex and Nellie Camfoo* (Canberra: Aboriginal Studies Press, 2000); G. Cowlishaw, *The City's Outback* (Sydney: NewSouth Books, 2009); M. Jackson, *The Wherewithal of Life: Ethics, Migration, and the Question of Well-Being* (Berkeley: University of California Press, 2013); E. Vincent, *Against Native Title: Conflict and Creativity in Outback Australia* (Canberra: Aboriginal Studies Press, 2017).

19 James Clifford, for example, reads Marjorie Shostak's *Nisa: The Life and Words of a !Kung Woman* as an experiment in ethnographic writing framed by American feminist concerns, and ultimately as an allegory of female humanity. J. Clifford, "On Ethnographic Allegory," in *Writing Culture: The Poetics and Politics of Ethnography*, ed. J. Clifford and G. Marcus (Berkeley: University of California Press, 1986), 98–121. Crapanzano observes that an explosion of biographical writing in American anthropology coincided with the publication of Foucault's declaration of the "new man-less science of man." Crapanzano, "Review: Life-Histories," 953.

20 Rapport, *Transcendent Individual*, 24.

21 Rapport, *Transcendent Individual*, 25.

22 Rapport, *Transcendent Individual*, 57.

23 Abu-Lughod, "Writing against Culture," 154; L. Abu-Lughod, *Dramas of Nationhood: The Politics of Television in Egypt* (Chicago: University of Chicago Press, 2008).

24 L. Abu-Lughod, "The Interpretation of Culture(s) after Television," *Representations* 59 (1997): 126.

25 J. Biehl, *Vita: Life in a Zone of Social Abandonment* (Berkeley: University of California Press, 2005).

26 Biehl, *Vita*, 8.

27 Biehl, *Vita*, 23.

28 Biehl, *Vita*, 23.

29 A. Kleinman, V. Das, and M. Lock, eds., *Social Suffering* (Berkeley: University of California Press, 1997); V. Das et al., eds., *Violence and Subjectivity* (Berkeley: University of California Press, 2000); V. Das et al., eds., *Remaking a World: Violence, Social Suffering, and Recovery* (Berkeley: University of California Press, 2001).

30 "Break Up Indigenous Paedophile Rings: Brough," *ABC News*, May 17, 2006, https://www.abc.net.au/news/2006-05-17/break-up-indigenous-paedophile-rings-brough/1755274.

31 This paper received significant public attention when it was later published as a part of *The Politics of Suffering: Indigenous Australia and the End of the Liberal Consensus* (Melbourne: Melbourne University Press, 2009).

32 J. Robbins, "Beyond the Suffering Subject: Toward an Anthropology of the Good," *Journal of the Royal Anthropological Institute* 19, no. 3 (2013): 447–62.

33 Robbins tracks this change by way of arguments made by Michel-Rolph Trouillot, observing seismic shifts both in empirical circumstances and "in the broader symbolic organization that defines the West and the savage." Robbins, "Beyond the Suffering Subject," 449; M.-R. Trouillot, "Anthropology and the Savage Slot: The Poetics and Politics of Otherness," in *Global Transformations: Anthropology and the Modern World* (New York: Palgrave Macmillan, 2003), 7–28.

34 D. Fassin, *Humanitarian Reason: A Moral History of the Present* (Berkeley: University of California Press, 2011), 6.

35 L. Boltanski, *Distant Suffering: Morality, Media and Politics* (Cambridge: Cambridge University Press, 1999); R. Silverstone, *Media and Morality: On the Rise of the Mediapolis* (Cambridge: Polity, 2007); J. Lydon, *Flash of Recognition: Photography and the Emergence of Indigenous Rights* (Sydney: NewSouth Books, 2012).

36 Fassin, *Humanitarian Reason*, 27.

37 L. Wacquant, *Punishing the Poor: The Neoliberal Government of Social Insecurity* (Durham, NC: Duke University Press, 2009).

38 J. Brimblecombe and M. Ferguson, "Food Price Gap Shows Need for Subsidies and Promo Deals for Remote Areas," *Journal of the Home Economics Institute of Australia* 22, no. 2 (2015): 36–37.

39 Robbins, "Beyond the Suffering Subject."

40 S. Boym, *The Future of Nostalgia* (New York: Basic Books, 2001).

41 Boym, *The Future of Nostalgia*, 10.

42 Boym, *The Future of Nostalgia*, xiii.

43 Boym, *The Future of Nostalgia*, xiv.

44 Boym, *The Future of Nostalgia*, 10.

45 B. Kapferer and D. Theodossopoulos, eds., *Against Exoticism: Towards the Transcendence of Relativism and Universalism in Anthropology* (New York: Berghahn Books, 2016), 13.

46 G. Marcus, "The Uses of Complicity in the Changing Mise-en-Scène of Anthropological Fieldwork," *Representations* 59 (1997): 101; P. Rabinow, *Marking Time: On the Anthropology of the Contemporary* (Princeton, NJ: Princeton University Press, 2008).

47 Marcus, "The Uses of Complicity," 96.

48 Marcus, "The Uses of Complicity," 97.

49 Marcus, "The Uses of Complicity," 97.

50 Marcus, "The Uses of Complicity," 98.

51 R. Gomberg-Muñoz, "The Complicit Anthropologist," *Journal for the Anthropology of North America* 21, no. 1 (2018): 36.

52 Berlant, *Cruel Optimism*; H. Vigh, "Motion Squared: A Second Look at the Concept of Social Navigation," *Anthropological Theory* 9, no. 4 (2009): 419–38; Fassin, *Humanitarian Reason*; A. Muehlebach, "On Precariousness and the Ethical Imagination: The Year 2012 in Sociocultural Anthropology," *American Anthropologist* 115, no. 2 (2013): 297–311; M. Hinkson, "Precarious Placemaking," *Annual Reviews of Anthropology* 46 (2017): 49–64.

53 M. Jackson, *In Sierra Leone* (Durham, NC: Duke University Press, 2004); Jackson, *The Wherewithal of Life*.

54 See, for example, S. Ahmed, *Strange Encounters: Embodied Others in Post-coloniality* (London: Routledge, 2000), 61–74; D. Bell and T. Nelson, "Speaking about Rape Is Everyone's Business," *Women's Studies International Forum* 12, no. 4 (1989): 403–16; J. Huggins et al., "Letters to the Editors," *Women's Studies International Forum* 14, no. 5 (1991): 506–7.

55 D. Vessey, "Gadamer's Account of Friendship as an Alternative to an Account of Intersubjectivity," *Philosophy Today* 49, no. 5 (2005): 61.

56 H.-G. Gadamer, *Truth and Method* (New York: Seabury, 1975), 371.

57 I. Ramelli, *Hierocles the Stoic: Elements of Ethics, Fragments and Excerpts* (Atlanta: Society of Biblical Literature, 2009).

58 M. J. Collier, "Core Symbols in South African Intercultural Friendships," *International Journal of Intercultural Relations* 21, no. 1 (1999): 133–56; B. Beer and D. Gardner, "Friendship, Anthropology of," in *International Encyclopedia of the Social and Behavioral Sciences*, 2nd ed., vol. 9, ed. J. D. Wright (Oxford: Elsevier, 2015), 425–43; J. Pitt-Rivers, "The Kith and the Kin," in *The Character of Kinship*, ed. J. Goody (Cambridge: Cambridge University Press, 2015), 89–105.

59 This sequence of ethnography and its analysis are reproduced from M. Hinkson, "Locating a Zeitgeist: Displacement, Becoming and the End of Alterity," *Critique of Anthropology* 39, no. 3 (2019): 381–82.

60 E. Casey, *Remembering: A Phenomenological Study* (Bloomington: Indiana University Press, 2009).

61 The moment immortalized by legendary player Nicky Winmar in 1993 has recently been set in bronze. "Nicky Winmar: Statue of Footballer's Stand against Racism Unveiled in Perth," BBC, July 6, 2019, https://www.bbc.com/news/world-australia -48893928.

62 This sequence of ethnography is published in M. Hinkson, "Turbulent Dislocations in Central Australia: Exile, Placemaking and the Promises of Elsewhere," *American Ethnologist* 45, no. 4 (2018): 521–32.

63 P. Geschiere, *The Perils of Belonging: Autochthony, Citizenship, and Exclusion in Africa and Europe* (Chicago: University of Chicago Press, 2009); G. Hage, *Against Paranoid Nationalism: Searching for Hope in a Shrinking Society* (London: Pluto, 2003).

64 M. Herzfeld, *Cultural Intimacy: Social Poetics and the Real Life of States, Societies, and Institutions* (London: Routledge, 2016), 26; see also A. Feldman, *Formations of Violence: The Narrative of the Body and Political Terror in Northern Ireland* (Chicago: University of Chicago Press, 1991), 15.

65 P. Werbner, ed., *Anthropology and the New Cosmopolitanism: Rooted, Feminist and Vernacular Perspectives* (Oxford: Berg, 2008).

66 F. Myers, *Pintupi Country, Pintupi Self: Sentiment, Place, and Politics among Western Desert Aborigines* (Berkeley: University of California Press, 1991).

67 K. Hastrup, "Writing Ethnography: State of the Art," in *Anthropology and Autobiography*, ed. J. Okely and H. Callaway (London: Routledge, 1992), 122.

68 S. Boym, "On Diasporic Intimacy: Ilya Kabakov's Installations and Immigrant Homes," *Critical Inquiry* 24, no. 2 (1998): 498–524.

69 Boym, "On Diasporic Intimacy," 500.

2. STAKING NEW GROUND

Ethnographic material in this chapter is republished from M. Hinkson, "On the Edges of the Visual Culture of Exile: A View from South Australia," in *Refiguring Techniques in Digital Visual Research*, ed. S. Pink, S. Sumartojo, and E. Gómez Cruz (London: Palgrave Macmillan, 2017), 93–104.

1 Jeff Easter and Sheri Easter, *Over and Over* (Spring House Music Group, 2012. All rights reserved).

2 J. Bauer in discussion with the author, February 2016.

3 G. Williams, "A Decade of Australian Anti-terror Laws," *Melbourne University Law Review* 35, no. 3 (2011): 1137–51.

4 G. Hage, *Against Paranoid Nationalism: Searching for Hope in a Shrinking Society* (London: Pluto, 2003); G. Ramsay, "Humanitarian Exploits: Ordinary Displacements and the Political Economy of the Global Refugee Regime," *Critique of Anthropology* 40, no. 1 (2020): 3–27.

5 L. Griffiths, "Sharkie Savages Downers as 'Out of Touch,'" *Australian*, July 30, 2018, https://www.theaustralian.com.au/news/nation/rebekha-sharkie-savages-downers -as-being-out-of-touch/news-story/eaebe2eaf52b29ee9a711d148c85bf03.

6 F. Gale, *Urban Aborigines* (Canberra: ANU Press, 1972).

7 Gale, *Urban Aborigines*, 74.

8 Gale, *Urban Aborigines*, 167.

9 N. Mirzoeff, *The Right to Look* (Durham, NC: Duke University Press, 2011); P. Carter, *The Lie of the Land* (London: Faber and Faber, 1996).

10 J. Berger, *Berger on Drawing*, ed. Jim Savage (Cork: Occasional, 2005); J. Berger, *Bento's Sketchbook* (London: Verso, 2011).

11 H. Naficy, *An Accented Cinema: Exile and Diasporic Filmmaking* (Princeton, NJ: Princeton University Press, 2001).

12 L. Malkki, *Purity and Exile: Violence, Memory, and National Cosmology among Hutu Refugees in Tanzania* (Chicago: University of Chicago Press, 1995); M. Jackson, *The Wherewithal of Life: Ethics, Migration, and the Question of Well-Being* (Berkeley: University of California Press, 2013). The heading for this section of the chapter reverses the title of Gillian Cowlishaw's *The City's Outback* (Sydney: NewSouth Books, 2009).

13 Central Australian women produce fine white alkaline ash from the bark of river red gum eucalyptus tree that when mixed with tobacco aids the ingestion of nicotine through the lining of the mouth.

14 H. Keith, "Feminism and Pragmatism: George Herbert Mead's Ethics of Care," *Transactions of the Charles S. Peirce Society* 35, no. 2 (1999): 328–44.

15 Malkki, *Purity and Exile*, 4.

16 Malkki, *Purity and Exile*, 3.

17 Malkki, *Purity and Exile*, 209, 194.

18 Malkki, *Purity and Exile*, 253.

19 Malkki, *Purity and Exile*, 222.

20 E. Said, "Reflections on Exile," in *Reflections on Exile and Other Essays*, ed. E. Said (Cambridge, MA: Harvard University Press, 2002), 173–86.

21 J. Deger, "Imprinting on the Heart: Photography and Contemporary Yolngu Mournings," *Visual Anthropology* 21, no. 4 (2008): 292–309; S. Coutin, *Exiled Home: Salvadoran*

Transnational Youth in the Aftermath of Violence (Durham, NC: Duke University Press, 2016); M. Taussig, *The Nervous System* (New York: Routledge, 1992); D. Lumsden, "Broken Lives: Reflections on the Anthropology of Exile and Repair," *Refuge* 18, no. 4 (1999): 30–39.

22 U. Beck and N. Sznaider, "Unpacking Cosmopolitanism for the Social Sciences," *British Journal of Sociology* 57, no. 1 (2006): 391.

23 P. Geschiere, *The Perils of Belonging: Autochthony, Citizenship, and Exclusion in Africa and Europe* (Chicago: University of Chicago Press, 2009), 222–23.

24 Geschiere, *The Perils of Belonging*, 223.

25 D. Harvey, "Cosmopolitanism and the Banality of Geographic Evils," *Public Culture* 12, no. 2 (2000): 543.

26 Harvey, "Cosmopolitanism and the Banality of Geographic Evils," 546.

27 Harvey, "Cosmopolitanism and the Banality of Geographic Evils," 555–56.

28 Harvey, "Cosmopolitanism and the Banality of Geographic Evils," 560 (emphasis added); see also C. Besteman, *Making Refuge: Somali Bantu Refugees and Lewiston, Maine* (Durham, NC: Duke University Press, 2016).

29 M. Hinkson, *Remembering the Future: Warlpiri Life through the Prism of Drawing* (Canberra: Aboriginal Studies Press, 2014), 71–72.

30 S. Wild, "Recreating the Jukurrpa: Adaptation and Innovation in Songs and Ceremonies in Warlpiri Society," in *Songs of Aboriginal Australia*, ed. M. Clunies Ross, T. Donaldson, and S. Wild (Sydney: University of Sydney, 1987); Hinkson, *Remembering the Future*, 124–26.

31 K. A. Appiah, *The Lies That Bind: Rethinking Identity* (London: Profile Books, 2018).

32 B. Sansom, *The Camp at Wallaby Cross: Aboriginal Fringe Dwellers in Darwin* (Canberra: Australian Institute of Aboriginal Studies, 1980), 137.

33 M. Brady, "Giving Away the Grog: An Ethnography of Aboriginal Drinkers Who Quit without Help," *Drug and Alcohol Review* 12, no. 4 (1993): 401–11; D. McKnight, *From Hunting to Drinking: The Devastating Effects of Alcohol on an Australian Aboriginal Community* (London: Routledge, 2002).

34 Jackson, *The Wherewithal of Life*.

35 S. Hall, "Cosmopolitanism, Globalization and Diaspora: Stuart Hall in Conversation with Pnina Werbner," in *Anthropology and the New Cosmopolitanism*, ed. P. Werbner (Oxford: Berg, 2008), 346.

36 J. Berger and J. Mohr, *A Seventh Man: A Book of Images and Words about the Experience of Migrant Workers in Europe* (London: Verso, 1975).

37 Berger and Mohr, *A Seventh Man*, 117.

38 H. Vigh, "Motion Squared: A Second Look at the Concept of Social Navigation," *Anthropological Theory* 9, no. 4 (2009): 422.

39 Vigh, "Motion Squared," 423.

40 G. Vizenor, "Aesthetics of Survivance," in *Survivance: Narratives of Native Presence*, ed. G. Vizenor (Lincoln: University of Nebraska Press, 2008), 1–24.

3. BETWEEN HERE AND THERE

1 A. Barwick, "NT Police Apologise for Refusing to let NSW Woman Buy Six-Pack of Beer in Alice Springs," *ABC News*, August 30, 2019, https://www.abc.net.au/news /2019-08-30/nt-police-apologise-nsw-woman-blocked-buying-beer-alice-springs

/11462950; J. Haynes and D. Keane, "Presenter Karla Grant 'Shocked' after Being Questioned by Police in Alice Springs While Buying Alcohol," *ABC News*, September 13, 2019, https://www.abc.net.au/news/2019-09-13/indigenous-tv-host-karla -grant-highlights-racial-profiling/11509940.

2   Y. Musharbash, "Monstrous Transformations: A Case Study from Central Australia," in *Monster Anthropology in Australia and Beyond*, ed. Y. Musharbash and G. H. Presterudstuen (New York: Palgrave Macmillan, 2014), 33–55; see also V. Burbank, "The Embodiment of Sorcery," *Australian Journal of Anthropology* 28, no. 3 (2017): 286–300.

3   Musharbash, "Monstrous Transformations."

4   M. Meggitt, "Djanba among the Walbiri, Central Australia," *Anthropos* 50 (1955): 375–403.

5   M. Taussig, *The Devil and Commodity Fetishism in South America* (Chapel Hill: University of North Carolina Press, 1980).

6   See, for example, J. Comaroff and J. Comaroff, "Occult Economies and the Violence of Abstraction: Notes from the South African Postcolony," *American Ethnologist* 26, no. 2 (2003): 279–303; L. Bessire, *Behold the Black Caiman: A Chronicle of Ayoreo Life* (Chicago: University of Chicago Press, 2014); D. Jorgensen, "Preying on Those Close to Home: Witchcraft Violence in a Papua New Guinea Village," *Australian Journal of Anthropology* 25, no. 3 (2015): 280; P. Geschiere, *The Modernity of Witchcraft: Politics and the Occult in Postcolonial Africa* (Charlottesville: University of Virginia Press, 1997).

7   B. Kapferer, "Outside All Reason: Magic, Sorcery and Epistemology in Anthropology," in *Beyond Rationalism: Rethinking Magic, Witchcraft and Sorcery*, ed. B. Kapferer (New York: Berghahn Books, 2003), 14, 17.

8   Kapferer, "Outside All Reason," 14.

9   J. Torpey, "Coming and Going: On the State Monopolization of the Legitimate 'Means of Movement,'" *Sociological Theory* 16, no. 3 (1998): 239–59.

10 T. Lea et al., "Being Moved (On): The Biopolitics of Walking in Australia's Frontier Towns," *Radical History Review* 114 (2012): 139–63; R. Lippert and K. Walby, "Introduction: How the World's Cities Are Policed, Regulated and Securitized," in *Policing Cities: Urban Securitization and Regulation in a Twenty-First Century World*, ed. R. Lippert and K. Walby (London: Routledge, 2013), 5.

11 D. Harvey, "The Right to the City," *International Journal of Urban and Regional Research* 27, no. 4 (2003): 939–41; Lea et al., "Being Moved (On)."

12 J. Lear cited in A. Dowd, "Finding the Fish: Memory, Displacement Anxiety, Legitimacy and Identity: The Legacy of Interlocking Traumatic Histories in Postcolonial Australia," in *Placing Psyche: Exploring Cultural Complexes in Australia*, ed. T. Singer et al. (New Orleans: Spring Journal Books, 2011), 126.

13 Lea et al., "Being Moved (On)," 140.

14 Dowd, "Finding the Fish," 126–27.

15 K. Gelder and J. Jacobs, *Uncanny Australia: Sacredness and Identity in a Postcolonial Nation* (Carlton South: Melbourne University Press, 1998).

16 Dowd, "Finding the Fish," 137.

17 M. Jackson, *At Home in the World* (Durham, NC: Duke University Press, 1995); A. Lems, *Being-Here: Placemaking in a World of Movement* (New York: Berghahn Books, 2018).

18   F. Myers, *Pintupi Country, Pintupi Self: Sentiment, Place, and Politics among Western Desert Aborigines* (Berkeley: University of California Press, 1991), 149–55.

19   Å. Ottosson, "To Know One's Place: Belonging and Differentiation in Alice Springs Town," *Anthropological Forum* 24, no. 2 (2014): 115–35; Å. Ottosson, "Don't Rubbish Our Town! 'Anti-social Behaviour' and Indigenous-Settler Forms of Belonging in Alice Springs," *City and Society* 28, no. 2 (2016): 152–73. On white antiracists, see E. Kowal, *Trapped in the Gap: Doing Good in Indigenous Australia* (New York: Berghahn Books, 2015).

20   Northern Territory of Australia, Department of the Attorney-General and Justice, "Northern Territory Correctional Services Annual Statistics, 2016–17," 2018, https://justice.nt.gov.au/__data/assets/pdf_file/0004/599107/2016-17-ntcs-annual-statistics.pdf.

21   T. Rowse, *White Flour, White Power: From Rations to Citizenship in Central Australia* (Melbourne: Cambridge University Press, 1998); W. Rubuntja and J. Green, *The Town Grew Up Dancing: The Life and Art of Wenton Rubuntja* (Alice Springs: Jukurrpa Books, 2002).

22   Torpey, "Coming and Going."

23   D. Fisher, "An Urban Frontier: Respatializing Government in Remote Northern Australia," *Cultural Anthropology* 30, no. 1 (2015): 160.

24   J. Altman and M. Hinkson, eds., *Culture Crisis: Anthropology and Politics in Aboriginal Australia* (Sydney: UNSW Press, 2010).

25   Lea et al., "Being Moved (On)," 143.

26   D. Wilson and L. Weber, "Surveillance, Risk and Preemption on the Australian Border," *Surveillance and Society* 5, no. 2 (2008): 132; Torpey, "Coming and Going"; Lea et al., "Being Moved (On)."

27   E. Chlanda, "Cops at Bottle Shops: Expensive Bluff?," *Alice Springs News*, May 27, 2019, https://www.alicespringsnews.com.au/2019/05/27/cops-at-bottle-shops-expensive-bluff/.

28   D. Fassin, "Policing Borders, Producing Boundaries: The Governmentality of Immigration in Dark Times," *Annual Reviews of Anthropology* 40 (2011): 213–26.

29   Refugee Council of Australia, "Offshore Processing Statistics," October 25, 2020, https://www.refugeecouncil.org.au/operation-sovereign-borders-offshore-detention-statistics/7/.

30   J. Byrd, *The Transit of Empire: Indigenous Critiques of Colonialism* (Minneapolis: University of Minnesota Press, 2011).

31   V. Turner, "Betwixt and Between: The Liminal Period in *Rites de Passage*," in *The Forest of Symbols: Aspects of Ndembu Ritual* (Ithaca, NY: Cornell University Press, 1967), 95–96.

32   R. Benaduce, "Undocumented Bodies, Burned Identities: Refugees, Sans Papiers, Harraga—When Things Fall Apart," *Social Science Information* 47, no. 4 (2008): 505–27.

33   Benaduce, "Undocumented Bodies," 506.

34   Benaduce, "Undocumented Bodies," 509.

35   Benaduce, "Undocumented Bodies," 510.

36   Benaduce, "Undocumented Bodies," 511.

37 F. Myers, "Unsettled Business: Acrylic Painting, Tradition, and Indigenous Being," in *The Power of Knowledge, the Resonance of Tradition,* ed. L. Taylor et al. (Canberra: Aboriginal Studies Press, 2005), 21.

38 A. Honneth, "Integrity and Disrespect: Principles of a Conception of Morality Based on the Theory of Recognition," *Political Theory* 20, no. 2 (1992): 189.

39 B. Sansom, *The Camp at Wallaby Cross: Aboriginal Fringe Dwellers in Darwin* (Canberra: Australian Institute of Aboriginal Studies, 1980).

40 T. Rowse, *Remote Possibilities: The Aboriginal Domain and the Administrative Imagination* (Brinkin: North Australia Research Unit, 2002); R. Folds, *Crossed Purposes* (Randwick: UNSW Press, 2001).

41 T. Ingold, *Being Alive: Essays on Movement, Knowledge and Description* (London: Routledge, 2011).

42 Y. Musharbash, *Yuendumu Everyday: Contemporary Life in Remote Aboriginal Australia* (Canberra: Aboriginal Studies Press, 2008); Myers, *Pintupi Country, Pintupi Self.*

43 Honneth, "Integrity and Disrespect," 193–94.

44 L. Burney, "Cuts Can Lead to Bruises and Far Worse for Women," *Australian,* October 11, 2016.

45 ABC, "Australia's Shame," *Four Corners,* July 25, 2016.

46 P. Callaghan quoted in H. Davidson, "Juvenile Detention Royal Commission Told Use of Force 'Routine' at Don Dale," *Guardian,* October 11, 2016, https://www .theguardian.com/australia-news/live/2016/oct/11/northern-territory-juvenile -detention-royal-commission-hearing-begins-in-darwin-live.

47 E. Povinelli, *Economies of Abandonment: Social Belonging and Endurance in Late Liberalism* (Durham, NC: Duke University Press, 2011), 70–73.

4. TIES THAT BIND

1 T. Tatofi, "Don't Say Goodbye," *Stylin,' Kapena* (Kaneohe: KDE Records, 1990).

2 "Statistics," *Kidney Health Australia,* accessed June 27, 2019, https://kidney.org.au /advocacy/guidance-and-tools/indigenous-health/health-statistics.

3 Australian Institute of Health and Welfare, "Aboriginal and Torres Strait Islander Health Performance Framework 2017" (report, Canberra, 2017), ix.

4 F. Dussart, "'It Is Hard to Be Sick Now': Diabetes and the Reconstruction of Indigenous Sociality," *Anthropologica* 52, no. 1 (2010): 77–87.

5 Dussart, "'It Is Hard to Be Sick Now,'" 80.

6 See "Purple House Provides Dialysis in the Most Remote Parts of Australia," Purple House, accessed December 4, 2019, https://www.purplehouse.org.au/.

7 V. Burbank, "The Embodiment of Sorcery," *Australian Journal of Anthropology* 28, no. 3 (2017): 293.

8 See also E. Saethre, "Conflicting Traditions, Concurrent Treatment: Medical Pluralism in Remote Aboriginal Australia," *Oceania* 77, no. 1 (2007): 95–110.

9 V. Burbank, *An Ethnography of Stress* (New York: Palgrave Macmillan, 2011), 156.

10 L. Malkki, *Purity and Exile: Violence, Memory, and National Cosmology among Hutu Refugees in Tanzania* (Chicago: University of Chicago Press, 1995); G. Hage, *Against Paranoid Nationalism: Searching for Hope in a Shrinking Society* (London: Pluto, 2003);

M. Herzfeld, *Cultural Intimacy: Social Poetics and the Real Life of States, Societies, and Institutions* (London: Routledge, 2016).

11 M. Warin and T. Zivkovic, *Fatness, Obesity, and Disadvantage in the Australian Suburbs: Unpalatable Politics* (Cham, Switzerland: Palgrave Macmillan, 2019); M. Peel, *Good Times, Hard Times: Past and Future in Elizabeth* (Melbourne: Melbourne University Press, 1995).

12 N. Asher, "Tanya Day's Family Call for Criminal Investigation on Final Day of Coronial Inquest," *ABC News*, September 13, 2019, https://www.abc.net.au/news /2019-09-13/tanya-days-family-speaks-at-final-day-of-coronial-inquest/11508920.

13 A. Honneth, "Integrity and Disrespect: Principles of a Conception of Morality Based on the Theory of Recognition," *Political Theory* 20, no. 2 (1992): 187–201.

14 A. Honneth, ed., *Reification: A New Look at an Old Idea* (Oxford: Oxford University Press, 2008).

15 M. Jackson, *The Wherewithal of Life: Ethics, Migration, and the Question of Well-Being* (Berkeley: University of California Press, 2013).

16 G. Ramsay, "Humanitarian Exploits: Ordinary Displacements and the Political Economy of the Global Refugee Regime," *Critique of Anthropology* 40, no. 1 (2020): 3–27.

17 F. Myers, "Reflections on a Meeting: Structure, Language, and the Polity in a Small-Scale Society," in *The Matrix of Language: Contemporary Linguistic Anthropology*, ed. D. Brenneis and R. Macaulay (Boulder, CO: Westview, 1996), 234–57.

18 Burbank, *An Ethnography of Stress*; Dussart, "'It's Hard to Be Sick Now.'"

19 L. Stevenson, *Life Beside Itself: Imagining Care in the Canadian Arctic* (Berkeley: University of California Press, 2014), 70.

20 Saethre, "Conflicting Traditions, Concurrent Treatment."

21 Stevenson, *Life Beside Itself*.

22 P. Geschiere, *The Modernity of Witchcraft: Politics and the Occult in Postcolonial Africa* (Charlottesville: University of Virginia Press, 1997), 25, 99.

23 Geschiere, *The Modernity of Witchcraft*, 127.

24 H. Arendt, *Eichmann in Jerusalem: A Report on the Banality of Evil* (New York: Viking, 1965).

25 T. Anthony, "Growing Up Surplus to Humanity: Aboriginal Children in the Northern Territory," *Arena Journal* 51/52 (2018): 48.

26 Anthony, "Growing Up Surplus to Humanity."

27 M. Hinkson and T. Anthony, "Three Shots," *Arena Magazine*, no. 163 (December 2019): 16–21, https://arena.org.au/three-shots-by-melinda-hinkson-and-thalia -anthony/.

28 J. Hunyor, "Imprison Me NT: Paperless Arrests and the Rise of Executive Power in the Northern Territory," *Indigenous Law Bulletin* 8, no. 2 (2015): 3.

29 D. Fisher, "Running Amok or Just Sleeping Rough? Long-Grass Camping and the Politics of Care in Northern Australia," *American Ethnologist* 39, no. 1 (2012): 171–86.

30 Coroners Court of the Northern Territory, "Inquest into the Death of P Japanangka Langdon," NTMC 016, Coroner's report, Coroners Court, Darwin, August 14, 2015, 4.

31 Coroners Court of the Northern Territory, "Inquest into the Death of P Japanangka Langdon," 26.

32 Quoted in Hunyor, "Imprison Me NT," 4.

33 Hunyor, "Imprison Me NT," 6.

34 H. Davidson, "High Court Upholds Northern Territory's Paperless Arrest Laws," *Guardian*, November 11, 2015, https://www.theguardian.com/australia-news/2015/nov/11/high-court-upholds-northern-territory-paperless-arrest-laws.

35 Hunyor, "Imprison Me NT," 4.

36 D. Fassin, *Prison Worlds: An Ethnography of the Carceral Condition*, trans. R. Gomme (Cambridge: Polity, 2017), xii.

37 Fassin, *Prison Worlds*, 54.

38 A. L. Stoler, *Duress: Imperial Durabilities in Our Times* (Durham, NC: Duke University Press, 2016), 348.

39 Stoler, *Duress*, 350 (emphases in original).

40 S. Bielefeld, "Compulsory Income Management, Indigenous People and Structural Violence: Implications for Citizenship and Autonomy," *Australian Indigenous Law Review* 18, no. 1 (2014): 99–118; P. Mendes, "Compulsory Income Management: A Critical Examination of the Emergence of Conditional Welfare in Australia," *Australian Social Work* 66, no. 4 (2015): 495–510.

41 Stoler, *Duress*; E. Povinelli, *Economies of Abandonment: Social Belonging and Endurance in Late Liberalism* (Durham, NC: Duke University Press, 2011).

42 L. Wacquant, *Punishing the Poor: The Neoliberal Government of Social Insecurity* (Durham, NC: Duke University Press, 2009).

43 Y. Musharbash, "Boredom, Time and Modernity: An Example from Aboriginal Australia," *American Anthropologist* 109, no. 2 (2007): 307–17.

44 M. Hinkson, "What's in a Dedication? On Being a Warlpiri DJ," *Australian Journal of Anthropology* 15, no. 2 (2004): 143–62.

45 M. Hinkson, *Remembering the Future: Warlpiri Life through the Prism of Drawing* (Canberra: Aboriginal Studies Press, 2014), 151.

46 Hinkson, *Remembering the Future*, 152.

5. FORCES OF CONTAINMENT

1 See Y. Musharbash, *Yuendumu Everyday: Contemporary Life in Remote Aboriginal Australia* (Canberra: Aboriginal Studies Press, 2008).

2 W. E. H. Stanner, "The Dreaming," in *White Man Got No Dreaming: Essays 1938–73* (Canberra: ANU Press, 1979 [1956]), 23–40.

3 F. Myers, "Ways of Placemaking," *La Ricerca Folklorica* 45 (2002): 103.

4 P. Carter, *Meeting Place: The Human Encounter and the Challenge of Coexistence* (Minneapolis: University of Minnesota Press, 2013); P. Carter, *Places Made after Their Stories: Design and the Art of Choreotopography* (Crawley, Western Australia: UWA Press, 2015).

5 N. Peterson, "'What Was Dr Coombs Thinking?': Nyirrpi, Policy and the Future," in *Experiments in Self-determination: Histories of the Outstation Movement in Australia*, ed. N. Peterson and F. Myers (Canberra: ANU Press, 2017), 161–80.

6 F. Myers, "Emplacement and Displacement: Perceiving the Landscape through Aboriginal Australian Acrylic Painting," *Ethnos: Journal of Anthropology* 78, no. 4 (2012): 1–29.

7   U. Eickelkamp, "Finding Spirit: Ontological Monism in an Australian Aboriginal Desert World Today," *Journal of Ethnographic Theory* 7, no. 1 (2017): 258, 254 (emphasis added).

8   U. Eickelkamp, "Emplacing Christ: An Indigenous Australian Ethics of Placemaking across Borders," *Anthropological Forum* 28, no. 1 (2017): 55 (emphasis added).

9   G. H. Mead, *Mind, Self, and Society: From the Standpoint of a Social Behaviorist*, ed. and with an introduction by C. W. Morris (Chicago: University of Chicago Press, 1934), 71.

10 See also B. Smith, "'More Than Love': Locality and Affects of Indigeneity in Northern Queensland," *Asia Pacific Journal of Anthropology* 7, no. 3 (2006): 221–35.

11 B. Glowczewski, "The Paradigm of Indigenous Australians: Anthropological Phantasms, Artistic Creations, and Political Resistance," in *La revanche des genres: Art contemporain Australian*, ed. Geraldine Le Roux and Lucienne Striva (Paris: Edition Ainu, Exhibition Catalogue, 2007), 95.

12 F. Myers, "Unsettled Business: Acrylic Painting, Tradition, and Indigenous Being," in *The Power of Knowledge, the Resonance of Tradition*, ed. L. Taylor et al. (Canberra: Aboriginal Studies Press, 2005), 3–33.

13 Eickelkamp, "Emplacing Christ," 49.

14 B. Sansom, *The Camp at Wallaby Cross: Aboriginal Fringe Dwellers in Darwin* (Canberra: Australian Institute of Aboriginal Studies, 1980); F. Myers, *Pintupi Country, Pintupi Self: Sentiment, Place, and Politics among Western Desert Aborigines* (Berkeley: University of California Press, 1991).

15 H. Keith, "Feminism and Pragmatism: George Herbert Mead's Ethics of Care," *Transactions of the Charles S. Peirce Society* 35, no. 2 (1999): 333.

16 Myers writes of a situation he observed in the late 1970s in which a senior Pintupi man set his own truck alight, destroying his most valuable asset, in order to resolve the intensifying conflict among kin over access to the vehicle. See F. Myers, "Burning the Truck and Holding the Country," in *We Are Here: Politics of Aboriginal Land Tenure*, ed. E. Wilmsen (Berkeley: University of California Press, 1989), 15–42.

17 L. Stevenson, *Life Beside Itself: Imagining Care in the Canadian Arctic* (Berkeley: University of California Press, 2014), 126.

18 J.-P. Deranty, "Injustice, Violence, and Social Struggle: The Critical Potential of Axel Honneth's Theory of Recognition," *Critical Horizons: A Journal of Philosophy and Social Theory* 5, no. 1 (2004): 302.

19 Deranty, "Injustice, Violence, and Social Struggle."

20 M. Hinkson, *Remembering the Future: Warlpiri Life through the Prism of Drawing* (Canberra: Aboriginal Studies Press, 2014), 95–102.

21 Australian Wildlife Conservancy, "Newhaven Wildlife Sanctuary Stage 1 Declared Feral-Free," May 17, 2019, https://www.australianwildlife.org/newhaven-wildlife -sanctuary-stage-1-declared-feral-free/.

22 Myers, "Unsettled Business," 21.

23 N. Munn, "Excluded Spaces: The Figure in the Australian Landscape," *Critical Inquiry* 22, no. 3 (1996): 462.

24 Myers, "Ways of Placemaking," 111.

25 R. Hogg, "Penality and Modes of Regulating Indigenous Peoples in Australia," *Punishment and Society* 3, no. 3 (2001): 366.

26 M. C. Hartwig, "The Coniston Killings" (honors thesis, University of Adelaide, 1960); J. Cribbin, *The Killing Times* (Sydney: Fontana/Collins, 1984).

27 These include rationing systems (T. Rowse, *White Flour, White Power: From Rations to Citizenship in Central Australia* [Melbourne: Cambridge University Press, 1998]); child removal (A. Haebich, *Broken Circles: Fragmenting Indigenous Families 1800-2000* [Fremantle: Fremantle Art Centre Press, 2000]); housing (P. Read, ed., *Settlement: A History of Australian Indigenous Housing* [Canberra: Aboriginal Studies Press, 2000]); education (K. Keefe, *From the Centre to the City: Aboriginal Education, Culture and Power* [Canberra: Aboriginal Studies Press, 1992]); church (C. Schwartz and F. Dussart, "Christianity in Aboriginal Australia Revisited," *Australian Journal of Anthropology* 21, no. 1 [2010]: 1-13); language (M. Christie, "Darkness into Light: Missionaries, Modernists and Aboriginal Education," *Australian Journal of Aboriginal Education* 23, no. 3 [1995]: 28-34); and styles of interaction (K. Liberman, "Intercultural Communication in Central Australia," in *Cultural Communication and Intercultural Contact*, ed. D. Carbaugh [New York: Taylor and Francis, 2009], 185-92).

28 Myers and Peterson have shown that decentralization of small Aboriginal communities was influenced by a variety of forces from the 1950s onward. See F. Myers and N. Peterson, "The Origins and History of Outstations as Aboriginal Life Projects," in *Experiments in Self-Determination: Histories of the Outstation Movement in Australia*, ed. N. Peterson and F. Myers (Canberra: ANU Press, 2016), 1-22; S. Kesteven, "A Sketch of Yuendumu and Its Outstations" (master's thesis, Australian National University, 1978).

29 See, for example, S. Cane, "People and Policy in the Development and Destruction of Yagga Yagga Outstation, Western Australia," in *Experiments in Self-Determination*, ed. N. Peterson and F. Myers (Canberra: ANU Press, 2016), 253-78.

30 J. Altman, "In Search of an Outstation Policy for Indigenous Australians" (CAEPR Working Paper No. 34, Centre for Aboriginal Economic Policy Research, Australian National University, Canberra, 2006).

31 P. Sutton, *Dreamings: The Art of Aboriginal Australia* (New York: Viking, 1988); F. Myers, *Painting Culture: The Making of an Aboriginal High Art* (Durham, NC: Duke University Press, 2002).

32 J. Walker, "Night Patrol," *Arena Magazine* 102 (2009): 31-33.

33 A. Stojanovski, *Dog Ear Café: How the Mt Theo Program Beat the Curse of Petrol Sniffing* (Melbourne: Hybrid, 2010).

34 Hogg, "Penality and Modes of Regulating Indigenous Peoples," 366.

35 Hogg, "Penality and Modes of Regulating Indigenous Peoples," 368.

36 C. San Roque, "A Glass Darkly," *Journal of Child Psychology and Psychiatry* 15, no. 2 (2018): 91-102.

37 S. Holcombe, "Human Rights, Colonial Criminality, and the Death of Kwementyaye Briscoe in Custody: A Central Australian Case Study," *Political and Legal Anthropology Review* 29, supp. 1 (2016): 113.

38 Holcombe, "Human Rights," III; see also D. Fisher, "An Urban Frontier: Respatial-izing Government in Remote Northern Australia," *Cultural Anthropology* 30, no. 1 (2015): 152.

6. SEE HOW WE ROLL

1   G. H. Mead, *Mind, Self, and Society: From the Standpoint of a Social Behaviorist*, ed. and with an introduction by C. W. Morris (Chicago: University of Chicago Press, 1962), 283.

2   L. Wacquant, "Three Steps to a Historical Anthropology of Actually Existing Neo-liberalism," *Social Anthropology* 20, no. 1 (2012): 66.

3   I. Bogle, "Centrelink: Incident at Adelaide Office Prompts Conversation about Deep Frustration," *ABC News*, March 22, 2018, http://www.abc.net.au/news /2018-03-22/centrelink-the-perfect-recipe-for-deep-frustration/9573078.

4   L. Wacquant, "Race, Class, and Hyperincarceration in Revanchist America," *Daedalus* 139, no. 3 (2010): 84.

5   R. Nixon, *Slow Violence and the Environmentalism of the Poor* (Cambridge, MA: Harvard University Press, 2011); K. Coddington, "The Slow Violence of Life without Cash: Borders, State Restrictions, and Exclusion in the UK and Australia," *Geographical Review* 109, no. 4 (2019): 527–43; G. Ramsay, *Impossible Refuge: The Control and Constraint of Refugee Futures* (Abingdon: Routledge, 2018).

6   B. Sansom, *The Camp at Wallaby Cross: Aboriginal Fringe Dwellers in Darwin* (Canberra: Australian Institute of Aboriginal Studies, 1980), 74.

7   Sansom, *The Camp at Wallaby Cross*, 132.

8   M. Taussig, *The Corn Wolf* (Chicago: University of Chicago Press, 2015), 58.

9   "Mobile Assistance Patrol (MAP)," Aboriginal Sobriety Group, 2020, asg.org.au /mobile-assistance-patrol-map/.

10 "Toddler Allegedly Raped in Same Tennant Creek Household as Fatal Dispute," *ABC News*, February 23, 2018, http://www.abc.net.au/news/2018-02-23/toddlers -alleged-rape-occurred-in-same-home-as-fatal-dispute/9477048.

11 J. N. Price, "The Truth and Children Just Swept under the Carpet," *Australian*, March 6, 2018, https://www.theaustralian.com.au/commentary/opinion/the-truth -and-children-just-swept-under-the-carpet/news-story/af049c0aa7dc447d155d0adc 014f5ca1.

12 A. Aikman, "Child Sex Abuse 'Like a Tsunami,'" *Australian*, March 5, 2018, https:// www.theaustralian.com.au/nation/protection-agencies-swamped-by-tsunami-of-sex -abuse/news-story/4c76aa2baab4f094943d35ce589a1d06.

13 Mead, *Mind, Self, and Society*, 271.

7. FREE TO THE WORLD

1   S. Vivian and K. Beavan, "Yuendumu Residents Grieve Loss of Teenager Kumanjayi Walker after Police Shooting," *ABC News*, November 10, 2019, https://www.abc.net .au/news/2019-11-10/yuendumu-residents-mourn-loss-after-nt-police-shooting /11690670.

2   L. Wacquant, "Three Steps to a Historical Anthropology of Actually Existing Neo-liberalism," *Social Anthropology* 20, no. 21 (2012): 76.

3   M. Hinkson and T. Anthony, "Three Shots," *Arena Magazine*, no. 163 (December 2019), 16–21, https://arena.org.au/three-shots-by-melinda-hinkson-and-thalia-anthony/.

4   J. Masco, "Comments: D. Goldstein, Toward a Critical Anthropology of Security," *Current Anthropology* 51, no. 4 (2010): 509; see also Z. Gluck and S. Low, "A Sociospatial Framework for the Anthropology of Security," *Anthropological Theory* 17, no. 3 (2017): 282.

5   D. Goldstein, "Toward a Critical Anthropology of Security," *Current Anthropology* 51, no. 4 (2010): 487.

6   L. Wacquant, "Race, Class, and Hyperincarceration in Revanchist America," *Daedalus* 139, no. 3 (2010): 74–90.

7   K. Beavan, "Yuendumu in Central Australia at 'Severe Risk' of Running Out of Water," ABC *News*, August 13, 2019, https://www.abc.net.au/news/2019-08-13 /remote-community-yuendumu-running-out-of-drinking-water/11405024.

8   H. Davidson, "Uranium in Remote Communities' Water Puts 'People's Lives at Risk,'" *Guardian*, June 20, 2018, https://www.theguardian.com/australia-news/2018 /jun/20/uranium-in-remote-communities-water-puts-peoples-lives-at-risk.

9   Wacquant, "Race, Class, and Hyperincarceration," 83.

10 Wacquant, "Three Steps to a Historical Anthropology," 74.

11 D. Fassin, "The Police Are the Punishment," *Public Culture* 31, no. 3 (2019): 558.

12 L. Nelson Nakamarra, "Wapurtarlikirli: The Battle at Yumurrpa," as told to Lee Cataldi, in *Warlpiri Dreamings and Histories: Yimikirli*, ed. P. Rockman Napaljarri and L. Cataldi (San Francisco: HarperCollins, 1994), 111–15.

13 D. Elias, "Golden Dreams: People, Place and Mining in the Tanami Desert" (PhD diss., Australian National University, 2001); M. C. Hartwig, "The Coniston Killings" (honors thesis, University of Adelaide, 1960); L. Watts and S. Fisher, "Pikilyi: Water Rights—Human Rights" (master's thesis, Charles Darwin University, 2000). On the idea that Aboriginals themselves cause these diseases, see F. E. Baume, *Tragedy Track: The Story of the Granites* (Adelaide: Hesperian, 1933).

14 M. Peel, *Good Times, Hard Times: The Past and the Future in Elizabeth* (Melbourne: Melbourne University Press, 1995), 156.

15 Peel, *Good Times, Hard Times*, 158–59.

16 E. Povinelli, *The Cunning of Recognition* (Durham, NC: Duke University Press, 2002).

17 S. Cane, "People and Policy in the Development and Destruction of Yagga Yagga Outstation, Western Australia," in *Experiments in Self-Determination: Histories of the Outstation Movement in Australia*, ed. N. Peterson and F. Myers (Canberra: ANU Press, 2016), 253–78.

18 P. Garvey, "Closures Vindicate My Stand: Barnett," *Australian*, March 10, 2020, 7.

19 E. Povinelli, *Economies of Abandonment: Social Belonging and Endurance in Late Liberalism* (Durham, NC: Duke University Press, 2011), 185.

20 Povinelli, *Economies of Abandonment*, 49; J. Biehl and P. Locke, "The Anthropology of Becoming," in *Unfinished: The Anthropology of Becoming*, ed. J. Biehl and P. Locke (Durham, NC: Duke University Press, 2017); A. Mbembe, *Necropolitics* (Durham, NC: Duke University Press, 2019).

21 M. Darwish, *Palestine as Metaphor*, trans. A. El-Zein and C. Forché (Northampton, MA: Olive Branch, 2019), 21.

22 F. Fanon, *The Wretched of the Earth* (Harmondsworth: Penguin, 1963); P. Freire, *Pedagogy of the Oppressed* (New York: Seabury, 1970).

23 G. Vizenor, "Aesthetics of Survivance," in *Survivance: Narratives of Native Presence*, ed. G. Vizenor (Lincoln: University of Nebraska Press, 2008), 11.

24 J. Lear, *Radical Hope: Ethics in the Face of Cultural Devastation* (Cambridge, MA: Harvard University Press, 2008).

25 N. Rothwell, *Quicksilver* (Melbourne: Text, 2017), 49.

26 Darwish, *Palestine as Metaphor*, 21.

27 Lear, *Radical Hope*, 146. This discussion is drawn from and further elaborated in M. Hinkson, "Beyond Assimilation and Refusal: A Warlpiri Perspective on the Politics of Recognition," *Postcolonial Studies* 20, no. 1 (2017): 86–100.

28 M. Taussig, *The Corn Wolf* (Chicago: University of Chicago Press, 2015), 145.

29 J. Berger and J. Mohr, *A Seventh Man: A Book of Images and Words about the Experience of Migrant Workers in Europe* (London: Verso, 1975); S. Boym, *The Future of Nostalgia* (New York: Basic Books, 2001); E. Said, "Reflections on Exile," in *Reflections on Exile and Other Essays*, ed. E. Said (Cambridge, MA: Harvard University Press, 2002), 173–86.

30 P. Carter, "Utopian Projections: Urban Spells against the Fury of Exile," in *Conversations on Utopia: Cultural and Linguistic Projects*, ed. C. Gualtieri (Oxford: Peter Lang, 2020), 62–91.

31 L. Ralph, "The Qualia of Pain: How Police Torture Shapes Historical Consciousness," *Anthropological Theory* 13, nos. 1 and 2 (2013): 104–5; see also A. Feldman, *Formations of Violence: The Narrative of the Body and Political Terror in Northern Ireland* (Chicago: University of Chicago Press, 1991).

32 On strategic essentialism, see G. Spivak, *A Critique of Postcolonial Reason: Toward a History of the Vanishing Present* (Cambridge, MA: Harvard University Press, 1999). On repressive authenticity, see P. Wolfe, *Settler Colonialism and the Transformation of Anthropology: The Politics and Poetics of an Ethnographic Event* (London: Cassell, 1999).

33 S. Cooper, "Regulating Hybrid Monsters? The Limits of Latour and Actor Network Theory," *Arena Journal* 29/30 (2008): 305–30.

34 The ethnography and analysis of this passage are reproduced from M. Hinkson, "Locating a Zeitgeist: Displacement, Becoming and the End of Alterity," *Critique of Anthropology* 39, no. 3 (2019): 371–88.

35 "Town Camp Drunks Attack Police, Ignore COVID Rules," *Alice Springs News*, April 15, 2020, https://www.alicespringsnews.com.au/2020/04/15/town-camps-drunks-attack-police-ignore-covid-precautions/.

36 M. de Certeau, *The Practice of Everyday Life*, trans. S. Rendall (Berkeley: University of California Press, 1984). It is striking that the authors of a recent ethnographic study of obesity and disadvantage set in the suburb where Nungarrayi lives also turn to this analysis. See M. Warin and T. Zivkovic, *Fatness, Obesity, and Disadvantage in the Australian Suburbs* (Cham, Switzerland: Palgrave Macmillan, 2019), 21.

AFTERWORD

1 G. H. Mead, *Mind, Self, and Society: From the Standpoint of a Social Behaviorist*, ed. and with an introduction by C. W. Morris (Chicago: University of Chicago Press, 1934), 332.

Bibliography

ABC. "Australia's Shame." *Four Corners*, July 25, 2016.

Abu-Lughod, L. *Dramas of Nationhood: The Politics of Television in Egypt.* Chicago: University of Chicago Press, 2008.

Abu-Lughod, L. "The Interpretation of Culture(s) after Television." *Representations* 59 (1997): 109–34.

Abu-Lughod, L. "Writing against Culture." In *Recapturing Anthropology: Working in the Present*, edited by R. Fox, 137–62. Santa Fe, NM: School of American Research, 1991.

Agier, M. *Borderlands: Towards an Anthropology of the Cosmopolitan Condition.* Cambridge: Cambridge University Press, 2016.

Ahmed, S. *Strange Encounters: Embodied Others in Post-coloniality.* London: Routledge, 2000.

Aikman, A. "Child Sex Abuse 'Like a Tsunami.'" *Australian*, March 5, 2018. https://www.theaustralian.com.au/nation/protection-agencies-swamped-by-tsunami-of-sex-abuse/news-story/4c76aa2baab4f094943d35ce589a1d06.

Allam, L., and N. Evershed. "Too Hot for Humans? First Nations People Fear Becoming Australia's First Climate Refugees." *Guardian*, December 18, 2019. https://www.theguardian.com/australia-news/2019/dec/18/too-hot-for-humans-first-nations-people-fear-becoming-australias-first-climate-refugees.

Altman, J. "In Search of an Outstation Policy for Indigenous Australians." CAEPR Working Paper No. 34, Centre for Aboriginal Economic Policy Research, Australian National University, 2006.

Altman, J., and M. Hinkson, eds. *Coercive Reconciliation: Stabilise, Normalise, Exit Aboriginal Australia.* Melbourne: Arena Publications, 2007.

Altman, J., and M. Hinkson, eds. *Culture Crisis: Anthropology and Politics in Aboriginal Australia.* Sydney: UNSW Press, 2010.

Anthony, T. "Growing Up Surplus to Humanity: Aboriginal Children in the Northern Territory." *Arena Journal* 51/52 (2018): 40–70.

Appiah, K. A. *The Lies That Bind: Rethinking Identity.* London: Profile Books, 2018.

Arendt, H. *Eichmann in Jerusalem: A Report on the Banality of Evil.* New York, Viking, 1965.

Asher, N. "Tanya Day's Family Call for Criminal Investigation on Final Day of Coronial Inquest." *ABC News*, September 13, 2019. https://www.abc.net.au/news/2019-09-13/tanya-days-family-speaks-at-final-day-of-coronial-inquest/11508920.

Auge, M. *Non-places: An Introduction to Supermodernity*. London: Verso, 1995.

Australian Institute of Health and Welfare. "Aboriginal and Torres Strait Islander Health Performance Framework 2017." Report, Canberra, 2017.

Barwick, A. "NT Police Apologise for Refusing to Let NSW Woman Buy Six-Pack of Beer in Alice Springs." *ABC News*, August 30, 2019. https://www.abc.net.au/news/2019-08-30/nt-police-apologise-nsw-woman-blocked-buying-beer-alice-springs/11462950.

Bates, D. *The Passing of the Aborigines: A Lifetime Spent among the Natives of Australia*. London: John Murray, 1938.

Baume, F. E. *Tragedy Track: The Story of the Granites*. Adelaide: Hesperian, 1933.

Beavan, K. "Yuendumu in Central Australia at 'Severe Risk' of Running Out of Water." *ABC News*, August 13, 2019. https://www.abc.net.au/news/2019-08-13/remote-community-yuendumu-running-out-of-drinking-water/11405024.

Beck, U., and N. Sznaider. "Unpacking Cosmopolitanism for the Social Sciences." *British Journal of Sociology* 57, no. 1 (2006): 381–403.

Beckett, J. "Frontier Encounter: Stanner's Durmugam." In *An Appreciation of Difference: WEH Stanner and Aboriginal Australia*, edited by M. Hinkson and J. Beckett, 89–101. Canberra: Aboriginal Studies Press, 2008.

Beckett, J. "George Dutton's Country: Portrait of an Aboriginal Drover." *Aboriginal History* 2 no. 1 (1978): 1–28.

Beckett, J. "Walter Newton's History of the World—or Australia." *American Ethnologist* 20, no. 4 (1993): 675–95.

Beer, B., and D. Gardner. "Friendship, Anthropology of." In *International Encyclopedia of the Social and Behavioral Sciences*, 2nd ed., vol. 9, edited by J. D. Wright, 425–43. Oxford: Elsevier, 2015.

Bell, D. *Daughters of the Dreaming*. Sydney: Allen and Unwin, 1983.

Bell, D., and T. Nelson. "Speaking about Rape Is Everyone's Business." *Women's Studies International Forum* 12, no. 4 (1989): 403–16.

Benaduce, R. "Undocumented Bodies, Burned Identities: Refugees, Sans Papiers, Harraga—When Things Fall Apart." *Social Science Information* 47, no. 4 (2008): 505–27.

Berger, J. *Bento's Sketchbook*. London: Verso, 2011.

Berger, J. *Berger on Drawing*. Edited by Jim Savage. Cork: Occasional, 2005.

Berger, J., and J. Mohr. *A Seventh Man: A Book of Images and Words about the Experience of Migrant Workers in Europe*. London: Verso, 1975.

Berlant, L. *Cruel Optimism*. Durham, NC: Duke University Press, 2011.

Berndt, R. M. "Areas of Research in Aboriginal Australia Which Demand Urgent Attention." *Bulletin of the International Committee on Urgent Anthropological and Ethnological Research* 2 (1959): 63–69.

Bessire, L. *Behold the Black Caiman: A Chronicle of Ayoreo Life*. Chicago: University of Chicago Press, 2014.

Besteman, C. *Making Refuge: Somali Bantu Refugees and Lewiston, Maine*. Durham, NC: Duke University Press, 2016.

Biddle, J. *Breast, Bodies, Canvas: Central Desert Art as Experience*. Sydney: UNSW Press, 2007.

Biddle, J. *Remote Avant-Garde: Aboriginal Art under Occupation*. Durham, NC: Duke University Press, 2016.

Biehl, J. *Vita: Life in a Zone of Social Abandonment*. Berkeley: University of California Press, 2005.

Biehl, J., and P. Locke. "The Anthropology of Becoming." In *Unfinished: The Anthropology of Becoming*, edited by J. Biehl and P. Locke, 37–56. Durham, NC: Duke University Press, 2017.

Biehl, J., and P. Locke. "Deleuze and the Anthropology of Becoming." *Current Anthropology* 51, no. 3 (2010): 317–51.

Biehl, J., and P. Locke. "Introduction: Ethnographic Sensorium." In *Unfinished: The Anthropology of Becoming*, edited by J. Biehl and P. Locke, 1–40. Durham, NC: Duke University Press, 2017.

Bielefeld, S. "Compulsory Income Management, Indigenous People and Structural Violence: Implications for Citizenship and Autonomy." *Australian Indigenous Law Review* 18, no. 1 (2014): 99–118.

Blanchard, C. A. *Return to Country: The Aboriginal Homelands Movement in Australia*. Canberra: Australian Government Publishing Service, 1987.

Bogle, I. "Centrelink: Incident at Adelaide Office Prompts Conversation about Deep Frustration." *ABC News*, March 22, 2018. http://www.abc.net.au/news/2018-03-22 /centrelink-the-perfect-recipe-for-deep-frustration/9573078.

Boltanski, L. *Distant Suffering: Morality, Media and Politics*. Cambridge: Cambridge University Press, 1999.

Bottoms, T. *Conspiracy of Silence: Queensland's Frontier Killing Times*. Sydney: Allen and Unwin, 2013.

Boym, S. *The Future of Nostalgia*. New York: Basic Books, 2001.

Boym, S. "On Diasporic Intimacy: Ilya Kabakov's Installations and Immigrant Homes." *Critical Inquiry* 24, no. 2 (1998): 498–524.

Brady, M. "Giving Away the Grog: An Ethnography of Aboriginal Drinkers Who Quit without Help." *Drug and Alcohol Review* 12, no. 4 (1993): 401–11.

"Break Up Indigenous Paedophile Rings: Brough." *ABC News*, May 17, 2006. https://www .abc.net.au/news/2006-05-17/break-up-indigenous-paedophile-rings-brough/1755274.

Brimblecombe, J., and M. Ferguson. "Food Price Gap Shows Need for Subsidies and Promo Deals for Remote Areas." *Journal of the Home Economics Institute of Australia* 22, no. 2 (2015): 36–37.

Buechler, H., and J. Buechler. *Carmen: The Autobiography of a Spanish Woman*. Cambridge, MA: Schenkman, 1981.

Burbank, V. "The Embodiment of Sorcery." *Australian Journal of Anthropology* 28, no. 3 (2017): 286–300.

Burbank, V. *An Ethnography of Stress*. New York: Palgrave Macmillan, 2011.

Burke, P. *An Australian Indigenous Diaspora: Warlpiri Matriarchs and the Refashioning of Tradition*. New York: Berghahn Books, 2018.

Burney, L. "Cuts Can Lead to Bruises and Far Worse for Women." *Australian*, October 11, 2016.

Byrd, J. *The Transit of Empire: Indigenous Critiques of Colonialism*. Minneapolis: University of Minnesota Press, 2011.

Campbell, L. 2006. *Darby: One Hundred Years of Life in a Changing Culture*. Sydney: Australian Broadcasting Commission Books, 2006.

Cane, S. "People and Policy in the Development and Destruction of Yagga Yagga Outstation, Western Australia." In *Experiments in Self-Determination*, edited by N. Peterson and F. Myers, 253–78. Canberra: ANU Press, 2016.

Carter, P. *The Lie of the Land*. London: Faber and Faber, 1996.

Carter, P. *Meeting Place: The Human Encounter and the Challenge of Coexistence*. Minneapolis: University of Minnesota Press, 2013.

Carter, P. *Places Made after Their Stories: Design and the Art of Choreotopography*. Crawley, Western Australia: UWA Press, 2015.

Carter, P. "Utopian Projections: Urban Spells against the Fury of Exile." In *Conversations on Utopia: Cultural and Linguistic Projects*, edited by C. Gualtieri, 62–91. Oxford: Peter Lang, 2020.

Casagrande, J., ed. *In the Company of Man: Twenty Portraits by Anthropologists*. New York: Harper and Brothers, 1960.

Casey, E. *Remembering: A Phenomenological Study*. Bloomington: Indiana University Press, 2009.

Caton, S. "Coetzee, Agamben, and the Passion of Abu Ghraib." *American Anthropologist* 108, no. 1 (2006): 114–23.

Certeau, M. de. *The Practice of Everyday Life*. Translated by S. Rendall. Berkeley: University of California Press, 1984.

Chlanda, E. "Cops at Bottle Shops: Expensive Bluff?" *Alice Springs News*, May 27, 2019. https://www.alicespringsnews.com.au/2019/05/27/cops-at-bottle-shops-expensive -bluff/.

Christie, M. "Darkness into Light: Missionaries, Modernists and Aboriginal Education." *Australian Journal of Aboriginal Education* 23, no. 3 (1995): 28–34.

Clendinnen, I. "The Power to Frustrate Good Intentions: or, The Revenge of the Aborigines." *Common Knowledge* 11, no. 3 (2005): 410–31.

Clifford, J. "On Ethnographic Allegory." In *Writing Culture: The Poetics and Politics of Ethnography*, edited by J. Clifford and G. Marcus, 98–121. Berkeley: University of California Press, 1986.

Clifford, J., and G. Marcus, eds. *Writing Culture: The Poetics and Politics of Ethnography*. Berkeley: University of California Press, 1986.

Coddington, K. "The Slow Violence of Life without Cash: Borders, State Restrictions, and Exclusion in the UK and Australia." *Geographical Review* 109, no. 4 (2019): 527–43.

Collier, M. J. "Core Symbols in South African Intercultural Friendships." *International Journal of Intercultural Relations* 21, no. 1 (1999): 133–56.

Comaroff, J., and J. Comaroff. "Millennial Capitalism: First Thoughts on a Second Coming." *Public Culture* 12, no. 2 (2000): 291–343.

Comaroff, J., and J. Comaroff. "Occult Economies and the Violence of Abstraction: Notes from the South African Postcolony." *American Ethnologist* 26, no. 2 (2003): 279–303.

Commonwealth of Australia. "Our North, Our Future: White Paper on Developing Northern Australia." Department of Industry, Innovation and Science, Canberra, 2015.

Coombs, H. C. "The Future of the Outstation Movement." Working paper, Centre for Resource and Environmental Studies, Australian National University, 1979.

Cooper, S. "Regulating Hybrid Monsters? The Limits of Latour and Actor Network Theory." *Arena Journal* 29/30 (2008): 305-30.

Coroners Court of the Northern Territory. "Inquest into the Death of P Japanangka Langdon." NTMC 016, Coroner's report, Coroners Court, Darwin, August 14, 2015.

Coutin, S. *Exiled Home: Salvadoran Transnational Youth in the Aftermath of Violence*. Durham, NC: Duke University Press, 2016.

Cowlishaw, G. *The City's Outback*. Sydney: NewSouth Books, 2009.

Cowlishaw, G., ed. *Love against the Law: The Autobiographies of Tex and Nellie Camfoo*. Canberra: Aboriginal Studies Press, 2000.

Crapanzano, V. "Hermes' Dilemma: The Masking of Subversion in Ethnographic Description." In *Writing Culture: The Poetics and Politics of Ethnography*, edited by J. Clifford and G. Marcus, 51-76. Berkeley: University of California Press, 1986.

Crapanzano, V. "Review: Life-Histories." *American Anthropologist* 86, no. 4 (1984): 953-60.

Crapanzano, V. *Tuhami: Portrait of a Moroccan*. Chicago: University of Chicago Press, 1980.

Cribbin, J. *The Killing Times*. Sydney: Fontana/Collins, 1984.

Darwish, M. *Palestine as Metaphor*. Translated by A. El-Zein and C. Forché. Northampton, MA: Olive Branch, 2019.

Das, V. *Life and Words: Violence and Descent into the Ordinary*. Berkeley: University of California Press, 2006.

Das, V., A. Kleinman, M. Ramphele, and P. Reynolds, eds. *Violence and Subjectivity*. Berkeley: University of California Press, 2000.

Das, V., M. Lock, M. Ramphele, and P. Reynolds, eds. *Remaking a World: Violence, Social Suffering, and Recovery*. Berkeley: University of California Press, 2001.

Davidson, H. "High Court Upholds Northern Territory's Paperless Arrest Laws." *Guardian*, November 11, 2015. https://www.theguardian.com/australia-news/2015/nov/11/high-court-upholds-northern-territory-paperless-arrest-laws.

Davidson, H. "Juvenile Detention Royal Commission Told Use of Force 'Routine' at Don Dale." *Guardian*, October 11, 2016. https://www.theguardian.com/australia-news/live/2016/oct/11/northern-territory-juvenile-detention-royal-commission-hearing-begins-in-darwin-live?CMP=Share_iOSApp_Other.

Davidson, H. "Uranium in Remote Communities' Water Puts 'People's Lives at Risk.'" *Guardian*, June 20, 2018. https://www.theguardian.com/australia-news/2018/jun/20/uranium-in-remote-communities-water-puts-peoples-lives-at-risk.

Deger, J. "Imprinting on the Heart: Photography and Contemporary Yolngu Mournings." *Visual Anthropology* 21, no. 4 (2008): 292-309.

Deranty, J.-P. "Injustice, Violence, and Social Struggle: The Critical Potential of Axel Honneth's Theory of Recognition." *Critical Horizons: A Journal of Philosophy and Social Theory* 5, no. 1 (2004): 297-322.

Dowd, A. "Finding the Fish: Memory, Displacement Anxiety, Legitimacy and Identity: The Legacy of Interlocking Traumatic Histories in Post-colonial Australia." In *Placing Psyche: Exploring Cultural Complexes in Australia*, edited by T. Singer, C. San Roque, A. G. Dowd, and D. J. Tacey, 123-55. New Orleans: Spring Journal Books, 2011.

Dussart, F. "'It Is Hard to Be Sick Now': Diabetes and the Reconstruction of Indigenous Sociality." *Anthropologica* 52, no. 1 (2010): 77-87.

Dussart, F. *The Politics of Ritual in an Aboriginal Settlement: Kinship, Gender, and the Currency of Knowledge*. Washington, DC: Smithsonian Institution Press, 2000.

Dwyer, K. *Moroccan Dialogues: Anthropology in Question*. Baltimore: Johns Hopkins University Press, 1982.

Eickelkamp, U. "Emplacing Christ: An Indigenous Australian Ethics of Placemaking across Borders." *Anthropological Forum* 28, no. 1 (2017): 45–60.

Eickelkamp, U. "Finding Spirit: Ontological Monism in an Australian Aboriginal Desert World Today." *Journal of Ethnographic Theory* 7, no. 1 (2017): 235–64.

Elias, D. "Golden Dreams: People, Place and Mining in the Tanami Desert." PhD diss., Australian National University, 2001.

Fanon, F. *The Wretched of the Earth*. Harmondsworth: Penguin, 1963.

Fassin, D. *Humanitarian Reason: A Moral History of the Present*. Berkeley: University of California Press, 2011.

Fassin, D. "The Police Are the Punishment." *Public Culture* 31, no. 3 (2019): 539–61.

Fassin, D. "Policing Borders, Producing Boundaries: The Governmentality of Immigration in Dark Times." *Annual Reviews of Anthropology* 40 (2011): 213–26.

Fassin, D. *Prison Worlds: An Ethnography of the Carceral Condition*. Translated by R. Gomme. Cambridge: Polity, 2017.

Feldman, A. *Formations of Violence: The Narrative of the Body and Political Terror in Northern Ireland*. Chicago: University of Chicago Press, 1991.

Fisher, D. "Running Amok or Just Sleeping Rough? Long-Grass Camping and the Politics of Care in Northern Australia." *American Ethnologist* 39, no. 1 (2012): 171–86.

Fisher, D. "An Urban Frontier: Respatializing Government in Remote Northern Australia." *Cultural Anthropology* 30, no. 1 (2015): 139–66.

Folds, R. *Crossed Purposes*. Sydney: UNSW Press, 2001.

Freire, P. *Pedagogy of the Oppressed*. New York: Seabury, 1970.

Gadamer, H.-G. "Friendship and Solidarity." *Research in Phenomenology* 39, no. 1 (1999): 3–12.

Gadamer, H.-G. *Truth and Method*. New York: Seabury, 1975.

Gale, F. *Urban Aborigines*. Canberra: ANU Press, 1972.

Garvey, P. "Closures Vindicate My Stand: Barnett." *Australian*, March 10, 2020, 7.

Geertz, C. *Works and Lives: The Anthropologist as Author*. Cambridge: Polity, 1988.

Gelder, K., and J. Jacobs. *Uncanny Australia: Sacredness and Identity in a Postcolonial Nation*. Carlton South: Melbourne University Press, 1998.

Geschiere, P. *The Modernity of Witchcraft: Politics and the Occult in Postcolonial Africa*. Charlottesville: University of Virginia Press, 1997.

Geschiere, P. *The Perils of Belonging: Autochthony, Citizenship, and Exclusion in Africa and Europe*. Chicago: University of Chicago Press, 2009.

Glowczewski, B. *Desert Dreamers*. Minneapolis: University of Minnesota Press, 2000.

Glowczewski, B. "The Paradigm of Indigenous Australians: Anthropological Phantasms, Artistic Creations, and Political Resistance." In *La revanche des genres: Art contemporain Australian*, edited by Geraldine Le Roux and Lucienne Striva, 84–208. Paris: Edition Ainu, Exhibition Catalogue, 2007.

Gluck, Z., and S. Low. "A Sociospatial Framework for the Anthropology of Security." *Anthropological Theory* 17, no. 3 (2017): 281–96.

Goldstein, D. "Toward a Critical Anthropology of Security." *Current Anthropology* 51, no. 4 (2010): 487–517.

Gomberg-Muñoz, R. "The Complicit Anthropologist." *Journal for the Anthropology of North America* 21, no. 1 (2018): 36–37.

Grant, S. *Australia Day*. Sydney: HarperCollins, 2016.

Griffiths, L. "Sharkie Savages Downers as 'Out of Touch.'" *Australian*, July 30, 2018. https://www.theaustralian.com.au/news/nation/rebekha-sharkie-savages-downers-as-being-out-of-touch/news-story/eaebe2eaf52b29ee9a711d148c85bf03.

Haebich, A. *Broken Circles: Fragmenting Indigenous Families 1800-2000*. Fremantle: Fremantle Art Centre Press, 2000.

Hage, G. *Against Paranoid Nationalism: Searching for Hope in a Shrinking Society*. London: Pluto, 2003.

Hall, S. "Cosmopolitanism, Globalization and Diaspora: Stuart Hall in Conversation with Pnina Werbner." In *Anthropology and the New Cosmopolitanism*, edited by P. Werbner, 345–61. Oxford: Berg, 2008.

Hartwig, M. C. "The Coniston Killings." Honors thesis, University of Adelaide, 1960.

Harvey, D. "Cosmopolitanism and the Banality of Geographic Evils." *Public Culture* 12, no. 2 (2000): 529–64.

Harvey, D. "The Right to the City." *International Journal of Urban and Regional Research* 27, no. 4 (2003): 939–41.

Hastrup, K. "Writing Ethnography: State of the Art." In *Anthropology and Autobiography*, edited by J. Okely and H. Callaway, 116–33. London: Routledge, 1992.

Haynes, J., and D. Keane. "Presenter Karla Grant 'Shocked' after Being Questioned by Police in Alice Springs While Buying Alcohol." ABC News, September 13, 2019. https://www.abc.net.au/news/2019-09-13/indigenous-tv-host-karla-grant-highlights-racial-profiling/11509940.

Herzfeld, M. *Cultural Intimacy: Social Poetics and the Real Life of States, Societies, and Institutions*. London: Routledge, 2016.

Hill, B. *Broken Song: T. G. H. Strehlow and Aboriginal Possession*. Sydney: Vintage, 2002.

Hinkson, M. "Beyond Assimilation and Refusal: A Warlpiri Perspective on the Politics of Recognition." *Postcolonial Studies* 20, no. 1 (2017): 86–100.

Hinkson, M. "In and Out of Place: Ethnography as 'Journeying With' between Central and South Australia." *Oceania* 88, no. 3 (2018): 254–68.

Hinkson, M. "In the Name of the Child." In *Coercive Reconciliation: Stabilise, Normalise, Exit Aboriginal Australia*, edited by J. Altman and M. Hinkson, 1–13. Carlton: Arena Publications, 2007.

Hinkson, M. "Locating a Zeitgeist: Displacement, Becoming and the End of Alterity." *Critique of Anthropology* 39, no. 3 (2019): 371–88.

Hinkson, M. "Media Images and the Politics of Hope." In *Culture Crisis: Anthropology and Politics in Aboriginal Australia*, edited by J. Altman, and M. Hinkson, 229–48. Sydney: UNSW Press, 2010.

Hinkson, M. "On the Edges of the Visual Culture of Exile: A View from South Australia." In *Refiguring Techniques in Digital Visual Research*, edited by S. Pink, S. Sumartojo, and E. Gómez Cruz, 93–104. London: Palgrave Macmillan, 2017.

Hinkson, M. "Precarious Placemaking." *Annual Reviews of Anthropology* 46 (2017): 49–64.

Hinkson, M. *Remembering the Future: Warlpiri Life through the Prism of Drawing*. Canberra: Aboriginal Studies Press, 2014.

Hinkson, M. "Turbulent Dislocations in Central Australia: Exile, Placemaking and the Promises of Elsewhere." *American Ethnologist* 45, no. 4 (2018): 521–32.

Hinkson, M. "What's in a Dedication? On Being a Warlpiri DJ." *Australian Journal of Anthropology* 15, no. 2 (2004): 143–62.

Hinkson, M., and T. Anthony. "Three Shots." *Arena Magazine*, no. 163 (December 2019): 16–21. https://arena.org.au/three-shots-by-melinda-hinkson-and-thalia-anthony/.

Hogg, R. "Penality and Modes of Regulating Indigenous Peoples in Australia." *Punishment and Society* 3, no. 3 (2001): 355–79.

Holcombe, S. "Human Rights, Colonial Criminality, and the Death of Kwementyaye Briscoe in Custody: A Central Australian Case Study." *Political and Legal Anthropology Review* 29, supp. 1 (2016): 104–20.

Holcombe, S. E. *Remote Freedoms: Politics, Personhood and Human Rights in Aboriginal Central Australia*. Stanford, CA: Stanford University Press, 2018.

Honneth, A. "Integrity and Disrespect: Principles of a Conception of Morality Based on the Theory of Recognition." *Political Theory* 20, no. 2 (1992): 187–201.

Honneth, A. "On the Destructive Power of the Third." *Philosophy and Social Criticism* 29, no. 1 (2003): 5–21.

Honneth, A., ed. *Reification: A New Look at an Old Idea*. Oxford: Oxford University Press, 2008.

Huggins, J., J. Willmot, I. Tarrago, K. Willetts, L. Bond, L. Holt, E. Bourke, M. BinSalik, P. Fowell, J. Schmider, V. Craigie, and L. McBride-Levi. "Letters to the Editors." *Women's Studies International Forum* 14, no. 5 (1991): 506–7.

Hughes, H. *Lands of Shame: Aboriginal and Torres Strait Islander "Homelands" in Transition*. Sydney: Centre for Independent Studies, 2007.

Hunyor, J. "Imprison Me NT: Paperless Arrests and the Rise of Executive Power in the Northern Territory." *Indigenous Law Bulletin* 8, no. 2 (2015): 3–9.

Ingold, T. *Being Alive: Essays on Movement, Knowledge and Description*. London: Routledge, 2011.

Jackson, M. *At Home in the World*. Durham, NC: Duke University Press, 1995.

Jackson, M. *Critique of Identity Thinking*. New York: Berghahn Books, 2019.

Jackson, M. *In Sierra Leone*. Durham, NC: Duke University Press, 2004.

Jackson, M. *The Wherewithal of Life: Ethics, Migration, and the Question of Well-Being*. Berkeley: University of California Press, 2013.

Jorgensen, D. "Preying on Those Close to Home: Witchcraft Violence in a Papua New Guinea Village." *Australian Journal of Anthropology* 25, no. 3 (2015): 267–86.

Kapferer, B. "Outside all Reason: Magic, Sorcery and Epistemology in Anthropology." In *Beyond Rationalism: Rethinking Magic, Witchcraft and Sorcery*, edited by B. Kapferer, 1–30. New York: Berghahn Books, 2003.

Kapferer, B., and D. Theodossopoulos, eds. *Against Exoticism: Towards the Transcendence of Relativism and Universalism in Anthropology*. New York: Berghahn Books, 2016.

Keefe, K. *From the Centre to the City: Aboriginal Education, Culture and Power*. Canberra: Aboriginal Studies Press, 1992.

Keith, H. "Feminism and Pragmatism: George Herbert Mead's Ethics of Care." *Transactions of the Charles S. Peirce Society* 35, no. 2 (1999): 328–44.

Kesteven, S. "A Sketch of Yuendumu and Its Outstations." Master's thesis, Australian National University, 1978.

Khosravi, S. *Precarious Lives: Waiting and Hope in Iran.* Philadelphia: University of Pennsylvania Press, 2017.

Kleinman, A., V. Das, and M. Lock, eds. *Social Suffering.* Berkeley: University of California Press, 1997.

Kowal, E. *Trapped in the Gap: Doing Good in Indigenous Australia.* New York: Berghahn Books, 2015.

Langton, M. "Trapped in the Aboriginal Reality TV Show." *Griffith Review* 19 (2008): 143–62.

Latimore, J. "Steve Bunbadgee Hodder Watt: Jacinta Price under Fire from Aboriginal Women." *@indigenousX*, February 6, 2018. https://indigenousx.com.au/steve-bunbadgee-hodder-watt-jacinta-price-under-fire-from-aboriginal-women/.

Lea, T. "When Looking for Anarchy, Look to the State: Fantasies of Regulation in Forcing Disorder within the Australian Indigenous Estate." *Critique of Anthropology* 32, no. 2 (2012): 109–24.

Lea, T., M. Young, F. Markham, C. Holmes, and B. Doran. "Being Moved (On): The Biopolitics of Walking in Australia's Frontier Towns." *Radical History Review* 114 (2012): 139–63.

Lear, J. *Radical Hope: Ethics in the Face of Cultural Devastation.* Cambridge, MA: Harvard University Press, 2008.

Lems, A. *Being-Here: Placemaking in a World of Movement.* New York: Berghahn Books, 2018.

Liberman, K. "Intercultural Communication in Central Australia." In *Cultural Communication and Intercultural Contact*, edited by D. Carbaugh, 185–92. New York: Taylor and Francis, 2009.

Lippert, R., and K. Walby. "Introduction: How the World's Cities Are Policed, Regulated and Securitized." In *Policing Cities: Urban Securitization and Regulation in a Twenty-First Century World*, edited by R. Lippert and K. Walby, 1–8. London: Routledge, 2013.

Long, J. *The Go-Betweens: Patrol Officers in Aboriginal Affairs Administration in the Northern Territory 1936–74.* Darwin: North Australia Research Unit, Australian National University, 1992.

Lumsden, D. "Broken Lives: Reflections on the Anthropology of Exile and Repair." *Refuge* 18, no. 4 (1999): 30–39.

Lydon, J. *Flash of Recognition: Photography and the Emergence of Indigenous Rights.* Sydney: NewSouth Books, 2012.

Malkki, L. *Purity and Exile: Violence, Memory, and National Cosmology among Hutu Refugees in Tanzania.* Chicago: University of Chicago Press, 1995.

Manne, R. "W. E. H. Stanner: The Anthropologist as Humanist." In W. E. H. Stanner, *The Dreaming and Other Essays*, 1–18. Melbourne: Black Inc., 2010.

Marcus, G. "The Uses of Complicity in the Changing Mise-en-Scène of Anthropological Fieldwork." *Representations* 59 (1997): 85–108.

Masco, J. "Comments: D. Goldstein, Toward a Critical Anthropology of Security." *Current Anthropology* 51, no. 4 (2010): 509–10.

Mayberry-Lewis, D. *The Savage and the Innocent.* Boston: Beacon, 1968.

Mbembe, A. *Necropolitics.* Durham, NC: Duke University Press, 2019.

McKnight, D. *From Hunting to Drinking: The Devastating Effects of Alcohol on an Australian Aboriginal Community.* London: Routledge, 2002.

Mead, G. H. *Mind, Self, Society: From the Standpoint of a Social Behaviorist.* Edited and with an introduction by C. W. Morris. Chicago: University of Chicago Press, 1934.

Meggitt, M. *Desert People.* Sydney: Angus and Robertson, 1962.

Meggitt, M. "Djanba among the Walbiri, Central Australia." *Anthropos* 50 (1955): 375–403.

Mehta, S. *This Land Is Our Land: An Immigrant's Manifesto.* New York: Farrar, Straus and Giroux, 2019.

Mendes, P. "Compulsory Income Management: A Critical Examination of the Emergence of Conditional Welfare in Australia." *Australian Social Work* 66, no. 4 (2015): 495–510.

Michaels, E. *For a Cultural Future: Francis Jupurrurla Makes TV at Yuendumu.* Sydney: Artspace, 1987.

Mirzoeff, N. *The Right to Look.* Durham, NC: Duke University Press, 2011.

Miyarrka Media. *Phone and Spear: A Yuta Anthropology.* London: Goldsmiths University Press, 2019.

"Mobile Assistance Patrol (MAP)." Aboriginal Sobriety Group, 2020. asg.org.au/mobile-assistance-patrol-map/.

Muehlebach, A. "On Precariousness and the Ethical Imagination: The Year 2012 in Sociocultural Anthropology." *American Anthropologist* 115, no. 2 (2013): 297–311.

Munn, N. "Excluded Spaces: The Figure in the Australian Landscape." *Critical Inquiry* 22, no. 3 (1996): 446–65.

Munn, N. *Walbiri Iconography: Graphic Representation and Cultural Symbolism in a Central Australian Society.* Ithaca, NY: Cornell University Press, 1973.

Musharbash, Y. "Boredom, Time and Modernity: An Example from Aboriginal Australia." *American Anthropologist* 109, no. 2 (2007): 307–17.

Musharbash, Y. "Monstrous Transformations: A Case Study from Central Australia." In *Monster Anthropology in Australia and Beyond*, edited by Y. Musharbash and G. H. Presterudstuen, 33–55. New York: Palgrave Macmillan, 2014.

Musharbash, Y. "Sorry Business Is Yapa Way: Warlpiri Mortuary Rituals as Embodied Practice." In *Mortality, Mourning and Mortuary Practices in Indigenous Australia*, edited by M. Tonkinson and V. Burbank, 34–56. London: Routledge, 2017.

Musharbash, Y. *Yuendumu Everyday: Contemporary Life in Remote Aboriginal Australia.* Canberra: Aboriginal Studies Press, 2008.

Myerhoff, B. *Number Our Days.* New York: Simon and Schuster, 1978.

Myers, F. "Burning the Truck and Holding the Country." In *We Are Here: Politics of Aboriginal Land Tenure*, edited by E. Wilmsen, 15–42. Berkeley: University of California Press, 1989.

Myers, F. "Emplacement and Displacement: Perceiving the Landscape through Aboriginal Australian Acrylic Painting." *Ethnos: Journal of Anthropology* 78, no. 4 (2012): 1–29.

Myers, F. *Painting Culture: The Making of an Aboriginal High Art.* Durham, NC: Duke University Press, 2002.

Myers, F. *Pintupi Country, Pintupi Self: Sentiment, Place, and Politics among Western Desert Aborigines.* Berkeley: University of California Press, 1991.

Myers, F. "Reflections on a Meeting: Structure, Language, and the Polity in a Small-Scale Society." In *The Matrix of Language: Contemporary Linguistic Anthropology*, edited by D. Brenneis and R. Macaulay, 234–57. Boulder, CO: Westview, 1996.

Myers, F. "Unsettled Business: Acrylic Painting, Tradition, and Indigenous Being." In *The Power of Knowledge, the Resonance of Tradition*, edited by L. Taylor, G. Ward, G. Henderson, R. Davis, and L. Wallis, 3–33. Canberra: Aboriginal Studies Press, 2005.

Myers, F. "Ways of Placemaking." *La Ricerca Folklorica* 45 (2002): 101–19.

Myers, F., and N. Peterson. "The Origins and History of Outstations as Aboriginal Life Projects." In *Experiments in Self-Determination: Histories of the Outstation Movement in Australia*, edited by N. Peterson and F. Myers, 1–22. Canberra: ANU Press, 2016.

Naficy, H. *An Accented Cinema: Exilic and Diasporic Filmmaking*. Princeton, NJ: Princeton University Press, 2001.

Nelson Nakamarra, L. "Wapurtarlikirli: The Battle at Yumurrpa," as told to Lee Cataldi. In *Warlpiri Dreamings and Histories: Yimikirli*, edited by P. Rockman Napaljarri and L. Cataldi, 105–18. San Francisco: HarperCollins, 1994.

"Nicky Winmar: Statue of Footballer's Stand against Racism Unveiled in Perth." BBC, July 6, 2019. https://www.bbc.com/news/world-australia-48893928.

Nixon, R. *Slow Violence and the Environmentalism of the Poor*. Cambridge, MA: Harvard University Press, 2011.

Northern Territory of Australia, Department of the Attorney-General and Justice. "Northern Territory Correctional Services Annual Statistics, 2016–17." 2018. https://justice.nt.gov.au/__data/assets/pdf_file/0004/599107/2016-17-ntcs-annual-statistics.pdf.

Okely, J., and H. Callaway. *Anthropology and Autobiography*. London: Routledge, 1992.

Om, J. "Another Yuendumu Exodus to Adelaide." *ABC News*, February 12, 2011. https://www.abc.net.au/news/2011-02-15/another-yuendumu-exodus-to-adelaide/1943676.

Ottosson, Å. "Don't Rubbish Our Town! 'Anti-social Behaviour' and Indigenous-Settler Forms of Belonging in Alice Springs." *City and Society* 28, no. 2 (2016): 152–73.

Ottosson, Å. "To Know One's Place: Belonging and Differentiation in Alice Springs Town." *Anthropological Forum* 24, no. 2 (2014): 115–35.

Pearson, N. *Our Right to Take Responsibility*. Cairns: Noel Pearson and Associates, 2000.

Peel, M. *Good Times, Hard Times: Past and Future in Elizabeth*. Melbourne: Melbourne University Press, 1995.

Peterson, N. "An Expanding Aboriginal Domain: Mobility and Initiation Journey." *Oceania* 70, no. 3 (2000): 205–18.

Peterson, N. "'What Was Dr Coombs Thinking?': Nyirrpi, Policy and the Future." In *Experiments in Self-Determination: Histories of the Outstation Movement in Australia*, edited by N. Peterson and F. Myers, 161–80. Canberra: ANU Press, 2017.

Pitt-Rivers, J. "The Kith and the Kin." In *The Character of Kinship*, edited by J. Goody, 89–105. Cambridge: Cambridge University Press, 2015.

Povinelli, E. *The Cunning of Recognition*. Durham, NC: Duke University Press, 2002.

Povinelli, E. *Economies of Abandonment: Social Belonging and Endurance in Late Liberalism*. Durham, NC: Duke University Press, 2011.

Powdermaker, H. *Stranger and Friend: The Way of an Anthropologist*. New York: W. W. Norton, 1966.

Price, J. N. "The Truth and Children Just Swept under the Carpet." *Australian*, March 6, 2018. https://www.theaustralian.com.au/commentary/opinion/the-truth-and-children-just-swept-under-the-carpet/news-story/af049c0aa7dc447d155d0adc014f5ca1.

Rabinow, P. *Marking Time: On the Anthropology of the Contemporary*. Princeton, NJ: Princeton University Press, 2008.

Rabinow, P. *Reflections on Fieldwork in Morocco*. Berkeley: University of California Press, 1977.

Ralph, L. "The Qualia of Pain: How Police Torture Shapes Historical Consciousness." *Anthropological Theory* 13, nos. 1 and 2 (2013): 104–5.

Ramelli, I. *Hierocles the Stoic: Elements of Ethics, Fragments and Excerpts*. Atlanta: Society of Biblical Literature, 2009.

Ramsay, G. "Humanitarian Exploits: Ordinary Displacements and the Political Economy of the Global Refugee Regime." *Critique of Anthropology* 40, no. 1 (2020): 3–27.

Ramsay, G. *Impossible Refuge: The Control and Constraint of Refugee Futures*. Abingdon: Routledge, 2018.

Ramsay, G. "Incommensurable Futures and Displaced Lives: Sovereignty as Control over Time." *Public Culture* 29, no. 3 (2017): 515–38.

Rapport, N. *Transcendent Individual: Towards a Literary and Liberal Anthropology*. London: Routledge, 1997.

Read, P., ed. *Settlement: A History of Australian Indigenous Housing*. Canberra: Aboriginal Studies Press, 2000.

Refugee Council of Australia. "Offshore Processing Statistics." October 25, 2020. https://www.refugeecouncil.org.au/operation-sovereign-borders-offshore-detention -statistics/7/.

Robbins, J. "Beyond the Suffering Subject: Toward an Anthropology of the Good." *Journal of the Royal Anthropological Institute* 19, no. 3 (2013): 447–62.

Roberts, T. *Frontier Justice: A History of the Gulf Country to 1900*. Brisbane: University of Queensland Press, 2005.

Rosaldo, R., S. Lavie, and K. Narayan. "Introduction: Creativity in Anthropology." In *Creativity/Anthropology*, edited by R. Rosaldo, S. Lavie, and K. Narayan, 1–8. Ithaca, NY: Cornell University Press, 1993.

Rothwell, N. *Quicksilver*. Melbourne: Text, 2017.

Rowse, T. *Remote Possibilities: The Aboriginal Domain and the Administrative Imagination*. Brinkin: North Australia Research Unit, 2002.

Rowse, T. *White Flour, White Power: From Rations to Citizenship in Central Australia*. Melbourne: Cambridge University Press, 1998.

Rubuntja, W., and J. Green. *The Town Grew Up Dancing: The Life and Art of Wenton Rubuntja*. Alice Springs: Jukurrpa Books, 2002.

Saethre, E. "Conflicting Traditions, Concurrent Treatment: Medical Pluralism in Remote Aboriginal Australia." *Oceania* 77, no. 1 (2007): 95–110.

Said, E. "Reflections on Exile." In *Reflections on Exile and Other Essays*, edited by E. Said, 173–86. Cambridge, MA: Harvard University Press, 2002.

San Roque, C. "A Glass Darkly." *Journal of Child Psychology and Psychiatry* 15, no. 2 (2018): 91–102.

Sansom, B. *The Camp at Wallaby Cross: Aboriginal Fringe Dwellers in Darwin*. Canberra: Australian Institute of Aboriginal Studies, 1980.

Schwartz, C., and F. Dussart. "Christianity in Aboriginal Australia Revisited." *Australian Journal of Anthropology* 21, no. 1 (2010): 1–13.

Sexton, J. *Son of Tecún Umún: A Maya Indian Tells His Life Story*. Tucson: University of Arizona Press, 1981.

Shostak, M. *Nisa: The Life and Words of a !Kung Woman*. Cambridge, MA: Harvard University Press, 1981.

Silverstone, R. *Media and Morality: On the Rise of the Mediapolis*. Cambridge: Polity, 2007.

Simpson, A. *Mohawk Interruptus: Political Life across the Borders of Settler States*. Durham, NC: Duke University Press, 2014.

Smith, B. "'More Than Love': Locality and Affects of Indigeneity in Northern Queensland." *Asia Pacific Journal of Anthropology* 7, no. 3 (2006): 221–35.

Spivak, G. *A Critique of Postcolonial Reason: Toward a History of the Vanishing Present*. Cambridge, MA: Harvard University Press, 1999.

Standen, S., and T. Joyner. "Squalid Homes Demolished, Residents Relocated from Aboriginal Reserves, in Shadow of Big-Money Mines." *ABC News*, July 13, 2019. https://www.abc.net.au/news/2019-07-13/squalid-indigenous-housing-in-shadow-of-big-money-mines/9940500.

Stanner, W. E. H. "The Dreaming." In *White Man Got No Dreaming: Essays 1938–73*, 23–40. Canberra: ANU Press, 1979 [1956].

Stevenson, L. *Life Beside Itself: Imagining Care in the Canadian Arctic*. Berkeley: University of California Press, 2014.

Stojanovski, A. *Dog Ear Café: How the Mt Theo Program Beat the Curse of Petrol Sniffing*. Melbourne: Hybrid, 2010.

Stoler, A. L. *Duress: Imperial Durabilities in Our Times*. Durham, NC: Duke University Press, 2016.

Sutton, P. *Dreamings: The Art of Aboriginal Australia*. New York: Viking, 1988.

Sutton, P. *The Politics of Suffering: Indigenous Australia and the End of the Liberal Consensus*. Melbourne: Melbourne University Press, 2009.

Swain, T. *A Place among Strangers: Towards a History of Australian Aboriginal Being*. Cambridge: Cambridge University Press, 1993.

Taussig, M. *The Corn Wolf*. Chicago: University of Chicago Press, 2015.

Taussig, M. *The Devil and Commodity Fetishism in South America*. Chapel Hill: University of North Carolina Press, 1980.

Taussig, M. *The Nervous System*. New York: Routledge, 1992.

Taylor, P. "Remote Communities Making the Move to Town." *Australian*, July 16, 2019. https://www.theaustralian.com.au/nation/remote-communities-making-the-move-to-town/news-story/ac74fcdfab0c34968f02d2a9f1aeffic.

"Ten Things You Need to Know about Jacinta Price." *Welcome to Country*, February 9, 2019. https://www.welcometocountry.org/things-need-to-know-jacinta-price/.

"Toddler Allegedly Raped in Same Tennant Creek Household as Fatal Dispute." *ABC News*, February 23, 2018. http://www.abc.net.au/news/2018-02-23/toddlers-alleged-rape-occurred-in-same-home-as-fatal-dispute/9477048.

Torpey, J. "Coming and Going: On the State Monopolization of the Legitimate 'Means of Movement.'" *Sociological Theory* 16, no. 3 (1998): 239–59.

"Town Camp Drunks Attack Police, Ignore COVID Rules." *Alice Springs News*, April 15, 2020. https://www.alicespringsnews.com.au/2020/04/15/town-camps-drunks-attack-police-ignore-covid-precautions/.

Trouillot, M.-R. "Anthropology and the Savage Slot: The Poetics and Politics of Otherness." In *Global Transformations: Anthropology and the Modern World*, 7–28. New York: Palgrave Macmillan, 2003.

Tuck, E., and K. W. Yang. "Decolonization Is Not a Metaphor." *Decolonization: Indigeneity, Education and Society* 1, no. 1 (2012): 1–40.

Turner, V. "Betwixt and Between: The Liminal Period in *Rites de Passage*." In *The Forest of Symbols: Aspects of Ndembu Ritual*, 93–111. Ithaca, NY: Cornell University Press, 1967.

Tyler, S. A. "Post-modern Ethnography: From Document of the Occult to Occult Document." In *Writing Culture: The Poetics and Politics of Ethnography*, edited by J. Clifford and G. Marcus, 122–40. Berkeley: University of California Press, 1986.

Vaarzon-Morel, P. "Pointing the Phone: Transforming Technologies and Social Relations among Warlpiri." *Australian Journal of Anthropology* 25, no. 2 (2014): 239–55.

Vaarzon-Morel, P., ed. *Warlpiri karnta karnta-kurlangu yimi / Warlpiri Women's Voices: Our Lives, Our History*. Alice Springs: Institute of Aboriginal Development, 1995.

Vanstone, A. "Beyond Conspicuous Compassion: Indigenous Australians Deserve More Than Good Intentions." In *A Passion for Policy: Essays on Public Sector Reform*, edited by J. Wanna, 39–46. Canberra: ANU Press, 2005.

Vessey, D. "Gadamer's Account of Friendship as an Alternative to an Account of Intersubjectivity." *Philosophy Today* 49, no. 5 (2005): 61–67.

Vigh, H. "Motion Squared: A Second Look at the Concept of Social Navigation." *Anthropological Theory* 9, no. 4 (2009): 419–38.

Vincent, E. *Against Native Title: Conflict and Creativity in Outback Australia*. Canberra: Aboriginal Studies Press, 2017.

Virilio, P. *The Great Accelerator*. Translated by Julie Rose. Cambridge: Polity, 2012.

Virilio, P. *Speed and Politics*. Translated by Mark Polizzotti. Los Angeles: Semiotext(e), 2006.

Vivian, S., and K. Beavan. "Yuendumu Residents Grieve Loss of Teenager Kumanjayi Walker after Police Shooting." *ABC News*, November 10, 2019. https://www.abc.net .au/news/2019-11-10/yuendumu-residents-mourn-loss-after-nt-police-shooting /11690670.

Vizenor, G. "Aesthetics of Survivance." In *Survivance: Narratives of Native Presence*, edited by G. Vizenor, 1–24. Lincoln: University of Nebraska Press, 2008.

Wacquant, L. "Crafting the Neoliberal State: Workfare, Prisonfare, and Social Insecurity." *Sociological Forum* 25, no. 2 (2010): 197–220.

Wacquant, L. *Punishing the Poor: The Neoliberal Government of Social Insecurity*. Durham, NC: Duke University Press, 2009.

Wacquant, L. "Race, Class, and Hyperincarceration in Revanchist America." *Daedalus* 139, no. 3 (2010): 74–90.

Wacquant, L. "Three Steps to a Historical Anthropology of Actually Existing Neoliberalism." *Social Anthropology* 20, no. 21 (2012): 66–79.

Wahlquist, C. "Fears Western Australia Will Close Remote Indigenous Communities by Stealth." *Guardian*, July 14, 2016. https://www.theguardian.com/australia-news/2016 /jul/14/fears-western-australia-will-close-remote-indigenous-communities-by-stealth.

Walker, J. "Night Patrol." *Arena Magazine* 102 (2009): 31–33.

Warin, M., and T. Zivkovic. *Fatness, Obesity, and Disadvantage in the Australian Suburbs: Unpalatable Politics*. Cham, Switzerland: Palgrave Macmillan, 2020.

Watts, L., and S. Fisher. "Pikilyi: Water Rights—Human Rights." Master's thesis, Charles Darwin University, 2000.

Werbner, P., ed. *Anthropology and the New Cosmopolitanism: Rooted, Feminist and Vernacular Perspectives*. Oxford: Berg, 2008.

Wild, S. "Recreating the Jukurrpa: Adaptation and Innovation in Songs and Ceremonies in Warlpiri Society." In *Songs of Aboriginal Australia*, edited by M. Clunies Ross, T. Donaldson, and S. Wild, 97–120. Sydney: University of Sydney, 1987.

Williams, G. "A Decade of Australian Anti-terror Laws." *Melbourne University Law Review* 35, no. 3 (2011): 1137–51.

Willis, P. "Patrons and Riders: Conflicting Roles and Hidden Objectives in an Aboriginal Development Programme at Kununurra (WA)." Master's thesis, Australian National University, 1980.

Wilson, D., and L. Weber. "Surveillance, Risk and Preemption on the Australian Border." *Surveillance and Society* 5, no. 2 (2008): 124–41.

Wolfe, P. *Settler Colonialism and the Transformation of Anthropology: The Politics and Poetics of an Ethnographic Event*. London: Cassell, 1999.

Wright, A. *Tracker*. Sydney: Giramondo, 2017.

Wright, A. "What Happens When You Tell Someone Else's Story?" *Meanjin*, Summer 2016. https://meanjin.com.au/essays/what-happens-when-you-tell-somebody-elses-story/.

"Yuendumu Campers Pack Up and Go." *ABC News*, March 14, 2011. https://www.abc.net.au/news/2011-03-11/yuendumu-campers-pack-up-and-go/2661492?site=alicesprings.

Index

kinship: citizenship and, 84; demands of, 84; family, recognition, and misrecognition, 126; friendship and, 37; hyperkinship, 82, 92; identification, containment, and policing vs., 74–81; moral particularism and affirmation of, 99–100; mosaic of relatedness, 91–92; placemaking and, 121; sorcery and, 103; The Troubles and, 74; web of extended kin, 5; welfare citizenship demands vs., 107–8; work of, 125–26

kinship riding, 9, 83, 89

Kleinman, Arthur, 29

kunta (shame), 139

land rights: Aboriginal Land Rights Act (Northern Territory), 77, 159; domestic violence advocates and, 86; legal recognition of, 134; movement and, 10–11; reversal of moral sentiment of, 160; traditional ownership, 2, 7, 10–11, 76–78, 120, 128, 159

Langdon, Kumunjayi, 46, 104–6, 124

Law, Warlpiri, 119–20

Lear, Jonathan, 174

life writing. *See* anthropology and ethnographic writing

liminality, 57, 76, 80–82

Locke, Peter, 17–18

Malkki, Liisa, 57

Marcus, George, 34–35

marlpa (company/kin), 74, 103

Masco, Joseph, 160

Mbembe, Achille, 15

Mead, George Herbert, 16, 18–19, 56, 121, 143, 155–56

medical services, 94–96, 98, 103

Meggitt, Mervyn, 72–73, 113

memorials, roadside, 76

memory: COVID-19 pandemic and, 180; interrogated, 81; Mead on environment and, 180–81; movement and, 39; nostalgia and, 33–34; placemaking and, 121–22

mining royalties, 11, 56, 84–85, 121, 123–24, 127, 163. *See also* extractive capitalism

mirlalypa (guardian spirits), 130, 180

Miyarrka Media, 20

mobile phones, 19, 23, 74, 176

mobility: "becoming" analytic and, 176; COVID-19 pandemic and, 171; criminalization

and, 78; as dangerous, 75; dreams and, 56; globalization and transnational mobility, 63; history of, 7–11; hypermobility, 36, 96, 100, 109, 132–33; for improvement, narratives of, 6; memory and, 39; mobile phones, social media, and, 19; rupture vs. continuity and, 79; Walker killing and, 159; welfare regime and restrictions on, 146. *See also* relocation

monsters, 72–73, 88

mortality rates, 95

movement: 8–11; containment and, 17, 134; COVID-19 pandemic and, 171; memory and, 39; migration and "force of circumstance," 49; as morally inflected, 83; policing of, 76–78, 134, 159, 177; public transport, 97–98; resource pursuit and, 83–84; Torpey on modern state and, 74–75; in Warlpiri iconography, 8. *See also* mobility

"Move to Town" program (Western Australia), 5–6

Munn, Nancy, 8, 132–33

Musharbash, Yasmine, 72

Myers, Fred, 40, 75, 101, 119–21, 125

national emergency declaration, 29–30

Nature Conservancy, 128–30

navigation, 50–51, 64

neoliberalism, 13, 31, 59, 144, 159–60

Nepalese immigrants, 58, 62–63, 69–70, 99, 170

NeverEnding Story, The (film), 173–74

ngankari healers, 60, 81, 94, 127

Nietzsche, Friedrich, 163

night patrols, women's, 135

Northern Territory Emergency Response (the Intervention), 13–14, 24, 77, 153, 159–60, 170, 177

nostalgia, 33–34, 50, 121–22, 175

obituary mode, 26–29

Ottosson, Åse, 76

outstations, 5, 84, 120, 127–31, 134–35, 172

ownership, traditional: emplacement and, 76–78; invoking, 128, 149; of Jukurrpa, 2; under land rights law, 7, 159; movement and, 10–11; Tiny Town and, 120

paperless laws, 104–6

parklands, Adelaide, 14, 40–41, 50–52, 98, 109–10, 148–52, 151f

www.ingramcontent.com/pod-product-compliance
Lightning Source LLC
Chambersburg PA
CBHW071738270326
41928CB00013B/2730